C000246605

ONE WING HIGH

Halifax Bomber –
the Navigator's Story

HARRY LOMAS

ONE WING HIGH

**Halifax Bomber –
the Navigator's Story**

Airlife
England

Copyright © 1995 by Harry Lomas

First published in the UK in 1995
by Airlife Publishing Ltd

British Library Cataloguing in Publication Data
  A catalogue record for this book
  is available from the British Library

ISBN 1 85310 320 9

Typeset by Hewer Text Composition Services, Edinburgh
Printed by Biddles Ltd, Guildford and King's Lynn

Airlife Publishing Ltd
101 Longden Road, Shrewsbury SY3 9EB

CONTENTS

Author's Foreword

I n the years since the last bomb was dropped on Germany in 1945, many excellent and authoritative books have been written about Bomber Command. They have, naturally enough, tended to dwell on the more publicised epics, like the Dambuster's raid, the Battle of Berlin or the bombing of the *Tirpitz*.

Bomber Command consisted literally of thousands of small integrated fighting units, the bomber crews, each of which was a tiny component of a vast war machine. Each crew was made up of a small group of ordinary young men, gathered together in the casual lottery which was the crewing-up process. These ordinary men sometimes did their duties in extraordinary ways. In spite of heavy losses, their numbers increased as the war progressed and without them the war would not have been won. This is basically the true story of one such crew.

After nearly fifty years since the end of the war in Europe, what can my story add to what has already been written?

I think the answer lies in the question itself. For one thing, writing about events of the distant past inevitably produces a degree of objectivity, which other accounts may lack. I have been fortunate in that my memory of wartime years remains clear, helped by the fact that at the time I was a compulsive compiler of diaries, notebooks, letters and logbooks. As a result, I can offer an unusually detailed and very authentic account of aircrew life.

Another factor is that the period between then and now is so great, the change in people's lifestyles, motivations and attitudes so pronounced, that we are in effect looking at a slice of social history. Take one example. Today's teenagers (itself not a word in use in wartime) generally enjoy extended education and involvement in current pop culture. Fifty years ago a nineteen-year-old could well be the captain of a heavy bomber, with seven lives in his hands, or an eighteen-year-old gunner could have completed a hazardous first tour of ops. Thankfully, such a scenario is unthinkable today.

In recent years, the hindsight strategists, the historical revisionists, the

7

modern-day iconoclasts have all had their say – generally denigrating Bomber Command's efforts. On the very day I read an article decrying the systematic bombing of German cities, I watched a TV documentary which displayed the piles of emaciated corpses after the liberation of a Nazi death camp. Maybe it should be made compulsory viewing once a year. A total of 55,000 aircrew lost their lives in their efforts to bring the war to a speedy and successful conclusion. Their sacrifice must always be remembered. I hope this book helps.

Looking back, various points of significance come to mind regarding the men involved.

First of all, the strange incongruity of a lifestyle which could find young men drinking beer in the peaceful setting of an English village pub, only hours after fighting for their lives in the battle-scarred skies five hundred miles distant. It called for a continuing process of adjustment which few other combatants have ever had to perform. It says much for their natural resilience that the only outward manifestations were a certain boisterousness of behaviour and a more than average indulgence in cigarette smoking and beer drinking. Secondly, the diversity of nationalities involved in the bombers' war, and the large proportion of those who were operating far from their homeland. On my own 158 Squadron, the number of flyers from Canada, Australia and New Zealand, and particularly those bearing the responsibilities of aircraft captaincy, was quite remarkable. Apart from their distinctive accents, they brought their national characteristics of toughness, determination and plain speaking, and I sometimes wonder if we properly acknowledged the debt we all owed them.

I happened to be the navigator of the crew of which I write, so it is perhaps appropriate that I should be the storyteller. Like a lot of navigators, I was a year or so older than most of the other crew members, due to a longer training period, and as such was often their confidant. I was also crew scribe, statistician, keeper of records, arbiter of fair play, and the one expected to stay sober enough at crew booze-ups to navigate the party safely back to billets.

In writing this book I have attempted to describe anything of a technical nature in layman's terms. As in all the services, day-to-day life in the Royal Air Force revolves around abbreviations and initials. Ex-airmen will not be confounded by the likes of DROs, SWOs, SPs or 252s, but to save others the tedious business of referring to a 'glossary of terms' I have tried to avoid such contractions wherever possible. Within these limits, I think the book gives an accurate representation of the way we used to talk, think and act.

Finally, if you should ever happen to hear the elderly gentleman in the corner mention 'I was on Lancasters' or 'I flew in Halifaxes', and he is ready to talk of it – then lend him your ear. He will be remembering the tremendous spirit and comradeship of the time, and may even be recalling what he now considers to be his golden days . . .

1

THE MAN WHO HATED GERMANS

I was sitting on a bench in Leicester Square, studying a street map and sharing my breakfast sandwiches with the pigeons.

It was not my first visit to the capital. Some ten years ago, as a very young and excited schoolboy, I had taken part in the local schools' one-day organised outing. We had boarded a special train at our nearest railway station, and three hours later transferred to a fleet of sightseeing buses outside Euston Station. Those of us who had been unfortunate enough to sample the cold pork pie for lunch on the train had spent the next hours lying groaning in our bus seats and vomiting into paper bags. When back at school, and called upon to write our essays on 'My impressions of London', my contribution took up only five lines of my exercise book, I remember.

This time, though I had only arrived hours previously, my impressions were already formed. In the aftermath of the bombing, London was certainly not looking her best. Her face was scarred, her complexion blotched, her smile gap-toothed. Yet I was already captivated by her. To my uncritical provincial eyes she conveyed an unusual vitality, a deep sense of history. Her charm was undiminished by the blemishes of wartime visible all around me – the boarded windows, the sandbagged entrances and the ugly brick and concrete air raid shelters. I felt stongly the aura of a place which was the focus of the war, the hub of the empire. The great profusion of different uniforms of every allied nation on view in the streets was alone sufficient to augment that feeling.

My view was no doubt influenced by the feeling of near euphoria which held me. I was well aware that this was the first day of a completely new life for me. A life which would offer excitement and challenge – the very antithesis of the one I had been leading. Since leaving school at the beginning of the war, I had been employed in a boring job in a gloomy office in an insalubrious part of Manchester. Now it was goodbye to all that, and good riddance.

In my pocket was a buff-coloured directive from the Air Ministry which was my personal passport to these new horizons. It instructed me

11

to report to the Aircrew Reception Centre, Lord's Cricket Ground, St John's Wood, by 1200 hours on 4 May 1942, to commence the full-time aircrew training for which I had volunteered. It was the summons for which I had been waiting four long months.

I was, I think, a fairly typical representative of my generation – earnest, untravelled, quietly patriotic, respectful of authority and amenable to discipline. None of these qualities was liable to conflict with the normal concepts of life in the armed forces. In that sense, at least, we were the right generation for the times.

During the waiting period I had done what I could to prepare myself for my new vocation. I brushed up on my maths from my old school books, and devoured countless books on aviation subjects from the library. I learned to recognise the silhouettes of all known RAF and Luftwaffe aircraft. I even taught myself the Morse Code with the aid of a home-made buzzer. I must have been pretty dull company at home.

Having finished the last of my packed sandwiches, I was about to move on for an hour or two of sightseeing when I was joined on the bench by a young fellow of about my own age.

'Would you be heading for Lord's, by any chance?' he asked me.

I looked at him with some surprise. Tall, with keen blue eyes and fair hair, he was smartly turned out in a tweed jacket and grey flannels. He was carrying a small suitcase similar to my own.

'I am, as a matter of fact,' I replied.

'Thought so. I noticed your suitcase, and spotted you were wearing a VR badge. I'm going there myself.'

I saw then that he too wore the silver RAF Volunteer Reserve badge in his jacket lapel. This common bond established, we were soon chatting freely. His name was Michael Brown, and he was a Londoner and proud of it. He seemed a friendly and articulate fellow, with an accent which would have been considered rather posh where I came from. We had other things in common, it transpired. We were exactly the same age, and smoked the same brand of cigarette. The contents of our suitcases were identical – pyjamas, shaving kit, ration book, gas mask, spare packets of cigarettes – except that my mother I found had slipped in an envelope containing a contingency fund of five one pound notes, and a packet of stamped postcards. During the course of our conversation I brought up the inevitable recruits' question: 'What made you volunteer?'

He answered with another question: 'What do you think of the Germans?'

I didn't understand the relevance, and gave a noncommital reply:

'Oh, I suppose they're the same as everybody else, really, There's good and bad. Maybe they're a bit more easily led than we are.'

In a tone of some bitterness, he said unequivocally:

'I hate the bastards. All of them. I lost my home and family in the blitz. Since then, I've had one big ambition – to be a bomber pilot. You can keep your Spitfires and your tally-hos and victory rolls. I'll take the bombers, and the bigger the better. I can't wait to give them a taste of what they've given the Smoke. During the raids when their bombers were overhead I've stood in the street shaking my fist at the sky and shouting: Your day will come, you murdering swine! It's a wonder they didn't lock me up. I volunteered for pilot training on my eighteenth birthday, and was accepted. They said I was highly motivated, and they were dead right.'

I was a little taken back by this vehement outburst, especially considering our short acquaintanceship. On the other hand, I had already discovered that in matters concerning the war some people had extremely deep feelings very near the surface. In comparison, my own motivation seemed a little mundane.

I had always been fascinated by flying. It probably stemmed from the time I had experienced the exhilaration of a short five-shilling flight in a biplane, when Sir Alan Cobham's flying circus had visited my locality some years previously. It must be remembered that in those days flying was an experience denied to all but a tiny minority. I had always considered the RAF's flyers to be a breed apart; men of such mental prowess, physical perfection and sheet guts as to be supermen when compared with the likes of me – an average grammar school product, subject to petty ailments of adolescence, and whose courage or endurance had never been put to the test. This image had been dented when I heard that an old school acquaintance, one Frosty Winterbottom, had been accepted for training as an observer. Frosty was no great physical specimen, nor were his scholastic attainments any better than mine. The RAF, I figured, must have lowered their standards in this the third year of the war, and consequently there must be a chance for me to join the élite band.

I knew my limitations well enough. I had little in the way of technical knowledge. I had never driven a car, nor did I understand the functioning of the internal combustion engine. And I certainly didn't have the lightning reactions nor the ready co-ordination of hand and eye which I realised must be the prerequisite of a prospective pilot.

But an observer – that was something different. He was the man in the aircraft who sat at a table, with the awesome responsibility of navigating

13

to and from the target, and dropping the bombs in the right spot. Surely these were things which could be taught in a classroom or trainer, without any great need of special aptitudes. It was something I would willingly work at, given the chance. I remembered reading a magazine article about a bomber crew. They all appeared extremely photogenic and happy with their lot, but it was the observer who caught the eye. He was pictured as a handsome young officer in a stylish fur-trimmed leather jacket, looking up from his chart with a confident smile for the camera. The caption stated, in the journalese of the time:

'This is the Observer – the man they all rely on to get them there and back. If the Pilot is the Heart of the aircraft, the Gunner is the Eyes, the Wireless Operator is the Ears, then this man must certainly be the Brain.'

It must be very satisfying, I felt, to be considered the brain of anything. I had done my best to explain all this to the officer on the subsequent selection board when he asked me why I did not want to be a pilot like everybody else, and I must have succeeded.

Since I would be called up for military service eventually anyway, my parents had no great objection to my volunteering for aircrew duties. My mother accepted it with the quiet resignation of mothers everywhere. My father, an ex-serviceman himself, thought I had done rather well in ensuring I kept well away from the poor bloody infantry. I wasn't too sure how my boss at the office would take it. A man of high-minded principles, we considered him a bit of an old woman, and I knew that he had been a conscientious objector in the First World War. In the event, after predictably grumbling about ever-decreasing staff and ever-increasing workload, he wished me well. He realised I had been hankering for a more adventurous life than the office provided. Once I left home, I would be subject to various temptations – like drink and women – which I must stoutly resist. He made my prospects sound very attractive.

As far as Michael's expressed Germanophobia was concerned, it was a very personal thing, and not a factor in my own case. Nor, I might add, was I ever to find a lot of evidence of it elsewhere in the forces. The British serviceman, I was to find, has a tendency to blame his superiors rather than his enemies for his misfortunes. Oddly enough, one of the last people to whom I had said my goodbyes was my Aunt Elfreide, a German born and bred, who was currently living at home with my parents. She had married my father's younger brother, a Merchant Navy officer, shortly before the war. Now her husband was dead, killed by U-Boat action in the Atlantic, and her home and possessions had been destroyed by the

Luftwaffe during the Liverpool blitz. Her parents in Hamburg were suffering bombing raids by the RAF crews, and now her young nephew was going to join them. She was as much a victim of Hitler's war as anyone could be, and surely one could only sympathise, whatever her nationality. I put this point to Michael in the course of our conversation.

'Fair enough,' he acknowledged. 'I don't expect everyone to feel as I do. I know I have a bee in my bonnet, I admit it.'

Since we had ample time to spare before we needed to report in, he offered to show me around the sights in the West End, and we moved off together.

My new acquaintance proved to be a lively and knowledgeable companion. He also proved to be, by my standards at least, a most sophisticated young man. As we passed various theatres, and I was impressed by some of the star names billed, he dismissed them with a metaphorical sniff.

'Most of the fellows are nancies, you know. That's why they're not in uniform.'

Again, strolling in Mayfair, and occasionally passing an elegant young woman exercising her pekinese. 'She's on the game, you know, and too expensive for the likes of us.'

I passed no comment. I was not sure he was altogether serious. I can say that I learned a good deal more about central London than I ever would have done from a lone stroll with my street map.

In due course we travelled together by tube to Lord's having established a rapport like we had known each other for months rather than hours. There were others on the train heading for the same place, readily identifiable by their small cases, short haircuts and rather bewildered looks common to recruits everywhere.

Many others were converging on the main gates at Lord's. Here two service policemen inspected our papers and directed us to the pavilion, which was our reporting centre. We handed in our badges and ration books, and began the long process of form filling.

Since the war I have visited Lord's many times for test matches, and find it increasingly difficult to reconcile the impressive present-day cricketing Mecca with the place I remember of old. In those days, it had survived the bombings and the military takeover at the cost of a genteel shabbiness, like a sadly rundown stately home. Everywhere there was need for structural repairs and coats of paint. The centre of the sacred turf had been cordoned off, but the rest of the ground swarmed with bodies in and out of uniform, and the air rang with the cries of sergeants and corporals marshalling their charges. The famous pavilion had long been stripped of all its cricketing memorabilia, and was converted into

15

offices and classrooms. A large Naafi canteen had been established under the main stand, and it was here we took our lunch. Having taken care to stick together throughout the processing procedures, Michael and I were eventually grouped together into a flight of fifty bodies and marched away to our billet. This proved to be a multi-storeyed block of what had once been luxury flats. The RAF had taken over the building, removed all fittings and furniture, and re-equipped with service beds and lockers. The one-time underground car park was now our cook-house and dining room. We shared a large room with a pleasant young man from a remote corner of Scotland, whose accent I found almost incomprehensible.

I lay abed that night pondering the events of a long day. It was good to feel that one had already made a friend, someone to talk to and to ease the strangeness of new surroundings. I had not yet however accepted that this was a real lasting friendship. Being fairly reserved by nature, I was used to a process of assimilation – a period of gentle probings and gradually shared confidences leading to a slowly deepening relationship. I hadn't yet the experience to realise that service life brings a telescoping of these processes. Often, mere proximity rather than shared interests breeds the common bond; the mutual realisation that we are in this together – us against them. It is without doubt the most important factor in service life. It is, of course, called comradeship.

No doubt my experience the previous night on the midnight train from Manchester helped cause me to reserve judgment on my new friend . . .

I had said my goodbyes on the platform, then managed to gain a corner seat in a compartment full of servicemen. The blackout blinds were drawn on all the windows, and the shaded bulbs shed little light. Two soldiers and an airman had already begun a game of pontoon, using a stack of suitcases as a table. As the train eventually pulled out of the dark cavernous station, the airman improved the interior lighting by the simple expedient of removing a bulb and scraping off its blue paint coating with his penknife.

I found myself casting a critical eye over this airman, a young fellow not much older than me, who was sitting directly opposite. It was warm inside the compartment, and he had already shed his tunic, displaying thick service braces over a crumpled shirt. For a serviceman, his hair was over-long, and his shoes were unshined. Comparing him with the soldier sitting alongside, a Grenadier Guardsman in a crisply-pressed battle-dress, I felt he was letting our service down. Not only that, but as the game progressed he was prone to an occasional outburst of profanity, which had me glowing with embarrassment considering there were two

16

Waafs within earshot in the corridor outside. Later in the game there was some badinage between him and the guardsman regarding their prospective services, and I heard him say:

'Discipline's one thing mate, but bullshit's something else entirely. And when it comes to pure unadulterated bullshit your mob has a lot to answer for.'

I held my breath. I had a momentary expectation of a flurry of fisticuffs as the guardsman upheld the honour of his regiment. I felt quite disappointed when he merely dismissed the remark with a good-natured grin.

Eventually the card game ended, and the soldiers stretched out in repose. The airman looked at me for the first time, and spotted my RAFVR badge. 'Hello,' he said. 'Just called up? What trade are you going in for?'

'I've been accepted for training as an observer,' I replied, stiffly.

'Ah, a flying arse-hole man. Did they tell you about the aircrew chop rate?'

I wished desperately for a suitable reply, something to cut him down to size, but I couldn't think of anything and didn't reply. He didn't pursue the conversation. Instead, he settled down in the corner opposite, closed his eyes, and announced to nobody in particular:

'I'm getting off at Bletchley. If I fall asleep, will someone give me a nudge when we get there.'

I sat there, quietly brooding. What did this scruffy erk know about it all? Flying arse-hole indeed. What a way to describe the observers' brevet, that badge of responsibility and dependability, upon which I had set such store. What the hell did chop rates concern him. What bloody presumption!

I didn't really sleep, but I must have dozed off and on. I opened my eyes as the train juddered to a halt. Outside in the darkness a voice was calling:

'Bletchley. This is Bletchley station. Next stop Euston.' The feckless fellow opposite, and indeed the whole compartment, was fast asleep. I hurriedly leaned over and shook him vigorously.

'Thanks, mate,' he said, grabbing his case and tunic from the rack above. I opened the carriage door for him and he slipped into his tunic. It bore sergeants' stripes on the sleeves, and beneath the air gunners' brevet was the distinctive diagonally-striped ribbon of the Distinguished Flying Medal. As he stepped onto the platform, he turned to me:

'All the best, mate. And Nil Illegitima Carborundum.' He grinned, and translated: 'Don't let the bastards grind you down.' With that he was gone.

17

I was left to brood again, this time on the fact that I had made a fool of myself. In the space of a few seconds I had had to revise completely the first impressions I had formed. Here was a young man, little older than myself, who had already proved himself. A hero, no less, whom I had condemned on the strength of his unpolished shoes and a few harmless expletives. I resolved there and then that in this strange new world I was entering I would have to reserve judgement on anyone I met.

However, the next few weeks left me in no doubt that my chance meeting up with Michael had been fortuitous indeed. His general liveliness and larger than life personality was a great help in easing me into this new life-style. Someone once said that recruit training in the armed forces is a process of disabusing them of any notions that life is fair. I think that just about sums it up. The end product is meant to be the firm establishing of who is in charge, and a reaction of automatic obedience to him. The system only worked to a limited extent with Michael, who never really became submerged in the morass of petty restriction, tight discipline and general bloody harassment.

Most of our time was spent under the sharp eyes of the drill instructors. The corporal in charge of our flight was a cropped-haired ramrod with large jutting ears and the face of a prizefighter. The toecaps of his boots reflected light like twin mirrors, the creases of his trousers looked too knife-like to touch, and the polishing his buttons had sustained had all but worn away their crown and eagle insignia. Michael was the only one of our company who refused to be over-awed. In fact, from the beginning he set out to wage a minor war of wills with our corporal: a war of course which he could not hope to win. Michael's rapier of wit would always be out-weaponed by the big bludgeon of authority. I don't know whether his attitude was a determination to preserve a spark of individuality in a world of regimentation, or merely his inherent liking for getting in the last word. Whatever it was, we were grateful for the light relief he so often provided.

It was strange at first to find ourselves carrying out our military training amid the ambience of a big city, in full view of the public. We did our drilling and marching in the quiet streets of St John's Wood, and took our exercises in the open spaces of Regent's Park. We attended lectures in the Rudolph Steiner Hall, and Morse tests in the Long Room at Lord's. As we marched along the streets, our corporal at the head, and happened to pass a presentable female, Michael from the rear would give a quiet 'Eyes Left' and fifty leering faces would ogle her, to her utter embarrassment. After half an hour's drilling, he would remind our custodian that he was a heavy smoker by calling 'Ready for your fag yet, corporal?' and receive abuse for talking in the ranks. Within minutes

however would come the order 'Halt. Ten minutes break. For a smoke –
dismiss!' To be followed immediately by Michael's *sotto voce* parody
'Non-smokers, through the motions – go!'

Because we drilled in the open streets, and possibly because we were all
embryo officers or NCOs, our drill instructors were not encouraged to
spur us on by the use of oaths or obscenities. In times of stress our corporal
would sometimes call upon the word bastard, but used as an adjective
rather than a personal epithet. Hence such exhortations as 'Swing them
arms higher. Let's have some bastard swank!' In the early days, I recall
his haranguing us all on account of some sloppy drill. He ended,
witheringly, 'Call yourselves the bastard cream . . .'

Michael playfully took the opportunity of taking the words literally.
'We are the bastard cream,' he called.

A roar: 'Who said that?'

'Wasn't it Winston Churchill, corporal?'

A scream: 'Gimme your name and number. You're on a bastard
fizzer!'

He was put on a charge for insolence, and received five days full pack
jankers. Even then, he got his own back by originating an unkind
nickname for the corporal – 'Wingnut', on account of his large protrud-
ing ears. We liked it.

I suppose there was a good measure of youthful hero worship involved
in my relationship with him. He seemed to embody all those qualities I
didn't have myself but wished I had – worldliness, ready wit, confidence
with women and the strength of character to be different. Even in other
ways he stood out in a crowd. He was one of the few to withstand the
various vaccinations and inoculations without any drastic ill effects. And
when we were taken to the clothing stores, he alone emerged in a
smoothly-fitting uniform, unadorned with tailors' chalk. He had that
quality so seldom associated with an eighteen-year-old – style.

He had his faults of course. Certainly a lack of patience, and definitely
a tendency to exaggeration, plus the Londoner's traditional disdain of
anything originating beyond the northern suburbs. He had by this time
taken me under his wing, and professed to be exasperated by my
northern naivety.

'Stone the crows,' he would say. 'You bleeding northerners aren't fit to
be let out alone. Don't they teach you anything up there except how to
make hotpots and black puddings?'

I once asked him why he always seemed compelled to preface the word
north or northerner with the adjective bleeding.

'Because I once promised my mother I would never use really bad
language,' was the reply.

Our free time was restricted, since most evenings were taken up with polishing sessions, picket and guard duties, and occasional punishment fatigues. Weekends however brought welcome relief from routine, and we made the most of them.

One Sunday morning, Hamish, our dour Scottish room-mate, and I accompanied Michael on another sightseeing tour, to prove his point that there was a lot of free entertainment in the city, even on the Sabbath. We watched a demonstration in Trafalgar Square by a lot of earnest civilians, who were enthusiastically demanding 'A Second Front Now' in support of the Russians. We moved on to Hyde Park, where a military band in full regalia were giving a concert. At Speakers' Corner we joined the curious servicemen gathered around an excitable old man in clerical grey, who was telling the world that London's brothels were operating in church-owned property, and what were we doing about it? We ended with a stroll round the back streets of Soho, where black marketeers, pimps and prostitutes abounded. Hamish, who had been brought up in the atmosphere of a strict Presbyterian sect, was spellbound by the amount of sin on display.

Hamish's culture shock was only slightly lessened the following week, when we visited a local music hall to see Michael's favourite entertainer, Max Miller. We crammed ourselves on the shilling benches, way up in the gallery among the other servicemen. The Cheeky Chappie bounced onto the stage, holding aloft his notebooks.

'Come on then,' he leered. 'Which book do you want?'

'The blue book, Maxie,' the audience roared.

'Right, you asked for it.' And we got it. Unremarkable by today's standards perhaps, but to us it was a display of innuendo, double entendre and drawing back from the brink such as we had never heard before. We enjoyed it enormously. Afterwards, Hamish was understood to remark that if the Wee Frees knew how he had spent the evening, they would be praying for his soul.

I was privileged on another occasion to see Michael's technique with the opposite sex. His propounded theory was that although a pilot's wings were the ultimate aphrodisiac as far as the girls were concerned, the cadets' white cap flash wasn't a bad substitute, and should be exploited whenever possible. We had called in a cafe one Saturday for a cup of tea, and were served by an attractive blonde waitress. There followed some mutual banter each time she passed our table. When she finally came to make out our bill, Michael addressed her:

'I suppose you've been told a hundred times that you're a dead ringer for Veronica Lake, except that you're younger and better looking.'

'I'm sure I haven't,' she replied, tossing the long lock of blonde hair from her eyes. Her tone was disdainful, but she remained standing at our table. 'Does that white band in your cap mean that you are training to be an officer?'

'No,' said Michael, 'It means we are still virgins.'

'Oo,' she said, pretending to be shocked. 'You air force boys will say anything.'

'The thing is,' Michael persisted, 'we've been allowed away from the war until midnight tonight. Can we meet you about seven o'clock, and can you bring along your best looking friend for my mate here?'

She could, and she would, and she did. I was in luck. Her friend was another film star – a slinky young version of Hedy Lamarr. We took them to a dance where the floor was ringed with girls, outnumbering the servicemen. As we danced round the hall, girls cut in to excuse us several times, and we had difficulty in maintaining contact with our partners. We thoroughly enjoyed ourselves. Later, we took them home, and engaged in some heavy snogging. We failed to make the midnight deadline back at our billet, and collected three extra fire pickets each, but considered it well worth it.

Within a surprisingly short time we all seemed to have undergone a strange metamorphosis. We had suddenly acquired the look of real airmen, instead of an awkward ungainly rabble. We confidently swung through the streets in unison – a phalanx of swinging arms and stamping feet, buttons gleaming, webbing blancoed and faces aglow with open air freshness. Wingnut marched alongside, in what now seemed like proud approbation. There were positive signs that his attitude towards us was changing.

He had marched us to a nearby cinema, where a special film showing had been laid on. It was a Canadian instructional film, in glorious technicolour, on the evils of venereal diseases. It had such an impact that one of our number fainted during the showing, and afterwards induced us all to thoughts of total celibacy. As we formed up outside, ready to be marched away, Wingnut added his little homily:

'I hope that warns you randy lot to keep away from dirty women. There's no place in the air force for poxed-up pilots.'

'Oh, I don't know,' came Michael's muttered tones. 'They'd make good drill instructers.'

It was only meant to be heard by those in close proximity, but it was heard by us all, including Wingnut. We waited for the explosion, as we looked at his face. Was that the momentary trace of a smile?

'Get fell in, you lot.' Two weeks ago, it would have been five days jankers. No question about it.

Sometimes in the evenings, as we lay on our beds resting our throbbing feet, Michael and I would talk about the future. This extended no further than the realisation of our present ambitions regarding our flying careers. I remember on one occasion discussing news of the RAF's newest bomber, the wooden-framed Mosquito, which carried a crew of only two, could fly faster than a fighter and could reach as far as Berlin carrying a 4,000 pound bomb. This appealed strongly to Michael. He would have me as his observer, and to keep him on a steady path, and together we would become the twin scourges of the Third Reich. It was purely fanciful talk; we both knew that our chances of even meeting again after leaving the recruit centre were remote in the extreme. Eventually came the time for the postings.

I found my name listed, along with fifty other prospective observers (or navigators, as we were henceforth to be known) for initial training at Babbacombe in South Devon. Michael, to his disgust, found he was bound for a similar pilot's course up bleeding north. Before we all left there was a cash collection amongst the flight for Wingnut, strictly against King's Regulations. It was organised by Michael, no less, who assured us that it was the done thing – a thank you for all his efforts to turn us into efficient airmen. We all coughed up a shilling or so, though personally I couldn't help thinking it was rather like asking the early Christians to contribute towards the lions. With a disciple as collector!

I never saw Michael again.

I spent the summer months on ground training at delightful Babbacombe. It was more like a large university campus than an RAF garrison town, with the cadets' white cap flash and blue uniform in lieu of students' cap and gown. It seemed very remote from the war, in spite of the odd occasion when we were visited by a hit-and-run Messerschmitt. I enjoyed my stay immensely. I didn't know it at the time, but it was here I started a love affair with the RAF which would persist throughout the next twenty-seven years of my life as a navigator.

I heard once from Michael. A picture postcard of Scarborough arrived, to say that he was enjoying the course, and to confirm that civilised life existed even so far bleeding north. From there he sailed to Canada for pilot training, and we lost touch.

He never did get his own back on the Germans. It was by mere chance, a long time later, that I heard that he had been killed in a flying accident.

I have always felt that Michael would have gone a long way had he lived. He seemed to have all the qualities the RAF looked for in its leaders – determination, intelligence, aggressiveness, personality. What a terrible waste it all seemed. On occasion, the thought also intrudes that his other qualities – self-confidence, impulsiveness, impatience – may in the end have weighed against him. Do we sow the seeds of our own destruction? Is it all sheer bad luck? Who can say?

I knew him for exactly one month, and that was more than fifty years ago, but I have never forgotten him. I have attended the Rememberance Day service every year since the war. When the poignant words of the Exhortation are spoken, beginning: 'They shall grow not old, as we that are left grow old . . .' who else would I think of but my unforgettable friend Michael?

2

TROOPSHIP

The troop train delivered us right onto the Liverpool dockside itself. As we climbed out and paraded for roll-call, we were swept by a chilling February wind. It brought with it the musty sooty smell of a much bombed city. We gazed up at the ship towering alongside, awed by the sheer bulk of her. We noted the anti-aircraft turrets amidships by the twin funnels, and the large gun at the stern. In place of lifeboats, she carried steel landing-craft slung along the upper decks. She had a worn and weathered look, and gave the impression that she had already seen her share of action in this war. It was our first view of His Majesty's Troopship *Orontes*, former P&O liner, 40,000 ton displacement, and our home-to-be for an unknown duration.

As we prepared to embark, a number of army types gathered at the ship's rails above us, and the whistling and catcalling began. We, of course, were the butt:

'Here come the Brylcreem Boys. Why should England tremble?'

'You won't like it here. Tell your mum to sell the pig and buy you out.'

'Where was the bleeding RAF at Dunkirk?'

We tried to ignore it all as we moved in single file to the gangplanks. We were dressed in greatcoats, full webbing and packs. On our back-packs were strapped the large old fashioned solar topees with which we had recently been issued, giving the odd appearance of a queue of waddling hunchbacks coming aboard.

'I see you've brought your piss-pots with you,' came a loud voice from above, accompanied by more raucous laughter.

I heard Tom Arundele's voice directly behind me: 'My bloody topee goes overboard the first chance I get. Even the pongos are taking the pee out of them.'

It didn't take much to get Tom going, even at the best of times.

Once aboard, we were led along a never-ending sequence of dark stairways and ill-lit corridors, grumbling and stumbling under the weight of our kit.

'How much further down are they taking us?' complained Tom. 'We must be way below the torpedo line by this time. What are we supposed to be – human ballast?'

We came finally into a gloomy mess-deck, almost entirely filled by twenty or so long tables, each with its double row of benches, and the whole securely bolted to the floor.

'Right,' said the NCO who had conducted us, 'I want all these seats filled up. Fourteen bodies to a table, seven on each side. These will be your permanent mess positions for the duration of the voyage.'

We slid obediently onto the benches, Tom and I, along with Ronnie Barstead, ensuring that we remained together on the same mess-table. It was a tight fit. We were so packed together it was difficult to move a limb, and as the packs, bags and greatcoats piled up on the table in front of us the fellows opposite became completely hidden from view.

Morale generally was at a very low ebb. Heaven knows, none of us had ever expected a pleasure cruise, but this was ridiculous. How on earth could three hundred airmen eat, sleep and live in a space about the size of a swimming pool for weeks on end? To add to the claustrophobic atmosphere, all the portholes were closed and shuttered, and there was a constant irritating drone of fan motors. We looked at each other in quiet dismay.

A senior officer now made an appearance at the entrance to the mess-deck.

'Your attention please,' he called. 'My name is Wing Commander Parsons, and I am the Officer Commanding Troops. Welcome aboard.'

We all gazed at him about as bleakly as I imagine Captain Bligh regarded the *Bounty* mutineers when they set him adrift in the longboat. With the suspicion of a smile, he continued:

'I can see from your faces that you are not impressed with your accommodation. Before you start comparing this place to the Black Hole of Calcutta, let me say to you just two things. Firstly, when you have properly stowed away your greatcoats and packs at the far end of the mess-deck, and stashed your personal kit in the racks provided, you'll find there is sufficient room for manoeuvre. Secondly, I have recently been trooping in the *Queen Elizabeth* on the North Atlantic crossing. There, the American troops are sleeping in four-tier bunks in eight hour shifts round the clock, and getting only two meals a day. I have also served recently in the *Mauretania*; it's a lousy ship, and I do mean that literally. Here on *Orontes* you'll get three meals a day – and no bugs. So count your blessings.'

He allowed the low murmur to die down, then continued:

25

'Shortly you'll all be issued with a personal lifejacket, to be worn at all times on the open deck. Lifeboat drill will be carried out daily, as from tomorrow – details on your notice board. Blackout regulations will be rigorously enforced. Anyone found smoking on deck after dark will be locked away for the rest of the voyage. Finally, may I ask you all to refrain from fooling around near the ship's rails. We are forbidden to stop to pick up anyone falling overboard, and drowning isn't a pleasant way to go. For the benefit of anyone who doesn't yet know, your draft will be disembarking in South Africa.'

We had of course long since guessed our destination, though we had never been told so in as many words. Under the auspices of the Empire Air Training Scheme, our navigator training would be carried out in the clearer skies of Canada or South Africa, and the issue to us of full tropical kit at the embarkation unit told us which one it was to be.

It was there, at Blackpool, that Tom, Ronnie and I had first been thrown together. It had come about in the usual impersonal manner by our service numbers coming in sequence on the list of draftees, and accordingly being detailed to share a billet in Mrs Eckersley's back street boarding house. On the face of it, we hadn't a lot in common. Ronnie was that rarity in our ranks, a regular and voluntary church-goer, who, rather paradoxically, was also handy with his fists and had a keen eye for the girls. In looks and manner he was the sort of young man any mother would be delighted for her daughter to bring home. Tom was a good deal less well favoured. A chronic grumbler, who was also determinedly atheistic and decidedly bolshie, his general belligerence tended to hide the good-natured fellow underneath. His down-to-earth humour however was always to the fore. My own qualities must have been quite compatible, since the three of us had formed a close friendship right from the start.

Dear Mrs Eckersley was almost a comic postcard caricature of a seaside landlady, with her long sharp nose, with tongue to match, and her hair tied up in a large bun. In our short stay with her she mothered us, smothered us, swore at us and generally straightened us out as well as any NCO could have done. She would harangue us for coming home late or tiddly, or both, then spend an hour darning our socks. She had a husband, whom we never saw. He lived a strange troglodytic existence down in the basement. He was activated by instructions from his wife shouted down the shaft of the dumb waiter, from whence he served up well-presented meals three times daily. On the day we finally left we had shouted down to him our thanks and goodbyes, and had heard a faint 'Good luck, lads,' in response – proving that he really existed.

As the Commanding Officer had predicted, the scene on our mess-deck changed quite remarkably in the next few hours. Most of our kit was now stowed away round the periphery, and we ourselves stripped down to slacks and sweaters. Many of us were reclining in hammocks slung from hooks in the ceiling, or lying on blankets on the floor. The congestion which had so depressed us now no longer seemed any great problem. In true service fashion we were settling in, making do. We were discovering, as countless prisoners or refugees had done before us, that man can live in a surprisingly confined space if he has to.

Creature comforts were now coming our way. A large carton of books arrived from the ship's library, and an even more welcome supply of corned beef sandwiches and hot sweet cocoa from the galley. Later, I managed to clamber into my hammock, prepared to renew acquaintances with Mr Pickwick and company, and surveyed the scene around me. Everyone seemed to be happily engaged, chatting, reading, writing, cardplaying. The soft glow of the lights made everything appear warm and cosy. It wasn't going to be bad after all.

Early next morning we sensed the ship's movement, and assumed we were on our way. We had merely been towed away from the dockside to the middle of the Mersey estuary, where we dropped anchor. A crew member told me we were now awaiting the convoy to form up, and our escort to arrive. We could be here a week.

We were there in fact for three days, with time hanging heavily on our hands. We were joined, one by one, by other troop-carrying ships of varying sizes. About an hour before dusk on the third day, a general vibration of the decks denoted our engine start-up. Soon afterwards, as we all rushed on deck, we moved slowly out to sea, eight ships in two columns line astern. Nobody waved us off, no military bands played; just a cacophony of ships' sirens and a screeching of seagulls. I couldn't help thinking about my home and family, especially my mother. Her only brother had been lost at sea in 1915 on his way to the Dardanelles: he had been exactly the same age then as I was now. How she would worry until I was able to write home at the end of the voyage.

By the next day the convoy had become established. Our original company had grown to more than twenty ships – troopers, merchantmen, tankers and escorts. The latter, as far as we could see, consisted of five destroyers and a smaller corvette. It was difficult to keep track of them as they fussed about on the perimeter of the convoy at about twice its speed. They were beautifully sleek craft, light grey in colour, and looked very business-like and reassuring.

Eventually the last spit of land on our port side faded behind us. This I decided, with reference to my atlas, was Malin Head, the northernmost headland of Ireland. We were now heading westwards into the open

27

Atlantic, and the convoy seemed to be spreading out in all directions. The sea was quite calm, and we all felt that we had already gained our sea legs. As I looked around, I tried hard not to associate the occasional white cap on the waves with the ripple from the periscope of a shadowing U-Boat.

The daily routine on board was also by now well established. One could rise as early or as late as one wished. All meals were served at our mess-tables. Two airmen, by roster from each table, collected the food in metal containers from the galley, and were responsible for serving it up to their mess-mates. This process was most vigorously scrutinised by us all, for whatever the quality of the grub the quantity was certainly a good deal less than we had hoped for. Bread, for instance, was rationed to four slices per day per man. The fellow who got the smallest baked potato had to be compensated with the largest spoonful of vegetables, and fourteen pairs of eyes were there to see fair play.

Sometime during the morning the alarm bells would sound for lifeboat drill; the set target time for everyone to scramble to their boat stations was four minutes, and this was easily achieved by the third day out.

Later, each mess-deck would be inspected for general cleanliness. Apart from an occasional lecture or organised PT exercise, the rest of the long day was our own. The more energetic amongst us would spend an hour jogging on one of the promenade decks cleared for the purpose, but most of us would settle down to reading, yarning, dozing or card-playing.

The congestion and discomfort of the mess-decks was equally evident on the open decks. If the weather was fine, hundreds of huddled bodies would cover every inch of hard deck board, since there was no other form of seating available. During the voyage, we would all have our various fantasies. No doubt these would focus on such delights as juicy steaks, foaming pints of beer or nubile nymphomaniacs; in my own case, I grew to crave the simple comfort of a soft padded armchair, or the absolute luxury of a well-sprung mattress.

By my estimate, we had aboard something like 4000 troops; the army were in the majority, but there was also a large contingent of RAF ground staff, and a sprinkling of naval personnel. The officers were berthed way above us, and beyond our ken. There wasn't a single woman on board. Most were going as reinforcements for the desert campaign in North Africa, sailing the longer but safer way via the Cape and Suez. In view of the catcalling which had greeted us aircrew cadets on embarkation, I had assumed that there would be a good deal of inter-service friction, but this did not prove to be the case. Everyone in fact was surprisingly well-behaved and self-disciplined. I learned quite a lot in my first week at sea.

I found, for instance, that a convoy is not the closely bound unit I had imagined it to be. Sometimes, if the visibility was not very good, it became difficult to spot any of our companions. I was told that a convoy such as ours could well occupy more than 400 square miles of ocean. I discovered too that whenever one of our destroyer escorts came into close view, soldier and airman alike gave an almost involuntary prayer:

'Thank God we've got a Navy!'

On a more personal note, I learned that the difference between a fresh-water and a salt-water shower was well worth the effort of rising before 0700 hours rather than later. I also shattered the myth that lying in a hammock is a comfortable way of spending the night. The agility and effort needed to climb in, the inhibitions caused by a fear of falling out, and the aches and pains it induced soon had me looking for alternative sleeping arrangements. I found myself a sheltered niche in the adjacent covered deck where I could settle down on my blankets surrounded by a network of steam pipes. There I was as warm and cosy as a fieldmouse in its nest amongst the straw.

The comparative serenity of our day-to-day existence was to be rudely shattered on our sixth day out. Early that morning, without any warning, we ran into a North Atlantic gale of extreme severity.

About 0200 hours I awakened to find myself rolling off my blankets as the deck took on an alarming tilt, before rolling me back in the opposite direction. The whole ship's structure seemed to be creaking and groaning in agony, and every few moments the deck shuddered violently as though the propellers were clean out of the water. In the nerve-tingling moment when the roll was at its peak, the loud crash of breaking crockery in the mess-decks could be heard. The stomach-churning pitching and rolling was intensifying by the minute. Further sleep was impossible: it was a case of hanging on, literally and figuratively, until daylight.

At first light I made my way back to the mess-deck. I was confronted by a scene which immediately put me in mind of a picture I had once seen by the allegorical painter Bosch – his representation of Hell!

The dim lighting enhanced the normal sepulchral air, making the suspended hammocks look like so many swinging shrouds. From each of them protruded nerveless limbs and pallid faces bearing expressions of utter misery. The floor was wet with sea-water, seeped through the portholes, and slippery with vomit, lying in malodorous pools beneath the hammocks. Broken plates and mugs were everywhere, with fallen salt

29

and pepper pots adding their contents to the general mess. Above the ship's noises came the sound of desperate retchings, and the overpowering stench of wet blankets and sour vomit.

I retreated hastily to gain fresh air on deck, but was unable to gain access due to the howling wind and blinding spray. Goodness knows what problems the commodore of the convoy was experiencing, trying to control his flock under such conditions. As for any U-Boats in the vicinity, they would be lying many fathoms deep, and would stay there if they had any sense.

For myself, I was happy to find that I was weathering the storm far better than I could have expected. I had survived so far without any feelings of the seasickness which had so stricken most of the others. I took this as an indication that I would not be particularly troubled by airsickness when I started my flying training.

The gale abated in the afternoon, and those of us who were fit enough began the long nauseous task of swabbing out the mess-deck, and generally cleaning up and drying out the place.

The cooks in the galley must have had their own problems. It was late evening before the first meal of the day became available. Fourteen stiff pieces of fried fish arrived at our table.

Ronnie had been particularly severely seasick, and was still confined to his hammock. In addition to his malady he had to bear the unsufferable smugness of those of us who were unafflicted. I offered him a portion of fish, and he nearly threw up over me.

'Take it away,' he groaned. 'And stuff it.'

'If it's any consolation,' I said brightly, 'most of the Navy lads in the next mess are as ill as you.'

'It isn't. Now go away, and let me die with dignity.'

The fourteen pieces of fish were not wasted. There were four of us on our table still capable of eating, and it worked out at three and a half pieces each. It was the first time I felt full since we boarded.

Within the next day or so the weather improved dramatically, and the casualties recovered likewise.

It was at about this time that I lost my comfortable sleeping spot. An inspection team from the ship's crew found me, and turfed me out. 'If one of those steam pipes was to spring a leak,' said the officer, 'you would have your flesh scalded off your bones. Find yourself somewhere else to kip.' I settled for the floor under our mess table.

We were all of us aware that our convoy, with its preponderance of troopships, would make a prime target for the Germans, especially at this particular time when their U-Boats were operating so successfully in the Atlantic. It was something one tried to put at the back of one's mind, whilst making sure that one's life-jacket was kept within grabbing distance at all times.

It was during our second week at sea that the first bit of excitement occurred. One of the destroyers on our beam was joined by two others, and the three of them proceeded to lay a pattern of depth charges. Great plumes of water arose in their wakes, as we all watched spellbound. The convoy sailed on, without any word of explanation from the ship's loudspeaker, and the escorts later rejoined us. Once more we turned to each other and thanked God we had a Navy.

The next incident was a sudden announcement:

'All troops clear the open decks. Gun crews close up. Possibility of air attack.'

It was a false alarm. The speck on the horizon proved to be a Coastal Command Sunderland flying boat, who winked his Aldis lamp before joining the convoy on close escort duty. I could picture the navigator in his commodious cabin busy drawing up his creeping line ahead patrol pattern, and how I envied him.

It was part of my routine each night before turning in to spend a few minutes on deck searching the clear northern sky for the Pole Star. I had learned to estimate its altitude quite accurately, and knew that this figure corresponded to our own latitude. This night my estimated latitude placed us on the same parallel as Lisbon in Portugal. As if to confirm it, the very next day part of the convoy turned eastwards, accompanied by a couple of destroyers which had just rendezvoused with us. They were on their way to Gibraltar, our Navy neighbours assured us, where there would be shore leave and night life. We meantime carried on with our southerly heading, with the likelihood of an eventual fuel stop at Freetown in Sierra Leone, where there would be neither.

As the weather grew warmer, our quality of life improved in various ways. For one thing, we could spend more time on the open deck, which, though dreadfully crowded, was infinitely preferable to the stuffy mess-decks. Another factor was more psychological: our fears of ending up in the icy water after a torpedo attack receded in proportion to the rapid increase in the temperature. Also, the ship's entertainment committee now came into their own, organising welcome open-air diversions like housey-housey sessions, quiz competitions and musical interludes. We aircrew cadets were sometimes invited to the officers' lounge on the top deck for general interest talks by whoever could be inveigled into giving them. I recall an Australian airgunner giving a modest account of his flying tour in the turret of a Wellington bomber, an army lieutenant telling us of life in a tank in the Western Desert, and a Royal Navy commander giving us an eye-witness report on the sinking of the *Bismark*.

There came the time when the weather was considered hot enough for the order to be given for the troops to stow away their normal uniforms and turn out in their issued tropical kit. It became a day of strange metamorphosis. What had been perfectly normal-looking military contingents were now transformed into an ill-assorted rabble in badly fitting khaki drill. Long confinement in kitbags had ensured that shirts had lost any crispness they might once have had, and slacks were creased from waist to hem. Small men sported baggy shorts hanging below their kneecaps, and tall ones appeared as leggy overgrown Boy Scouts, their white knees contrasting with their sunburnt faces. Those who had still retained their bulky topees merely added to this ill-assortment. Tom looked around the crowded deck and said for us all:

'What chance has the Afrika Korps against us lot? They'll die laughing.'

But as we had found when first boarding the ship, first impressions were not lasting ones. By the end of the voyage we had got our knees brown, and had sufficiently stitched, laundered and pressed our new rigout as to have restored some semblance of military smartness and uniformity.

On the morning of the sixteenth day at sea I went up on deck and noted that we were now heading approximately eastwards. Later we got our first glimpse of Africa, the cloud-tipped mountains behind the port of Freetown towards which we were now steering. A few hours later we had moved through the harbour boom, and were moored about a mile from the shore. We had been told that the area was extremely unhealthy, with malaria and yellow fever endemic, and nobody would be allowed ashore.

From where we were it all looked clean and colourful. After two weeks with nothing to look at except the dull grey seascape, our eyes had become positively starved of colour; it was a pleasure to feast them on the panoramic view of palm-fringed golden sands and the verdant slopes behind, speckled with white thatch-roofed huts.

We watched the approach of a fleet of small cigar-shaped bumboats, laden with fruit. We had been warned that it was a military offence to buy from these native vendors due to the risk of contamination, but one or two of the troops succumbed to temptation. After all, none of us had even seen a banana for three years. It proved a bad bargain for the customers. The bananas were not cheap at half a crown a bunch, payable in advance, and when the fruit came aboard it was immediately pounced on by the military police and thrown into the sea. It was not long before the fruit vendors left to try their luck with other ships at anchor.

We soon had another diversion. Our visitor was an ebony-black character wearing a battered top hat and waving a small Union Jack, who arrived in his little boat accompanied by two small black boys.

It would be impossible to reproduce his fractured English in print, but his greeting to us went something like this:

'Hello, soldiers and fly-force boys in blue khaki. Me British subject also. Speak good English. Oh yes. Bloody hell, bugger me, sod off. My name Mister Blackout. Me bring you good sing song. You throw me pennies and cigarettes. You all very good men. You win the war.'

With that, he launched into his version of *Kiss Me Goodnight Sergeant-Major*. It took several bars before we could recognise either the words or the tune.

This unexpected entertainment went down well with the troops at the ship's rails, and a hail of copper descended towards his boat. Most of the coins missed their target and fell into the sea. This was where the two youngsters got into the act. Quick as a flash, like a pair of little black dolphins, they were into the water, emerging with huge white-toothed grins and fistfuls of copper. More coins rained down, and hardly one reached the seabed. We received an encore from Mister Blackout – it might have been *Bless 'em All*.

For three uncomfortable days we sweated it out in the equatorial heat whilst the convoy was refuelled. Our portholes were opened up for the first time, but without the ship's movement there was no air circulation. It was too hot to sit on deck, and too sticky to rest below. We found whatever shade we could, looking and feeling as limp as our sweat-soaked shirts.

There came a pleasant interlude on our last night in harbour when a Grand Variety Show, involving volunteer entertainers, was staged on the flood-lit forward deck. A wooden stage was rigged up, with a backdrop of flags and fairy lights, featuring a piano and an eight-piece orchestra. Every inch of deck space was taken up by the audience, with others clinging to the rigging, perched on the booms and hanging from the lifeboat stations. A most welcome off-shore breeze brought to us the musky scent of Africa.

The show opened with a high-kicking chorus line of painted and padded crew members, with appropriate catcalls from the troops. There followed some blue comedy patter from an RAF corporal, a selection of

Australian songs from the Aussie aircrew contingent, knockabout comedy from two naval Laurel and Hardy lookalikes, and a very professional act from an army officer amateur magician. I joined in the tumultuous applause which followed every turn – which was quite a feat considering I was clinging to a steel ladder on the main mast about thirty feet above the deck. The show ended with community singing. I think we were already a little homesick, with most of the troops having no idea when they would see their homes again, and as the final strains of *Land of Hope and Glory* rang out over the water there was many a damp eye I can assure you.

The following morning we upped anchor and moved off in single file out of the harbour, on the last stage of our voyage. The portholes were closed and secured, and blackout regulations resumed. The eighteen-knot breeze generated by the ship's movement was very welcome. We noted that the escort had now been augmented by a Royal Navy cruiser; it was boldly camouflaged in green, blue and grey, and carried its own amphibious plane. It reminded us that there was still a war on.

The ship's speaker announced that in these equatorial regions sleeping on the open decks would be allowed. That night I moved my blankets yet again to the stern deck, and for the first time in my life lay down to sleep without a roof over my head. I looked up at the stars, which at sea always appear brighter and more significant. Polaris of course had long since disappeared from our skies; new stars and constellations were above, some of them familiar from my study of the star charts in our navigators' manual. The stern was crowded, but I slept soundly, and was awakened in the morning by the warning shouts of the seamen waiting to hose down the deck.

A mind-numbing boredom was now the chief factor in our circum-scribed existence. We had read most of the available reading matter, the card schools had lost their appeal, the food was dull and we felt shut off from the rest of the world. We had been at sea more than three weeks, with the daunting prospect of a similar period before we disembarked. Tom, as usual, summed it up when it was announced that to save time later we could hand in any letters for home, to be censored by the officers.

'Censored? What the hell is there to censor? All I've seen for the last month is seawater. And all I've got to write about is my bowel movements and my wet dream!'

However, the weather was becoming very pleasant as we moved away from the equator. Tom, Ronnie and I took to spending the balmy evenings in a quiet corner of the open deck. We observed such phenomena as shoals of flying fish, and, after dark, the startling phosphorescence in the ship's wake. Here we had arguments and discussions of great profundity. There is a convention in the services that though one may discuss one's intimate personal details or sex life, it is pretty bad form to offer a religious or political conviction. This convention we ignored completely, and many a ding-dong we had. I seemed to be the man in the middle, the one who held the balance of power in the arguments. For instance, Tom would hold that the most significant feature of the war was the Anglo-Russian alliance, whilst I would side with Ronnie that this was merely a freak of circumstances which would most likely fail to outlast the war. Then again I would find myself, as a lapsed church-goer, in support of Tom against some item of religious dogma propounded by Ronnie. We sometimes generated some heat, but never any animosity. And it all helped to pass the time away.

On some things we were in full agreement. One evening, for instance, we discussed the burial at sea we had witnessed earlier that day. A member of the ship's crew had collapsed and died soon after we had left Freetown, and his shrouded body had been committed to the sea by his crewmates. We all thought it an impressive ceremony, for different reasons. Ronnie found the simple service, conducted by the ship's master, appealed to his Noncomformist beliefs; Tom liked its sincerity and lack of religious trimmings; and I thought the whole thing entirely fitting and sensibly pragmatic.

Another surefire means of passing an hour or two was by joining the queue for the ship's canteen. This started to form a couple of hours before opening time, and would develop along passageways and up stairways until it stretched along the upper deck. Apart from the cigarette ration, there was always a glorious uncertainty as to what one was queueing for. On a good day there might be a chocolate bar or a tin of peaches on offer. On a bad day, one might come away bearing a bottle of Blanco or a tin of boot polish.

There was also an adjoining wet canteen, where the queue was usually even longer. Here one could purchase fourpennyworth of tepid beer – bring your own mug. If you wanted a refill, then you returned to the end of the queue – thus providing an effective damper against any thoughts of bacchanalian excess.

One afternoon, the committee came up with their final triumph of organised entertainment – an interservice boxing tournament held on the open deck before a packed audience. There were eight bouts arranged, each one Army versus Royal Air Force, with the protagonists in PT vests and shorts and coloured sashes to denote their service. Each bout proved to be an unscientific but vastly entertaining slogging match,

35

urged on by a partisan crowd. I'm sure they were relieving the frustrations and boredom of the long voyage as they tore into each other. The highlight was a sensational simultaneous knock-out by two heavyweights, which we thought was hilarious. Of the remaining seven bouts, the RAF won six, which delighted us. It helped to counter-balance the image the army always held of the RAF, the Brylcreem image.

Life went on, with each day exactly the same as the previous one. Conversation had long since lagged; the only new talking point was that the canteen had now run out of English cigarettes, though fortunately ample supplies of South African brands were available. We now had to get used to varieties like Springbok, Gold Leaf and C to C; the latter initials apparently stood for Cape to Cairo, which some wit soon dubbed Camel to Consumer. The majority of us were moderate smokers, and the loss of our cigarette ration would have sunk our morale to rock bottom. Smoking also helped curb our appetites during this time of restricted food rations.

Great excitement next morning, with a distant smudge of land discernible on our port quarter. Some hours later, a large alteration of course signified that we were rounding the Cape, where the waters of the Atlantic and the Indian Ocean meet. The flat plateau of Table Mountain became recognisable on the horizon as half a dozen ships left the convoy and headed north for Capetown. The rest of us sailed on, north-easterly. Our destination, we were now told, was Durban.

Three days later, exactly six weeks after boarding, we awoke to find in view Durban's impressive modern skyline, framed by dark green hills and fair-weather cumulus. The whole ship's complement massed on deck as we slowly nosed into the harbour, and eventually moored alongside a large landing stage.

Now, we stand with the hot sun on our faces, and the smell of over-ripe fruit borne in by the land breeze into our nostrils, taking stock of the colourful dockside ambience. There is an awesome contrast between this place and the bleak, blitzed and blacked-out port from whence we sailed. Above the bustle and clamour of the quayside I can hear the black dock workers soliciting us for cigarettes, and the small Indian boys offering for sale their trays of sweets and nuts and biscuits:

'How much, Johnny?'

'One ticky, sah.'

'How much is that?'

'Three English pennies, sah.'

We have learned our first peculiarly South African word – 'ticky', meaning a tiny threepenny coin.

There is a member of the ship's crew with us at the rails. 'Look out for the Lady in White,' he tells us. 'She'll be along any minute.'

'Who is the Lady in White?' we ask.

'Nobody knows exactly who she is. All we know is that whenever a troopship arrives at Durban she comes onto the dockside to greet the boys with a song. Good voice too. She'll be along, she never misses.'

He is right. Within minutes of our tying up a chauffeur-driven car arrives at the quayside, and out steps a matronly figure in a long white dress and picture hat. She begins to sing to us through a megaphone, in a strong clear voice: *Rule Britannia*, followed by *We'll Meet Again*.

There is total silence until she finishes. Then the troops respond with cheers and whistles, and the ship's siren blasts an acknowedgement. She waves to us all, blows a kiss, and departs as quickly as she had arrived.

There follows a buzz of conversation as we discuss our unknown songster and this novel introduction. Whether we see it in the context of well-wisher's greeting, a touch of friendly unorthodoxy or a bit of Hollywood-style razzmatazz, the message has come across loud and clear:

'Welcome to South Africa!'

3

A QUESTION OF COLOUR

L ong before the time came to set foot on South African soil, we had received a suitable briefing. The Officer Commanding Troops had visited our mess-deck to talk to the aircrew cadets, rather like a fond father addressing his young son before his first holiday away from parental control. His long and instructive talk may be summarised thus:

'You will soon be living, for the first time in your lives, in a multi-racial society, with all that this implies. The Union of South Africa is a self-governing dominion of the British Empire, but in fact among the white population the British are outnumbered by the Afrikaners – descendants of the early Dutch settlers. The older generation fought in the Boer War, and not all of them support Britain's war aims, in spite of the efforts of Prime Minister Jan Smuts – who, incidentally, is very much respected by both communities. At times you may encounter people who are openly hostile to you. I should mention, however, that although there is no conscription a very large number of South Africans, including a large percentage of Afrikaners, have volunteered for service, and are at present fighting in North Africa. The people here are extremely proud of their efforts.

'The important thing out here is that the total white population is out-numbered four or five to one by the coloureds and blacks. A colour bar, enforceable by law, is operated, and you will be expected to conform to its rules. This includes no consorting with black or coloured women, and whilst in Durban avoiding the shebeens – illegal native drinking dens. You will find that all the places you will be frequenting – bars, clubs, cinemas, etc, are all barred to blacks; even park benches are labelled Europeans Only. The black people are called many things – natives, Bantu, Kaffirs – but the word nigger should never be used: it is offensive.

'In spite of what we may consider some strange attitudes, the South Africans are amongst the most hospitable people in the world, and their country itself is beautiful. Behave yourselves, and I am sure you will have a most enjoyable stay here. Perhaps we will meet again next year when many of you will be returning home. Good luck.'

Afterwards, the three of us had discussed the talk at some length, especially the part concerning the colour bar. Tom made his position clear at once, his egalitarian instincts already aroused.

'I'm on the side of the blacks,' he said. 'They're exploited something shameful. As far as I'm concerned they can stick their colour bar, or any other discriminations they expect us to go along with.'

Then Tom always saw things in black and white – no pun intended. For myself, I felt that I knew so little about the country I should reserve judgement. What did I know about South Africans other than that they produced gold, grew fruit in abundance and fielded formidable rugby and cricket teams? I knew even less about black men. In fact, until reaching Freetown I had been one of the many who had never even met a black person. To the average insular Englishman of those days, blacks were people portrayed in countless films as either spear-carrying savages in the jungle or comical servants on the American domestic scene. Ronnie was inclined to agree with me that since we were here by kind invitation of the South African government, it was not up to us to try to undermine their system.

We disembarked in the late afternoon, spruced up in our khaki tunics, shorts and full webbing, and grateful beyond measure to be throwing off the confines of the troopship at last. We boarded a dockside train for the short journey to the Imperial Forces Transit Camp at Clairwood, a few miles from the city. Tom started his policy of fraternising with the natives by tossing cigarettes to the eager black dock labourers, and by over-tipping the young Indian vendors.

As it turned out, there was little more comfort on offer at Clairwood than we had experienced on board ship, as scores of thousands of allied troops will recall. The camp was a vast complex of open-sided brick huts and cookhouses, with a pervading sickly smell from a large neighbouring jam factory. We slept on the concrete floors, and took our ablutions in the open air. The toilets consisted of a series of round holes in a strip of concrete which covered a channel of running water; part of the morning ritual was to watch the frequent ripples of rising bottoms as balls of burning newspapers were playfully launched upstream!

Conditions on camp were of no great concern to us, since we spent almost all of our spare time in Durban, this splendid city long accustomed to catering for the requirements of the Navy and the troops from the convoys.

It would be difficult to over-exaggerate the impact Durban had on young men arriving after a long uncomfortable journey from cold, rationed and war-worn Britain. It was like reaching some semitropical Shangri-la. It had everything. Add to the natural charm of its wide tree-lined streets and golden beaches the bright lights, the well-stocked shops, cool bars, unlimited food, the pretty girls – and those wonderful servicemens' clubs. Run by such worthy organisations as the YMCA, Toc H, the Salvation Army and the Navy League, they vied with each other in the first-class facilities they offered. A shilling would buy a man-sized mixed grill and fruit salad, served with a smile by a young lady volunteer. The clubs offered baths, libraries, games rooms, dances and rest rooms; a notice board listed names and addresses offering hospitality and home comforts. Nothing seemed to be too much trouble.

A port which offered shore leave to untold thousands of troops of all nations bound for the war zones of North Africa and the Far East was bound to have its upsets. Not all the visitors were in search of tea and sympathy; drunkenness, assaults and street fights were sometimes part of the scene. The Australian soldiers in particular were prone to demonstrating their fighting capabilities before arriving at the desert. In spite of all this, Durban always seemed to cope. When I read that the island of Malta had been awarded the George Cross for the gallantry of its people, I thought that perhaps a modest mention in despatches might have been in order for the citizens of Durban, for efforts beyond the call of duty!

There seemed at this time to be a blockage in the pipeline to the air training schools, so our leisured life at Durban continued. We saw little of Ronnie these days. He had gone to a Sunday morning church service soon after our arrival, and seemed to have been adopted by a wealthy family he had met there. The attractive blonde daughter usually picked him up in her car after morning roll-call, and returned him in the evening.

Tom and I also experienced an example of the general goodwill towards us in this city where the British influence was strong. We were stopped on the street by an elderly lady, who insisted that we accompanied her home for dinner. Her son, it turned out, was a padre in the South African army who had recently been captured by the Germans in Libya. By a strange coincidence he had served before the war as curate of a parish near my home in Lancashire. We had a lovely dinner, and spent a pleasant evening talking and listening to records, with Tom on his best behaviour. It wasn't until we were on our way back to camp that he began to philosophise:

> 'Funny old world, isn't it? A god-fearing guy like Ronnie goes out and ends up with a millionaire's sexy daughter; you and I go out and we're

picked up by a vicar's elderly mother. We must be going wrong somewhere.'

I resolved to make the most of our extended stay in Durban by
seeing everything I possibly could of this fascinating country. I visited
most of the splendid beaches in the area, where the giant breakers
made for invigorating sea bathing.

One weekend I went by train to visit a native reserve, situated in the
picturesque Valley of a Thousand Hills. I wandered round the kraals
viewing the tribal life of black Africa on display. Just before nightfall I
returned alone to the railway halt to find that I had just missed the
Durban train, and had four hours to wait for the next one. Fortunately
there was a single small hotel for whites, situated on a nearby hilltop,
and to this I made my way in the darkness. There appeared to be no
residents, and I found myself to be the only customer in the small bar.
The black barman had a poor command of English, but indicated to
me that the bar did not stock beer; there was however a good selection
of the national drink, brandy. This, moreover, came in a variety of
flavours – lemon, cherry, apricot, ginger and orange, among others.
Eventually, out of curiosity and boredom, I began to sample a
selection. They all tasted innocuous enough, like strong fruit cor-
dials. It later seemed a good idea to sample every type on display.

At some stage of the evening, conscious memory went into abeyance. My state of complete mental oblivion continued until three
o'clock the following day. At that time I awoke, with a headache
which threatened to split my cranium, to find myself lying on the floor
in the non-European compartment of a still and empty train. I could
have been anywhere between Capetown and Mozambique. In fact, as
I found to my intense relief, I was in the railway sidings behind
Durban station. I checked my identity card and wallet, and found
them both intact. To this day, I don't know whether I was guided to
the train by the kindly hand of providence, or whether the black
barman saw me aboard, fearful lest he be blamed for my sorry state.
Anyway, I learned my lesson: it was the first and last time in my career
that I was every incapacitated through drink.

Shortly afterwards, about a hundred of us were informed that we
were to be posted the following day to No. 48 Airschool at East
London, Cape Province, where our navigator training would be
resumed in earnest. Not before time. It was now many months since
our initial training course at Babbacombe had ended, and some of our
learning already seemed gone beyond recall. Our new station was only
some three hundred miles down the coast, but due to the barrier of the

Drakensberg Mountains lying parallel to the coastline, the train journey would occupy three days.

So it proved, but we travelled in a style to which we had long been unaccustomed. The South Africans were justly proud of their railways, staffed mainly by Afrikaners – bilingual like most of the white population – and we could soon see why. The train had dining cars and bars, with an observation coach at the rear; each compartment had comfortable pull-down bunks for sleeping, and the washrooms had soft towels and scented soaps. The food was first class, served by efficient waiters. It could not possibly have been further removed from the old-fashioned troop train image – '*40 hommes/20 chevaux.*'

Some of the scenery was spectacular, particularly when winding our way through the Drakensbergs. Steep wooded slopes, deep ravines and leaping cataracts falling hundreds of feet; a sinuous track, with the rear of the train sometimes doubling back directly opposite our window; and the whole scene dramatically highlighted by jagged flashes of lightning as we ran into a tropical rainstorm. Later came the open grasslands of the veldt, hundreds of miles of it, dotted with an occasional homestead; small townships clustered round the railway halts, for all the world like the background of a wild west film.

No. 48 Airschool proved to be a large combined Royal Air Force and South African Air Force base, with extensive white barrack huts, parade grounds and sports fields. The CO was an RAF group captain, with a SAAF major as his second in command. The course was to be non-flying, and of fourteen weeks duration. After our long spell of idleness, we were to be flung in at the deep end, with a six-day working week, two evenings of compulsory lectures and two more voluntary study evenings. An exam failure in any subject would mean an end to the course, and a posting away to God knows where. The subjects previously studied at the Initial Training Wing would be enlarged upon, but the emphasis would be on navigational procedures and the air plot.

Perhaps at this stage I might be allowed to indulge in a paragraph concerning the technicalities of the navigators' job.

In those wartime days, the air navigational problem could be expressed quite simply in one word – wind. As anyone who has ever observed a light aircraft flying in a crosswind will testify, an aeroplane does not necessarily fly in the direction in which it is pointed. It drifts away from its heading by an amount dependent on the wind speed and direction. Unless the navigator could detect this wind, and apply a compensating correction to the heading, very large navigational and

42

timing errors would accrue. The navigator knew the aircraft's heading from the compass, and its airspeed from the airspeed indicator dial, so it was possible to plot these values continuously on a chart. At any time, therefore, he could plot a position on the chart where the aircraft would be if no wind was affecting it: in other words, an 'air position'. If he was also able to fix the aircraft's actual position at this particular time, the difference between the two positions represented the wind effect. It was a relatively simply matter then to calculate a wind for future use, expressed in direction and speed; for example, 270/25 knots. The tricky bit was in trying to actually fix the aircraft's position. The easiest way was by identifying a feature on the ground directly below by reference to a topographical map. This of course was not often possible, in which case other means had to be employed. A series of visual compass bearings on a known distant landmark, bearings taken on a radio beacon whose position was plotted on the chart, and sextant altitudes of heavenly bodies converted to position lines on the chart were the most usual means. It called for accuracy and judgement. The whole business I found always challenging, and certainly never less than interesting.

The navigational plot leaned itself readily to the classroom. Simulated flying exercises, known for some reason as 'gropes', we carried out regularly, with the required information of speeds, headings, bearings and fixes fed to us by the instructor as necessary. Later in the course, we found that some sadist had introduced refinements to these exercises. These included headphone interference and simulated flak bursts to teach us that we would eventually be plotting in less than ideal conditions, and a clock that moved through an hour in forty minutes to show that time is not on the side of the navigator.

There came the time of the exams. Five of our number failed, and were duly despatched. For the rest of us there was a week's leave, before posting to our flying training school.

I took the opportunity of accepting hospitality freely offered by the South Africans. My own particular host was a farmer living in the hills some fifty miles inland, who must have led an incredibly lonely life. A widower, he lived in his large farmhouse with two native servants, his nearest neighbour more than ten miles away. His native farmworkers lived in a collection of round mud huts nearby, and tended the maize fields with oxen-drawn ploughs. Like most lonely people, Mr Newey was an avid talker, given the company. I was surprised to hear that he had been a captain in the Coldstream Guards during the last war, serving in France. He had obviously been a man of some social standing, and it was difficult to reconcile this with his presence in this remote outback.

We got on well together, and I was given free rein on the farm, occupying myself pleasantly enough in various ways. One day I spent making a pen and ink sketch of the farmstead, which I presented to my host. Another day was spent on a long trek hunting jackals, armed with a .22 rifle. Nothing materialised, rather fortunately I thought, since I wouldn't have known a jackal from a farm dog. On my last day, the farmer gave me the rifle and suggested I tried shooting dassies – squirrel-like creatures living in holes on a nearby rock face. I duly expended the dozen bullets he had given me and reported back.

'I see you didn't manage to bag any of them,' said Mr Newey. 'Tricky little creatures, aren't they?'

'Oh yes,' I replied. 'I must have got about eight of them altogether.' He looked at me in disbelief: 'What have you done with them?'

'They're scattered on ledges all over the place. You said they were vermin, so I just left them.'

'So they are, but it's a pity you didn't bring some back with you. My Kaffirs consider them a delicacy – a nice change from their mealies.'

'Well,' I said, 'I can draw a sketch of the rock face, and mark on it where I think they lie. Then you can send someone to collect them.'

Late that evening I accompanied Mr Newey to the kraal, where eight skinned dassies were cooking appetisingly in iron pots over open fires. He talked to one of his men in the glotal Bantu language, then turned to me smilingly.

'They have given you a title,' he said. 'White man from over the water who has given us more meat than we have ever had before.'

A happy note on which to end my holiday. It also brings up the question of the relationship between blacks and whites, as it appeared in those days to a visitor from another continent.

In an era long before the word *apartheid* had become an emotive word in the world's vocabulary, the mild paternalism as demonstrated by Mr Newey seemed to me to express the general attitude of the whites. They considered the black man to be a simple fellow who had always lived in a primitive mud hut, and there was no reason why he should not continue to do so. The whites had brought peace and prosperity to this part of a dark continent, and they were the ones who should most benefit from it. Their European culture demanded a different and better standard of life, and the colour bar policy helped ensure this. There was no animosity involved as far as I could see. To most of us from Britain the idea of discrimination purely on racial grounds was wrong, whatever excuses were made for it. And yet, as we discovered, it was possible to go along with it. There were several reasons for this ambivalence. The white South Africans had shown themselves to be hospitable hosts, and it would have seemed churlish to be outspoken against their system. Again, although the black man was everywhere, he was also curiously remote. By this I mean that although the pavements may be crowded with blacks one never actually had contact with them, not even eye contact. One saw them around the camp, but they were always in the background, performing their menial tasks. It was, in fact, very difficult to gain any degree of contact, as Tom was discovering. Attempts to be friendly were usually met with incomprehension, or even suspicion. One could not help at times feeling exasperation at their apathy.

Feeling myself to be a fairly logical person, the thing which impressed itself most on my mind was that the colour bar was riddled with irrational anomalies. There was no distinction made between the coal-black negro and the man of mixed blood whose colour was no different from our own; it embraced alike the simple Bantu fresh from the tribal reserves and the wealthy Indian shop-owner. The black people were denied the white man's transport, entertainments and toilets, yet as servants seemed to have the run of his kitchens and his nurseries. As the wing commander had said, there were strange attitudes in evidence.

On returning from my leave I found that our course had been posted for the final flying stage of our training at No.42 Airschool at Port Elizabeth, a little further down the coast. This proved to be a large hutted camp on the fringe of a grass airfield, some three miles outside the Union's third largest port. Some twenty Avro Ansons, equipped as flying classrooms, were available for us to put into practice in the air the exercises so often sweated out in the ground trainers.

Within three days came the first entry in my flying logbook: two hours of air experience and map-reading, piloted by Lieutenant Smit, SAAF. South Africa's climate of course was ideal for year round flying training – little cloud, no fog and generally good visibility. Since the airfield was situated on the coast there was little danger of novice navigators becoming hopelessly lost; in any event the staff pilots were so familiar with the local topography they had the unerring homing instincts of racing pigeons. This was proved to me on a later exercise. After an hour's flying over the sea on wind-finding exercises I passed my final course to the pilot for the return to base. I moved forward and stood beside him to await our landfall, and it was with much gratification that I eventually saw our airfield coming up straight ahead. Then I looked down at the magnetic compass, to see that the pilot was flying some thirty degrees off the course I had passed him. He caught my glance: 'Not to worry, man. You underestimated the wind a little, so I just corrected for it.'

Flying over land provided unusual interest. Flying low and slow as we did, we once disturbed a herd of springbok, and they scattered with graceful bounds; buffaloes eyed us from the riverside, and native herdsmen waved to us from the hillsides.

I thoroughly enjoyed the flying, as did most of us. The exceptions were those who found themselves prone to airsickness. As the powerful African sun heated the ground, strong convection currents arose later in the day, creating bumpy flying conditions and consequent stomach queasiness. We trainee navigators flew in pairs; my partner was Ronnie, who was sometimes afflicted but always managed to do his job. Tom's partner, Andy Andrews, was undoubtedly the worst affected. He spent most of his flying hours retching at the Elsan toilet, whilst Tom sportingly carried out all his necessary log and chart work for him. In spite of Tom's heroic efforts, we didn't give Andy any chance at all of finishing the course.

Halfway through our flying course a tragic accident occurred, which saddened us all. Soon after take-off on a navigational exercise one of the Ansons unaccountably plunged into the sea, killing the staff pilot and wireless operator along with the two navigators. One of the latter was named Adams, and it so happened that we had another airman with the same surname on the course. Jim in fact was with me and half a dozen others on the following Saturday, sitting in a coffee bar in town. I happened to be reading a copy of the local newspaper, which carried a report of the accident.

'Looks like there's a misprint here,' I said, reading the names of the casualties from the paper. 'It says Leading Aircraftsman J D Adams. Surely those weren't his initials.'

'No,' said Jim. 'They're mine.'

There was a silence as we pondered the implications.

'Must be a misprint,' I ventured.

'One initial wrong, and I would agree. But not two. I don't like the sound of it at all. That newspaper report must have come from official sources, and it looks to me that there could have been an almighty cock-up with the names. What worries me is that my wife is expecting next month. Just imagine her getting a cable to say that I have got the chop out here. It doesn't bear thinking about.'

Jim's uneasiness prompted him to return to camp immediately, where he sought out the Orderly Officer to instigate a check. His worst fears were realised. As next of kin, his wife had been sent a cable three days previously regretfully informing her that her husband had been killed on active service.

There was, of course, an absolute furore on camp. The station commander was alerted, priority signals despatched, and a board of enquiry convened to instigate such gross negligence. Heads would roll, but nothing possible could be done to alleviate a further trauma for poor Jim's wife. Happily, as it turned out, she was able to cope with the double shock. Her baby daughter was born prematurely, but both were well, and she was able to cable her husband with reassurances. Jim, fortunately, was one of the more mature members of our course, and was able to put the unfortunate business behind him for the remaining weeks.

The flying carried on as per schedule, consisting of cross-country navigational trips. The first navigator would sit at the large plotting table, carrying out the chart plot and maintaining the navigation log. His partner would sit alongside the pilot, his first job after take-off being the manual cranking to lift the Anson's old-fashioned under-carriage, which usually generated a fair amount of sweat. Thereafter he would endeavour to map-read along the route, passing pinpoint fixes to the plotter as available, or maybe operate the drift sight. At our flying heights of around six thousand feet the temperature was just right. If the navigation was going well, the coffee was circulating, and the pilot was one of those who permitted an occasional cigarette, it was really something to write home about.

On the ground, we completed our lecture syllabus and were examined in each subject. We had an excellent course tutor, a former master mariner, and we all sailed through the exams. Now it was just a matter of building up the flying hours.

Our social life had become quite active by this time. Weekends in particular were very pleasant, with the beaches a great attraction during the day. In the evenings, although there were no English style pubs, many of the hotels offered public bar lounges, some with music and dancing. Every Saturday evening there was ballroom dancing in the large city hall, where the girls always outnumbered the men. The girls were generally well disposed towards the RAF boys, in the same way that many of our girls back home were attracted to the Americans. One exception, I recall, was a sunburnt brunette who was dancing with one of our number when she suddenly slapped his face and stalked off the floor. His offence? His innocent opening conversational gambit: 'Are you a native of this town?'

I had by this time acquired a girl friend in town, a slim blue-eyed blonde named Susie, whom I had met at a dance. At home she normally spoke Afrikaans, and I was fascinated by her English, which was clipped in the South African fashion, with curiously transposed vowel sounds. An expression such as: 'Yes, many thanks,' would come out like: 'Yiss, minnie thenks.' I would tease her about her accent, and she would respond by making fun of my own north-country vowels. We spent a lot of time together, chiefly at the beaches or the dances, and had a good relationship without either of us expecting it to be other than short-lived. She never took me home, and I got the impression that her father would not have approved of her going out with a visiting serviceman. I wouldn't have blamed him for that.

Only once throughout my stay in the Union did I experience an undercurrent of ill-will amidst the general sea of goodwill. The scene was set in the underground city centre toilets, late one Saturday night. The place was empty, but a sudden babel of voices speaking in Afrikaans heralded the approach of half a dozen civilians. The voices sunk to a whisper, and I sensed trouble. I turned to find two hefty white youths guarding the stairway, each one gripping a beer bottle by the neck, and the remainder gathering around me. Their spokesman, a huge fellow bursting out of his shirt and shorts, addressed me in accented English.

'You're on your own, Raf. We've got you where we want you. You're in big trouble, man.'

'Why? What have I done?' I was quite petrified, but obstinately determined not to show it.

'What have I done?' he mimicked my accent. 'I'll tell you what you have done Raf. You have come over here to take over our women, and to dodge the war while our boys are getting killed up north fighting your war for you. Now you can show us how you can fight.'

I knew I had to keep talking. They were expecting me to make a run for it, hence the two guards by the exit; it was equally clear that if I did I would be collecting a bottle over the head for starters.

'I'm no war-dodger,' I said, with as much indignation in my voice as I could muster. 'I didn't ask to come out here, I was sent. And next month I hope to be on my way home.' Then, gaining boldness: 'Anyway, does it take six of you to take me on?'

I knew I had pushed my luck as far as possible, but I had a sneaking feeling that since I was so heavily outnumbered none of them felt that he wanted to make the first move. There came a pause, which seemed a good deal longer to me than it was. One of them said something in Afrikaans, and pointed to the aircrew flash in my cap. Then suddenly the atmosphere changed, as it so easily can when people who have been drinking are involved. The big fellow grinned, and thrust at me a half filled bottle of brandy.

'Have a drink, man.'

It was a scenario which I suppose has happened countless times in countries with visiting troops from overseas; few can have ended so amicably, and I was suitably grateful to kind providence as I bemusedly went on my way.

The flying hours accumulated. My flying logbook eventually showed I had reached the hundred hour minimum, and my last trip arrived. This was a long straight haul at night, from Port Elizabeth to East London and back again, with little required in the way of navigation since both places were so brightly lit as to be visible over thirty miles away. The object was to gain practice in the art of shooting the stars with the bubble sextant, and plotting the results on the navigation chart. Some of these proved to be startingly wide of the mark. Naturally, in the way of navigators, I put this down to pilot error, in that he had failed to maintain the required precision of speed and heading whilst the shots were being taken.

We finally landed, with the pastel shades of the African dawn about us. It was a glorious feeling – a long held ambition finally realised. As we walked away from the aircraft Ronnie and I congratulated each other.

'How does it feel to be a real navigator?' I asked.

'Just great. And we're sergeants as well! Just imagine, we're on twelve and six a day as from next payday.'

The staff pilot and wireless operator walked alongside, smiling benignly. They had seen it all before.

Our passing-out parade was arranged for the following week, on the morning of Christmas Eve 1943. On the night before, we held our course dinner at a hotel in town, and really let our hair down. One of our guests, the least popular of the SAAF pilots, had more than that let down; his trousers were forcibly removed and hoisted high on the flagpole outside.

It was a sadly hungover course who paraded next morning in the heat of South Africa's Christmas, sweating in our best blue uniforms, to have our flying badge pinned on by a visiting senior officer. In the background the band of the Native Corps played what could have been *Take Me Back To Dear Old Blighty*. There followed a few words from the presenting officer – 'Well done, chaps, but remember you still have a lot to learn' – then a group photograph in front of a sturdy Anson. We marched off, to be stood down for the Christmas break.

The afternoon was spent in the barracks sewing on our sergeants' stripes and flying badges. Even though this was our big day, there was a lot of grumbling going on, as I recall. For one thing, although we had now all been promoted to the substantive rank of sergeant, we had just been informed that 'for administrative reasons' we would not be allowed to use the facilities of the Sergeants' Mess.

The other source of disaffection was the newly designed navigators' brevet, replacing the old observers' badge, which most of us were seeing for the first time today. It was a small cloth wing attached to an embroidered 'N', and none of us were particularly impressed with it. Tom was typically scathing:

'It's pathetic. Considering the blood and sweat we put into earning it, you would think they would have put a bit of imagination into its design. The Yanks have got it right; all their aircrew have a double-winged badge which anyone would be proud to wear. Who called it a wings parade? They've only given us half a wing!'

There was a murmur of approval, and he carried on:

'Shall I tell you why? Take a look at the RAF's top brass. Every one of them is a pilot, every one a double winger. Not a nav or a wop or a gunner in sight. It's just their way of telling you that if you aren't a pilot, you're nothing.'

He was in good form, and his last word on the subject was still to come. One of the fellows had finished the job of stitching on his brevet, and asked how it looked.

'From here, exactly like a blob of bird shit.' I wouldn't have put it so strongly, but he had a point.

Christmas in South Africa had a style of its own. In spite of the difference in climate, the European conventions were observed as far as possible. The messes were decorated, and carols came over the Tannoy. We sat down to a Christmas dinner at our special tables in the Airmens' Mess, traditionally waited on by the officers, and ploughed a way through the turkey with trimmings and the heavy plum pudding and mince pies. The temperature could not have been much less than a hundred degrees, and though we were dressed in shirts and shorts we were soon soaked in sweat. We couldn't wait to get down to the beaches to cool off. Our thoughts were with our families back home in foggy, ice-bound, rationed and bomb-scarred Britain. We had enjoyed our sojourn in the sun, but there was not one man amongst us who wasn't counting the days until we set off home.

Next day we had a final talk from our Chief Course Instructor, Flight Lieutenant Gardner. Our successors had already arrived, and he hoped they would turn out as good a course as we had been. He announced that four of our members would be granted commissions. Jim Adams had come top of the course, and was an automatic choice – and all credit to him. He had, in fact, been given the option of staying on as an instructor, but had declined. Two others named were the two oldest members of the course, both in their thirties. The fourth name was announced – Andy's! Our instructors apparently had heard all about Andy's airsickness problem, but had been impressed by the standard of work on his logs and charts handed in for assessment after each flight. The spirit and determination thus demonstrated had apparently been considered worthy of recognition. I took a look at Tom. This was the only time I found him speechless!

A few days later our course entrained in reserved coaches on the Durban train. I was amazed at the number of local people who turned up to see us off, and to wish us luck. The English-speaking South Africans still cherished their links with Britain, and for our part more than one of our company expressed intentions of emigrating here some day. Susie was on the platform, come to say goodbye; she pressed on to me a large envelope, which contained a recently-taken studio photograph of herself. We finally all climbed aboard, and the train pulled out to a great waving of arms and a chorus of goodbyes and not a few tears. 'Come back after the war,' someone shouted, 'You'll be welcome.' It seemed we had been better ambassadors than any of us had imagined.

Maybe the moment is now opportune to digress, to take a leap into the future, with the double objective of updating my narrative and showing how the bounds of probability may be stretched to their limit.

I have no doubt that many young men who served in the Union during the war returned afterwards to start a new life. I was not one of them, nor did I carry out an extended correspondence with anyone I met there. Some twelve years after the war I happened to be serving at a maritime airfield in the north of Scotland when a pilot and crew of the South African Air Force arrived. They had come to pick up a Shackleton aircraft purchased by their government and fly it back home. I was chatting to one of the crew in the mess bar, and mentioned that I had completed my navigator training in Port Elizabeth. He was interested, since this happened to be his home town, and asked me if I remembered the name of anyone living there. I mentioned Susie's name. He asked a question or two, then stared at me incredulously.

'She's married to my best friend,' he said. 'He's a flyer in the SAAF like myself. They have two children now. I was the best man at the wedding!'

I was as taken aback as he was, but remembered to ask him to pass on my best regards when he got home. To me it was a happy link with the long past.

Our stay in the transit camp at Durban was this time short-lived. The troopship, the four funnelled *Arundel Castle*, was already awaiting us at the dockside, and the familiar face of Wingco Parsons was there to welcome us aboard. We were again accommodated in large mess-decks, but, as senior NCOs, were a little higher above the water line than we had been on *Orontes*.

As we stood by the ship's rails watching other troops embarking, we were joined by two young RAF officers, resplendent in their brand new kit. I did what must have been a comical double take as I recognised them both. My last sight of them had been four months previously at East London Airschool: then they had been two of the woebegone airmen who had failed the course and been posted away. They explained this strange transfigurement. They had gone to some kind of holding unit, had there been remustered as trainee air bombers, and had then gone on to complete a short visual bombing course. After this they had been commissioned, since they were now in a relatively new trade and the officer quota was high. Good luck to them: they had managed to find themselves in the right place at the right time.

Even before we sailed it was announced that our journey home was to be via the Suez Canal and the Mediterranean. The war in North Africa had gone very much our way since we had first arrived out here, and the Med was now considered reasonably safe for convoys. The top deck of our ship was bristling with Oerlikon gun turrets, and it was announced that each would be manned by one trained gunner and two aircrew on a rostered anti-submarine watch. Anything to vary the tedium of normal troopship life was more than welcome.

The vast majority of troops aboard were reinforcements for South Africa's desert army, along with a contingent of RAF aircrew and ground crew heading for service with the Middle East Air Force. The remainder were some four hundred newly-trained pilots and navigators from the training schools of the Union and Rhodesia, bound for the UK.

We moved out in the early afternoon of our second day aboard to another good send-off. The departure of South Africa's Sixth Division was certainly no military secret. As the two tugs eased us away, the jetty was alive with a waving and a fluttering of handkerchiefs, and a dozen sirens blared. The Lady in White was there, her amplified voice piercing the hubbub. The plaintive words of *Carry Me Back To The Old Transvaal* followed us out to sea.

How sadly I look back at the events of the years which were to follow in this land so well endowed. The hardening of attitudes, the alienation, the ostracism, the bloodshed. I give the last word to Tom, who saw what was coming, and was always a quotable fellow. He said, in reply to my question, as the harbour receded:

'No I shan't be back. I've enjoyed my stay, but I don't see a big future. Can't they see the trouble they are storing up for themselves? They have a springbok as their national symbol: I think they should change it to an ostrich . . .'

4

A Period of Adjustment

I was wakened by an insistent shaking of my shoulder, and a voice in my ear: 'Wakey wakey, sarge. Your early call. Will you sign the book, please?'

I sat up in bed, and took the proffered pen from the young airman, who focused his torch on the wet notebook. As I signed my name, water dripped from the rubber cape he wore, to form a small pool at the bedside. I could hear the sound of rain drumming on the iron roof of the hut.

'The weather's bad,' said the airman, almost apologetically, as he prepared to leave. 'I expect your flying will be scrubbed anyway.'

As I dressed, I was conscious of that depressing smell well remembered by every serviceman who has ever awakened in a Nissen hut: an early morning miasma of stale smoke, cold ashes and damp blankets.

Was it really only six weeks ago since I had been sweating it out in the heat of a South African summer? Less than that since I had been on the equator itself, homeward bound aboard the *Arundel Castle*? Now here I was, shivering in the chilly pre-dawn of a Scottish winter, on a bleak coastal airfield in the back of beyond. The only possible reminder of those recent days in the sun lay gently snoring in the next bed. Cyril Keeton, one of the quieter members of the course, had been with me throughout my time out there at Port Elizabeth. We had occupied beds at opposite ends of the course hut, and I don't suppose we had exchanged a dozen words in all that time. Now we had by pure chance been thrown together, and had soon become firm friends.

We had both been instructed by telegram to report to our present location whilst enjoying home leave on our return from South Africa. What a terrific leave that had been. First, the delight of the family reunion, and their appreciative gasps at the luxuries I bore from the Durban emporia and the Port Said dockside – silk stockings, leather handbags, perfumes, cigars, brandy and tinned meats. Even a soggy pineapple, which I claimed may well have been the only one in England at that time. Then the pride of showing off my stripes and

54

flying badge, and the way they attracted the girls at the local dances. Aircrew casualties had been high during my absence. Several of my schoolmates, including Frosty Winterbottom, had been reported killed or missing. It helped to provide the RAF aircrews with a glamour the other servicemen could not hope to match. We had the image of hard drinking, womenising, devil-may-care fellows, and I am sure I did my bit to uphold it.

Now it was back to reality. Cyril and I and a dozen other newly fledged navigators had arrived at West Freugh, within sight of the Mull of Galloway, to be told the purpose of our stay. It was, basically, to carry out a series of navigational flying exercises, well away from the war, to accustom ourselves to the considerably different conditions of flying in the UK from those we had experienced abroad. For instance, whilst flying over the South African veldt or the Canadian prairies, the sight of a main road or a railway line would usually give a readily identifiable landmark to fix the aircraft's position. Over England, or the continent, the great profusion of such roads and networks of railways would tend to confuse, until the navigator had learned to read his maps with great fluency. The other main factor was the weather. Flying in South Africa's ideal climatic conditions tended to blind one to the vagaries of the weather in Europe. This was to be a period of adjustment for us before starting our serious pre-operational flying – a measure of the thoroughness of the RAF's navigator training.

The purpose of today's early morning foray was to undertake the first of these acclimatisation flights. I was keen to get cracking, and had spent the whole of the previous evening preparing for it. My plotting chart had become a thing of many-coloured splendour. Every radio beacon within fifty miles of our route had been plotted in green crayon, along with all possible diversion airfields. Restricted areas, such as coastal bird sanctuaries, had been outlined in blue; danger areas, like the artillery firing ranges off the Welsh coast, drawn in and shaded bright red. Yellow patches signified areas of high ground. I intended this to be a copy-book flight in every respect. When later the trip came to be assessed by the Navigation Leader, I did not intend to be found wanting under the heading of pre-flight preparation. When I eventually left this unit I intended going with a prestigious Above Average assessment entered in the back of my logbook. In that way, I figured, I might acquire myself an above average pilot and crew in due course.

It was still dark as I made my way to the Airmens' Mess for early breakfast. Since this was a non-operational flying station, the breakfast did not run to actual shellbound operational eggs: the wartime substitute, a yellow rubbery disc representing a dried egg omelette was served, along with a slice of fried Spam. I forced it down, and reported to the briefing room.

My crewmate, the staff wireless operator, was already there. A small hunched figure, enveloped in an oversized American-type flying jacket, he greeted me with eyes half closed from the smoke drifting up from the cigarette in the corner of his mouth. He reminded me of a diminutive Humphrey Bogart. He even sounded like him.

'Guess we're wasting our time, nav,' he said, ash falling from his drooping cigarette. 'They won't send us off in this weather. No way.'

I carried on with my flight planning. It would be good practice for me, anyway. It was to be a simple cross-country exercise on a triangular route, taking us across the Irish Sea to St David's Head in South Wales, then north-easterly to Newark and back to base. About three and a half hour's duration. I painstakingly worked out all the courses using the forecast winds displayed on a blackboard. These were strong westerlies, with speeds well in excess of any I had previously experienced. That was something else I would have to get used to.

We were presently joined by the staff pilot who had been detailed for the trip. He proved to be a Polish flight sergeant, his foreignness accentuated by his close-cropped hair, showing a hint of grey, and a gold front tooth. I wouldn't have been able to guess his age within ten years. His name, which I copied into my navigation log from the name-tag on his tunic, was an unpronounceable jumble of vowels and consonants. He had that undefinable air of a man with a tour of ops behind him.

'Looks like a scrub, eh Jan?' said the wireless op. The fellow seemed to be willing it so, I thought. Then he added: 'Shan't be sorry, either. Helluva thrash in the Mess bar last night. Didn't get to bed till two.'

The pilot, a man of few words, shrugged his shoulders. 'We see,' he said.

The met man arrived to give us his weather report. In the manner of meteorologists everywhere he hedged his bets with a host of ifs, maybes and perhaps's. The gist was that although we were experiencing fairly severe frontal conditions the complex was rapidly moving eastwards, and he was forecasting a steady improvement soon after our take-off time. He and the briefing officer held a short conference, then the decision was announced. We would carry on with our flight as planned; the wireless op was to maintain a careful listening watch at his briefed times, and if the expected weather improvement did not materialise we would be recalled back to base or diverted. It was not a situation I would have wished for on my first trip.

Soon after the gloomy dawn had broken, the three of us climbed aboard the Anson awaiting us in dispersal. As we did so, I noticed the Polish pilot crossing himself, and wondered if he knew something I didn't. We slipped and skidded on the wet floor as we moved forward to our crew positions. I had to use my handkerchief to mop up water on the navigation table before I could pin down my chart. I laid out the rest of my equipment, whilst the wireless op leaned over to load the colours of the day into the Very pistol, in case we were challenged en route. We completed our checks and taxied out. It was still raining heavily as we took off. Wryly, I recalled the day in South Africa when, having become airborne, the staff pilot spotted a thin and insignificant layer of stratus cloud in the distance. 'We're off back to base, navigator, until the weather improves,' he had said. This, it seemed, was an entirely different ball game.

We set course across the Irish Sea on the first leg of our trip. 'Ze weather not good,' commented our pilot. 'We press on.'

Press on we did. Our captain announced his intention of staying below the cloud base, and as this gradually lowered, so we lowered with it. I was instructed to make sure we remained over the sea as we were well below our safety height.

I needed no reminding. I was uneasily aware of our ever-decreasing altimeter reading, the ever-worsening outside visibility and the ever growing proximity of the Welsh mountains. Below us, the wind was whipping the white caps into sheets of spray, and the turbulence was making the aircraft pitch most uncomfortably. Our drift, that vital angle between the direction we were pointing and the direction we were actually travelling, was in the region of 25 degrees.

Happily, I was able to fix our position accurately as we flew abeam Bardsey Island; we were so low I could have peered through its lighthouse window had we been a little closer to it. In fact, we were far closer than we should have been, which indicated that either the wind was very much stronger than forecast or the pilot had been steering erratic courses. I had to assume the former, and the wind speed I calculated was a startling 70 mph.

Shortly afterwards, it seemed that the cloud base was nearly at sea level, and the pilot was forced to climb into it to reach a safe altitude. From now on we were flying blind. We turned on our estimated time of arrival at St David's Head, and set course for Newark, still in cloud.

I was becoming distracted by the layer of frost which was accreting on the windows and windscreen. Each time I looked it had thickened, until it fused into opaque ice which darkened the interior of the aircraft. There was also developing a most disconcerting vibration, sufficient to send my pencils tumbling to the floor. There came a sudden frightening clang, like a hammer hitting the side of the fuselage.

'No panic,' came the imperturbable voice up front. 'Is ice breaking off wings. We press on.' It seemed he had solved the language problem by communicating almost entirely in air force colloquialisms.

I was getting worried. I knew that really severe icing could eventually cause an aircraft to fall out of the skies. However, the problem resolved itself for the moment. We found ourselves suddenly clear of cloud, though below us stretched a continuous thick grey blanket, with a further extensive cloud layer above us.

The exercise called for a spell of map-reading on this leg, but though I stood optimistically with my half million scale map unfolded, there was no sign of even the smallest break in the cloud below. The alternatives were navigation by wireless bearings, to be obtained by the wireless op, or by sextant shots of the sun. Since the sun had yet to make an appearance today, the former was now my only option. I called up the wireless op for assistance.

'Sorry, nav,' came the reply, 'I'm having trouble with this receiver. All I'm getting at the moment is an earful of static. I'll call you back.'

I sat impatiently for some ten minutes. There was little else I could do. It would be an understatement to say that I was not enjoying this trip. The increasing turbulence was inducing a feeling of acute nausea, and my feet and fingers were feeling the cold. Rain from the cloud above us was seeping through the ill-fitting astrodome and dripping onto the navigation table. My chart was wet, and the carefully crayoned areas had merged into something like a tropical sunset. I looked back at my diminutive crewmate.

Even in the air he still maintained his image. Instead of a regulation helmet he wore American style earphones and headband worn over his forage cap, and a cigarette still dangled from the corner of his mouth. He had removed the metal cover from his wireless receiver, and was prodding its entrails with a screwdriver. 'No joy yet,' he said.

After another fifteen minutes I really began to worry. I desperately needed to fix our position. I had absolutely no idea what wind was affecting us at this height; the niggling feeling persisted that if in fact the previously strong wind had abated, then the course I had given the pilot would be taking us away from where we should be at the rate of some seventy miles every hour. Even a good deal more if the direction of the wind had changed as well.

There came one brief moment of hope. The pilot indicated that there seemed to be a gap in the cloud some way ahead. I moved forward rapidly with my map. Alas, there appeared a tantalising mirage-like glimpse of wet green countryside below, then the gap closed, never to re-open.

As I moved back, I noticed the wireless op now had a heap of valves and components on the table before him. He caught my eye, and the expressive shrug of his shoulders was exactly that of a young Bogart, faced with a situation which even he thought he might have difficulty in handling.

Meanwhile, it seemed, the pilot also had his problems. He had been trying for some time to contact local airfields on his short range VHF radio, so that if necessary they could relay messages to our base. His efforts had been unsuccessful; like the wireless op before him, he was able to raise only static and other interference. That worthy was called upon to check the equipment, and report. His technical diagnosis was as follows:

'The electrics are knackered, and no wonder. This bloody old crate is leaking like a sieve. Let's go home, Jan.'

We were, and had been for some time, completely out of communication with anyone. That meant that back at base they would probably by debating whether to press the panic button. The briefing officer, who had taken a bit of a chance with the weather, might already be preparing his story, in case we didn't return and it became a board of enquiry job. The book laid down very clearly what we ourselves should be doing – landing at the nearest suitable airfield. Not quite as simple as it sounds. There was an even more important injunction to aircrews, typified by a poster in the briefing room which I had looked at that very morning. It featured a contoured map of Britain with the high ground marked with tombstones; symbolic airmen with angels' wings and harps hovered above. The caption stated: 'They descended through cloud when unsure of their position!' At the present time, though I might not admit to being lost, I sure as hell would agree that I was unsure of our position. There was no way that I would condone a descent through cloud, whose base height was unknown, at this time, in search of a landing ground. We were all three in agreement on this.

'OK navigator,' said the pilot, 'we go home. Give me course for base.'

We were cutting short our trip, but we still had more than an hour's flying ahead. The minutes were ticking by, but still no signs of any breaks in the cloud. In fact, the clouds were thickening; dark solid banks loomed ahead, and soon we would be in the thick of it again. My mind buzzed with uneasy thoughts. Would we find ourselves icing up again? What would we do if we got back to base area without radio and found the predicted weather clearance had not materialised? How would we get down? What if we were actually a hundred miles from where I thought we were? I was experiencing that knotted-stomach feeling which, I was to learn, affects all navigators when things are going badly – a mingling of anxiety, frustration, depression and barely-suppressed panic.

I took a look at the pilot. There was something very reassuring about his firm grip on the control column, and his steady forward gaze. He seemed unperturbed. Maybe he had lots of experience of these situations. I suddenly remembered reading about a Polish crew who, in the earlier days of the war, had been sent on a practice bombing exercise on one of the inland bombing ranges. Instead, they had flown across the Channel and dropped their tiny practice bombs on Hitler's invasion barges moored off the French coast. Probably this fellow had the same spirit.

A few minutes later we were in cloud again. The turbulence increased, and my queasiness developed to such an extent that I had to make a rapid sortie to the Elsan in the rear. In a sudden surge I lost the greasy breakfast I had forced myself to eat a few hours earlier. I felt annoyed with myself, quite apart from feeling ill. Since the day I had survived a severe Atlantic gale aboard the troopship *Orontes* without any ill effects, I had assumed that I would always be immune to mere airsickness. Perhaps there was a psychological factor today. I felt better when, making my way forward, I was hurriedly passed by young Bogart, on his way to shedding the remains of the previous night's indulgence. I hoped our pilot had a stronger stomach than the pair of us.

I resumed my seat at the navigation table. The turbulence was now severe, and as the cloud thickened the light deteriorated rapidly. A loud tattoo of hailstones sounded on the upper fuselage. I was about to refasten my safety belt when it happened.

It was difficult to place events in sequence. I had the feeling that the floor had suddenly collapsed and the roof had come down to hit me on the head. Simultaneously came the sound of a violent explosion and a blinding violet light before my eyes. I was stunned by the shock of it, and completely dazzled by the brilliance of the flash. I sensed that the left wing had dropped alarmingly. There was a strong smell of burning. It seemed that all my senses were involved, in one way or another. My first coherent thought was that we had been involved in a midair collision.

In this moment of confusion came the voice of our captain over the intercom: 'We're OK. No panic. We're hit by lightning. Turning to port. Where are we, navigator?'

The sheer ecstasy of relief at the sound of this calm recital, and the knowledge that the aircraft was still in one piece and under control, had a wonderfully settling effect on me. I composed myself sufficiently to make a quick reference to the plotting chart.

'Somewhere over the Lake District by my reckoning.' Then, as a plea of mitigation: 'But I haven't been able to get a fix for over two hours.'

We were still turning. 'Give me a course to bring us over ze sea.'

'Turn on to due south, until I get organised,' I said.

I had to carry on with the navigational plot. First, I had to retrieve my protractor and other equipment which had been flung to the floor. As I searched under the table, another depressing thought struck me. We had just suffered a lightning strike; therefore the huge electrical charge thus generated had altered the whole magnetic field of the aircraft. That meant that the Anson's only compass, a simple bar magnet immersed in a bowl of dampening fluid, would now be dangerously inaccurate. At worst, instead of heading towards the Irish Sea, we could in fact be going the other way – towards the dangerously high Scottish mountains! I tried to push the thought to the back of my mind. I already had enough worries to be going on with.

I wasn't the only one with problems. The wireless op now announced that we had lost our wireless trailing aerial. It had been lowered when the lightning struck, and had been instantly vaporised. At least, that accounted for the strong smell of burning which still persisted.

But this was the point when the fates relented. We had reached the nadir of our discomfort, the final aggregate of misfortunes. This was when our luck changed.

It started when our captain settled down on his new course. Almost immediately, as we moved away from the storm centre, the turbulence eased and the light improved. The cloud became whispy, and a sudden shaft of sunlight transformed the interior. A magical moment later, we were in the clear. It came as a minor shock to find that the sun had been shining brightly in the heavens all the time! There was still a vast white vista of cloud way below us, but there seemed to be breaks in it here and there. The pilot headed for the largest one. As we overflew it, a patch of choppy grey sea was visible below. It was a welcome sight.

'We go down, navigator,' said the pilot, and swung the aircraft into a sharp spiralling descent. We levelled out at 1000 feet, below the cloud. At least, that was one problem solved – we were now in contact with the ground. All I had to do now was to try to find out where the hell we were.

If I had said a prayer, it could not have been more speedily or effectively answered. The pilot gave a shout, and pointed to the east. I looked through the astrodome in the direction indicated. On the distant horizon was a smudge of land – and on it, faintly but unmistakably, like a beckoning extended finger, was Blackpool Tower!

We both recognised it instantly. After all, I had been stationed in the town only a year previously; and the pilot, as I later learned, had been posted there when he first arrived in England. The third member of our crew, alerted by the excitement, came forward to take a look.

'Maybe it's the Eiffel Tower', he said. He had regained his Bogart image – cool and cynical.

Our problems were behind us. We were heading for Blackpool, and a diversion landing at Squires Gate aerodrome. We circled, whilst the wireless op requested permission to land with our one remaining means of communication, the Aldis lamp. A green flare from the Control Tower signified assent. A few minutes later we touched down on the grass strip in a faultless landing. I could have given the pilot a medal on the spot for his handling of the whole situation.

Two hours later there wasn't a cloud in the sky. It seemed to make a mockery of all our earlier problems.

Another Anson arrived from West Freugh to ferry us back, whilst our own aircraft was held for serviceability checks. By the time I had completed the formalities back at base it was late evening. I returned to the billet to find Cyril reading in bed, where I had left him early in this long day.

'How did the trip go?' he asked.

I dropped wearily onto my bed, and slowly gathered my thoughts. In the space of a few hours today I seemed to have gone through the full range of human feelings and emotions. Optimism, hope, doubt, discomfort, frustration, anger, pessimism, anxiety, nausea, fear, despair, terror, elation and thankfulness. In that order. Everything, in fact, except religious mania or sexual gratification. Now I just wanted to forget it all.

'Let me just say,' I replied, 'that I've realised today that you and I have opted for the wrong profession. And if this is what non-operational flying is all about, then God help us when the flak really starts.'

I meant it at the time.

Two days later I flew with the same crew on the second of our cross-country exercises. It was another triangular route, taking us over Wales and Northern Ireland. This time the weather was fine, the visibility good and the winds constant. We maintained our planned track the whole way, and hit each turning point right on the nose. I thoroughly enjoyed every minute of it.

It was all just part of the period of adjustment.

5

THE MATING GAME

E ngland abounds in pleasantly evocative place names. The mind cannot fail to conjure up an appropriate rural picture when confronted with the likes of Widecombe in the Moor, Milton under Wychwood, Walton on the Green or Bourton on the Water. My mind was no exception when I first discovered that our course of navigators were to be posted forthwith to No. 21 Operational Training Unit at a place called Moreton in the Marsh. I envisaged a makeshift airfield in the middle of some large soggy plain; a flat featureless wasteland where one would probably find oneself ankle deep in squelchy mud if one ventured off the concrete hard standing.

Of course, as is so often the case, reality proved to be nothing like the preconception. When we were eventually deposited on its flower-bordered railway platform, the place gave evidence of being a pleasant stone-built country town set amidst rolling Cotswold countryside, and not a single sign of marsh or bogland. The airfield, when we reached it in the waiting transport, seemed better appointed than the one we had just left, and was very conveniently situated about a mile from the town. It was the sort of place which appealed at first sight.

The rail journey down could not have been less stressful. We entrained in a special coach tacked on to the south-bound train awaiting us at Stranraer station. We spent the next twenty-four hours reading, sleeping, cardplaying and nibbling on our packed rations, whilst the coach underwent various bumpings and shuntings during the night before disgorging us at our destination.

Let me here and now offer my own personal tribute to a branch of the service generally unseen, unheard and unsung. I refer to those anonymous personnel of the wartime movements control whose job it was to arrange appropriate transport, from a 15 cwt. van to a 40,000 ton troopship, for all members of the armed forces going about their business. From my own experience of numerous postings and movements, never once did the system fail. Always there was waiting suitable transport, at the right time in the right place and in sufficient quantities. Today was a good example of their efforts. Not only were we navigators efficiently transported as described, but within the space of a few hours successive trains arrived bearing similar parties of pilots, bomb-aimers, wireless operators and air gunners. Each party had been plucked from its particular training school wherever it was located, and delivered punctually and without fuss to this rural backwater.

All of us had undertaken today's journey in a state of eager anticipation. A posting to an OTU meant a perceptible increase in our status. It signified that we were at last throwing off the constraints of Flying Training Command, and though we were still many months away from operational flying, it placed us on the outer fringes of Bomber Command. Our instructors would all be ex-operational types, and we would be taught the most up-to-date procedures with modern equipment. Most important of all, each of us here would join with others of a different aircrew category to form a crew, who would stick together for the foreseeable future. Each man would become a specialist in his own right; each crew would stand or fall on the efficiency of each member. It was an exciting and challenging prospect.

We had left behind one of our navigators at West Freugh. On the night the BBC had announced the startling loss of ninety-six of our bombers from the raid on Nuremburg, he had announced to the rest of us in the hut that he intended going no further along the road to operational flying. He had later reported sick feigning ear-ache and partial deafness, and intended to maintain the pretence as long as he could get away with it. I had heard of aircrew classed as L.M.F. – 'Lack of Moral Fibre' – when they had cracked under the stresses of flying over Germany, but had never expected to meet one who could be similarly classed whilst still six months short of operational flying. I am glad to say this was the only instance I was ever to encounter. Whilst none of us were like my friend Michael with his obsession about bombing the Germans, we certainly never contemplated anything other than doing the job for which we had trained so long.

On arrival at the airfield, we navigators were billeted in a long wooden hut, situated in a pleasant copse behind the Sergeants' Mess; eldertrees shaded the windows, and clusters of daffodils brightened the surrounds. Adjacent huts gradually filled up with the other aircrew parties as they arrived, and when the intake was complete it was announced over the Tannoy that the Chief Ground Instructor would address us all in the main briefing room in an hour's time.

Cyril and I took the opportunity of wandering round the dispersals to view the aircraft we would be flying here. The well-worn black painted Wellingtons had long since been relegated to the role of operational trainers, but still had the air of battle-hardened former front line veterans. In comparison with the Ansons on which we had been weaned, they appeared huge and formidable.

There was a beginning-of-term buzz in the briefing room as the hundred or so new arrivals gathered. We were a mixed bunch, with something like one in ten an officer and one in five bearing the shoulder flashes of Canada, Australia or New Zealand. The common factor was the extreme youthfulness of the assembly; one would have had to look carefully to spot anyone who looked over twenty-one.

The instructors filed in and lined the walls, and we eyed them surreptitiously. Slightly more mature in the face, slightly more casual in dress, they sported leather name tags on their battledress and whistles at their collar. Their peaked hats had the wire stiffeners removed, giving the floppy look favoured by Hollywood flyers. A surprisingly large number of them wore the ribbon of the DFC or DFM under their brevets. They all had that cool operational look about them, and we hoped that one day we would look the same.

The Chief Instructor welcomed us on behalf of the staff, and talked about the course syllabus. This would consist of an initial two weeks ground training, followed by ten weeks of flying exercises in which we would all participate as members of a permanent crew. To that end, the following day would be devoted to the crewing-up process. We would all gather inside the main hangar, and would not leave until we had sorted ourselves out into crews. Equal numbers of pilots, navigators, bomb-aimers and wireless ops, and twice that number of gunners, would be on display and open to offers. There would be no coercion of any kind. No matter what ranks were involved, the pilot would be the undisputed captain of the crew.

That gave us something to think about. As I said to Cyril, I had assumed that crewing-up would be done in the usual air force fashion – either by rank, seniority or assessment – and the method just announced seemed very much a hit or miss business. Cyril, always a man to reason things out, said:

'Oh, I don't know, Bomber Command isn't looking for super-crews. All they need is an average bunch of blokes who have reached a certain standard, and can work together as a team. And they can hardly complain about being incompatible when they've picked out each other in the first place.'

That evening I retired to bed early with a book. The hut was quiet, since most of the navigators had drifted off to the mess for a drink. Cyril returned early, with some interesting shop talk he had picked up from a navigator left over from a previous course. According to this fellow, Bomber Command were now navigating almost exclusively by the use of a marvellous new radar device, known as a Gee box. It could provide accurate fixing anywhere over Britain and part of the continent, quite irrespective of bad weather or darkness. We would be learning all about it on the course. It was still officially on the secret list, although it was known that the Germans had recovered intact sets from crashed bombers. It had certainly been kept a good secret from us. If this gadget did what this fellow claimed, then it was an invention which would do for us navigators what the invention of the wheel had done for the early travellers!

The half dozen of us in the hut began to discuss the implications of what we had just heard. No longer would we have to search desperately for gaps in the cloud, shoot hopefully at the stars with our sextants, or solicit wireless bearings of doubtful accuracy from our wireless ops. Now we could be virtually self-sufficient in our curtained-off navigation compartments. What a boost for our morale to start the course!

It was precisely at this moment that there came a knock on the door, and in walked a flight sergeant pilot wearing the dark blue uniform of the Royal Australian Air Force. He was a fair haired young man of my own age, with the sturdy open-air look of the typical dominion airman. He looked around, rather self-consciously.

'I'm looking for a navigator,' he said. 'Any of you fellows care to risk your lives flying in my crew?'

There was a silence. His request had taken us by surprise; we weren't expecting this process to start until the next day. I found the silence becoming embarrassing.

Then I heard myself say: 'Yes, I'll take you on, if you like.' He walked over to my bedside and held out his hand. 'My name's Anderson. Keith Anderson.'

'Harry Lomas. Pleased to meet you.' We shook hands. I felt a little foolish, formally greeting this stranger whilst lying in bed in my pyjamas. For the sake of saying something, I said the first thing that came to mind: 'That ties in with what I heard – that all Aussies are called either Keith or Bruce.'

'Not all of 'em. A fair number. Goodo, then. I'll look out for you tomorrow. Sorry to come busting in on you like this, but there's a rumour going round our pilots' hut that there aren't enough navigators on the course to go round. The last thing I want is to waste time hanging around waiting for a full crew, so I decided to jump the gun tonight.'

With that explanation he bade us goodnight and made to leave the hut.

'Don't worry,' my friend Cyril called out to him. 'You've got yourself a gen man.'

The incident sparked off conversation in the hut when he had left.

'Thanks for your testimonial,' I said to Cyril. 'What did you make of him?'

'Seemed a good type. Quiet too, for an Aussie.'

'Seems like a man who wants to get on with the war,' I said, and thought about the fellow we had left behind, busily lying his way out of it. 'Keen type. Is that a good thing or bad in a skipper?'

'Time will tell, my boy,' said Cyril. 'Only time will tell.'

Next morning, we were all assembled in the hangar by ten o'clock, as detailed. For a while we remained in five homogeneous huddles, displaying the Englishman's disinclination to form an association with people he hadn't met before, each group tentatively eyeing the others. Looking around, I thought I could detect characteristics in each one which somehow seemed appropriate to the particular aircrew role.

The assembled pilots seemed that little bit more cool and aloof, as befitting appointed leaders, men who fully realised that they would hold the very lives of us all at their fingertips, and would make all the important decisions. That knowledge alone, I figured, must do something for a man's self-esteem. Either that, or the responsibility of it all would overwhelm him; in which case he wouldn't have got this far, would he?

The characteristics of my own group I knew well enough. Navigators were essentially quiet and serious men, unless in drink, who often bore the abstracted look of those whose eyes are focused on faraway objects unseen by others in their company. Their trade had already taught them that facts are not facts until proved so, and conclusions are never ever leapt at. In this present process of assimilation they would be the ones who saw the most and said the least.

The bomb-aimers were a hybrid species, difficult to classify. Few of them had actually volunteered for the job they were doing. They were in the main fairly bright young men who had been selected for pilot training and found they couldn't judge a landing, or lacked the noses-to-the-table aptitude of the navigators. Here they formed a tight group, talking animatedly among themselves, offering no particular emanations. Their reactions to any situation would be unpredictable.

Not so the wireless operators. They came over to me as good solid tradesmen in the traditional mould, predictably down-to-earth fellows, with minds and fingertips long attuned to the peculiar metres of the

Morse Code, where accuracy is all. Crew members who would offer a cheerful reliability and good sense.

Since there would be two air gunners in each crew, their party was twice the size of the others, and ten times as noisy. They would be given the Herculean task of scanning the black night for many long hours whilst maintaining the capacity of instantaneous reaction. Volatile and uninhibited, they were already talking louder and laughing longer than necessary. However young we all were, this party was all of two years younger, and it showed.

Those were the characteristics of my fellow aircrew members as I saw them at the time, and I never had much cause to revise them in the future.

Very soon the process of intermingling and propositioning began. The pilots were expected to make the opening gambits, and they did indeed begin rather self-consciously to circulate. I soon spotted Keith, my pilot elect, and moved across to join him. He looked at me as I approached, then looked away.

'Don't you know me?' I asked.

He looked at me, then recognition registered on his face.

'Sorry, sport, I thought you were a little bloke when I met you last night. I was looking for someone about five foot tall.'

'I was curled up with a good book at the time,' I said.

'I hope you don't think I was pressurising you last night. Anyway, I had better start circulating, or I might still miss out. The rumour about the nav shortage was duff gen, I gather.'

As we spoke, a couple of young air gunners joined us. One was tall and slim, with evidence at wrist and ankle that he was still growing out of his uniform. His forage cap barely contained a mop of reddish curly hair, and the perfect image of a cheeky schoolboy was completed by a freckled face and a wide grin. His companion was in direct contrast. Neat, short and dark, he had the rather intense look of a young man to whom all this was a very serious business indeed.

The tall one had obviously taken on the role of spokesman, and he addressed himself to Keith in an unmistakable Midlands accent:

'Hi there, cobber. Would you by any chance be hoping to grab yourself a couple of ace gunners?'

'Yes, you could say that.'

'Then look no further. My name is Denis Till – 'Tail End Till' – and this is my best oppo George Tuohy. We've been together right through our training and want to join the same crew. George here will be your mid upper gunner, and I'll settle for the rear turret. That's if it's OK with you?'

'Fair enough. How old are you both, by the way? And does the other fellow talk as well?'

'We're both eighteen,' said George, in answer to both questions. Denis was not yet finished:

'By the way, if you aren't fixed up yet with a wireless op, we have one lined up for you. We met him in the Mess bar last night. He seemed a good type.'

'Bring him over,' said Keith, in a tone of good humoured resignation. 'We can't afford to miss out on a recommendation like that, can we?'

As they moved off together, he turned to me. 'I needn't have panicked last night, need I? At this rate we'll be fully crewed up in another five minutes.'

The two gunners returned, with another sergeant in tow. He was stocky and pale-faced, and looked no older than they did. His manner was shy.

Denis did the introduction: 'This is him. Les Lamb. Lives near Liverpuddle. Trainee alcoholic and scourge of the Waaf site.' Les blushed furiously as he solemnly shook hands all round.

So it was five down, one to go, and bring on the bomb-aimers. There was a bunch of half a dozen of them still talking among themselves in a corner of the hangar; the five of us eyed them critically, like patricians looking for bargains at an ancient Roman slave market.

One of them, a sergeant, looked a good deal older than the rest. He was tall and goodlooking, and had just made some quip which had the others laughing. I pointed him out to Keith.

'How about that older chap. The one cracking the jokes. Just what we need, a bit of maturity.' I was already using the collective pronoun.

'Yes,' said Keith, 'I'll have a word.'

He approached the group, and returned accompanied by this fellow. 'Meet our new bomb-aimer. The name's Ken.'

More handshakes. Ken seemed to be a bright and breezy fellow. 'I was beginning to feel like a wallflower. I thought it must be my armpits.'

Our new crew was now fully constituted. The whole mating process had taken exactly ten minutes, without the slightest fuss. From now on, as far as the RAF was concerned, we were no longer individuals: we were components of Flight Sergeant Anderson's crew. A pilot of the Royal Australian Air Force captaining an all-English Royal Air Force air crew – not a particularly unusual thing.

We were the first crew to leave the hangar, after handing in our list of names to the officer at the door. He told us we could stand down for the rest of the day. Someone suggested that we should celebrate the occasion by having a get-together drink in town that evening. We arranged to meet outside the guardroom at six o'clock. Approved unanimously.

Back in the navigators' hut, later in the day, we compared notes. The general lottery had thrown up some interesting combinations. By sheer coincidence, Cyril was now crewed up with Keith's friend, another Australian named Bill Strachan, who also hailed from Sydney. Another navigator had drawn a squadron leader pilot from Training Command; we considered that what he had gained in flying experience he would lose in general mateyness. One fellow had found a crew member from his own home town, and another was in the company of four different nationalities. The only one of us to express reservations was the navigator who found himself crewed up with another Australian pilot on the course, a rangy individual named Bluey. Bluey, he found out later, had arrived here direct from a short sharp spell at the aircrew correction centre at Sheffield – a place which to aircrews was synonymous with Alcatraz. He had been banished there on charges of drunkenness and general indiscipline. While this of course did not necessarily infer an inability to handle an aircraft, it did raise doubts as to whether one could happily put one's life in his hands.

There was one factor, unknown to us at the time, which was to pose problems regarding our proposed evening booze-up in the town. This was the fact that an armoured division of the United States Army had recently moved into the area, in readiness for the imminent invasion of Europe, and were now under canvas in the fields around Moreton in the Marsh. Not unnaturally, thousands of thirsty GIs had cleaned out the town's beer stocks, and those of the surrounding villages, in a very short time. As the six of us walked into town we passed scores of these troops, aimlessly wandering around looking for non-existent entertainment. Compared with our own soldiers, they had a curiously unmilitary look, at least to our eyes. Probably something to do with their smoothly tailored uniforms, soft-soled shoes and stylish haircuts.

In the town itself we found to our dismay that every pub was closed, with the explanatory notice 'Sorry, No Beer' in the windows. The one exception was a hotel in the main street whose doors were closed but which bore a notice saying 'Opening Tonight, 7.30pm till 9.00pm'. Outside this door a long queue of serviceman, mainly Americans, had already begun to form.

After due discussion the six of us decided to join the end of the beer queue. The doors opened eventually on time, and we patiently edged our way forward as the queue shortened. There were plenty of comments from the Americans.

'They sure as hell never told us we'd spend our nights queueing for a glass of warm limey beer.'

We eventually gained access to the bar, and only just in time. The soldiers directly behind us had the door closed in their faces by the landlord.

'Sorry lads,' he called. 'We've just run out of glasses.'

I heard the same disgruntled American voice:

'Man, this sure is one hell of a goddam war.'

Be that as it may, we were in, and the beer would flow freely for the next hour. We were out to enjoy ourselves, but we all knew we were also there both to assess each other and to present ourselves as worthy representatives of our individual trades. Under alcoholic lubrication, it wasn't long before tongues were loosened. I soon formed the impression that there would be no problems of incompatability; we all seemed to share a cheerful and optimistic outlook and a desire to get on with the job.

If Keith, as skipper, felt himself to be the one most under scrutiny, he didn't show it. What we had seen of him so far we liked. He seemed to be of a placid and sober disposition, but with a ready laugh, and just enough Aussie forthrightness to indicate he would be able to control us as firmly as need be. He had joined the air force while still studying engineering at university, not exactly to his parents' delight. The remarkable motivation of someone who had volunteered to join the air war from so far away when he didn't have to was common enough in those days not to be remarked upon, but it was another item on the credit side. The white wings on his chest contrasted nicely with his distinctive dark blue tunic, and if we wanted a captain who looked the part, we had got one.

Ken, our new bomb-aimer, proved himself a good man at keeping a party ticking over nicely. He had a ready wit and could tell a good tale, or cap anyone else's. In civilian life he had worked in a local government office. He had joined up to start training as a pilot, but at some stage had been washed out, reason unspecified. He was the only one married, and at twenty-seven he was six years older than Keith and myself. In view of this, we assumed he would become something of a father figure.

Denis, our self-appointed rear gunner, was a few weeks younger than George, his fellow gunner, and qualified as baby of the crew – if that is how one can describe a lively gangling youth well over six feet in height. In view of his general liveliness and his size, it was difficult for me to reconcile him with the fellow who would be held in the very close confines of a bomber turret for anything up to ten hours at a stretch. His home was in the Midlands, and he had joined up as soon as he could in search of excitement and adventure.

George obviously had a lot in common with his friend Denis, in spite of appearing different in every way. His was the trim and neat figure for which the turrets had been designed, and it was easy to picture him alert and watchful behind the guns, conscientiously carrying out his sky search. He came from Brighton, where he had met a girl with whom he was thinking of starting a serious relationship, to nobody's great surprise. Both gunners had gained their sergeant rank with a good deal less than a year's service behind them. No doubt they would be categorised as 'jumped-up aircrew' in some quarters, with no allowances made for the nature of the job.

Les, our wireless operator, spoke with the familiar broad vowels of a fellow Lancastrian, and had served an apprenticeship in the Lancashire coalfields. Sturdy and muscular, he kept himself fit by cross-country running, and had a practical man's interests like stripping down a motorbike. His manner was shy, without being awkward, and he had not yet come fully out of his shell.

As for my own part in the scheme of things, I got the impression that everyone had been gratifyingly indoctrinated as to the importance of the navigator's role in any crew. It seemed to be tacit that mine was the number two job, involving the most brainwork and hard graft, and my proficiency or lack of it would be of the greatest concern to all. Which was a boost for my ego right from the start.

During the course of the evening, three of the Americans near us at the bar had joined us in our general conversations. They had learned with interest that we were celebrating our coming together as a crew, and in the nicest possible way expressed surprise that our government was to entrust a heavy bomber to the care of such a young and lowly-ranking team. In their air force, they assured us, all the pilots, navigators and bombardiers were commissioned officers, and quite rightly so in their opinion.

The three were all army sergeants, and like most Americans were friendly and articulate. I asked them how they were enjoying life in this quiet English backwater. They said they were quite happy, having been well briefed about wartime conditions over here. They liked the fresh green countryside and the olde-worlde charm of the area, which more or less tied in with what they had expected from the movies. They found our pounds, shillings and pence completely baffling; when they ordered beers, they proffered a heaped handful of coins for the barman to take what he wanted. They were living in their temporary camps from day to day in anticipation of the cross-Channel invasion. They had been told that the great square stacks of ammunition boxes, which we had noticed on the grass verges lining all the country lanes, extended all the way down to the south coast. When the day came, it sure would be a Real Big Deal.

All too soon, the beer ration for the night ran out, and time was called. We had got along so well with the three Americans that Denis took it upon himself to invite them back to our Sergeants' Mess, where there was no shortage of beer. They accepted the invitation gratefully, since there were no bar facilities at their own tented camp. We all walked back to the aerodrome, and enjoyed a few further rounds at the mess bar. When it finally closed, they repaid our hospitality by inviting us back to their camp for a spot of late supper. We made our unsteady way there along the black country lanes, had our presence explained to the armed sentries who startled us by suddenly challenging us out of the darkness, then stumbled across the churned-up fields with their rows of blacked-out tents and adjacent parked armoured vehicles. We ended up inside a dimly-lit mess tent, happily eating American-style hamburgers and drinking real coffee. It all rounded the evening off very nicely.

We left in fairly good order, and made our merry way for the second time that night back to the aerodrome. Denis, in particular, was full of beer and bonhomie. He had his arm round Keith's shoulder, and was confiding in his ear: 'I reckon you're a good bloke, Andy. Not a bad bloke at all, for somebody descended from a long line of convicts.'

'Not the line about the convicts again,' groaned our skipper. 'I must have heard it a hundred times since I arrived over here. Don't they teach you anything else about Australia?' He raised his eyes in mock supplication. 'To think, when I joined up I saw myself zooming around in a Spitfire. What do I find now? Here I am, in charge of a bunch of drunken Poms, getting ready to fly clapped-out Wimpeys. Where did I go wrong?'

We made our way as decorously as possible through the main gate. There was a bit of a kerfuffle going on at the guardroom alongside. Apparently they had Bluey locked up inside, charged with being drunk and disorderly, and urinating in a public place, and he was making his presence felt. I wondered if he too had been celebrating his crewing-up.

It was a long time before I fell asleep that night. The day's events and impressions were still buzzing in my brain. It had already occurred to me that the morning's crewing-up ritual, so cosy, casual and light-hearted, held a deeper significance than was apparent at the time. Commitments had been made, conditions accepted, which were quite literally matters of life and death. One didn't have to be a fatalist to acknowledge that of all the young men involved, some would have condemned themselves to an early grave purely on the mischance of an ill-starred union, so willingly and unknowingly entered into today. It was a morbid thought, quickly put out of mind. Far better to think of the positive aspects. We were committed to live, work and play together as a bomber crew, the most integrated fighting unit of all. It would give us a comradeship like no other we had experienced. And at best it might cement deep bonds of friendship which would last us for the rest of our lives.

6

ALMOST THERE

W e had gone through the ritual of the crewing-up and the obligatory crew get-together. Now was the time for the hard graft, the moulding together, the interlocking of different skills, the proving process.

For the first two weeks we went our separate ways on the ground training programme. The pilots were introduced to the complexities of the Wellington's fuel, hydraulics, electrical, weapons and communication systems, in case they thought that piloting was just a matter of hurling an aircraft around the skies. For the rest of us, there were new procedures and new equipment to be mastered; and there were bombing, gunnery and navigation simulators to sharpen us up without having to lift a foot off the ground.

The navigators and bomb-aimers spent a lot of time in the Gee trainer. It was our first introduction to the new magic world of radar, and the equipment more than justified the high claims we had heard whispered. I gazed fascinatedly as the tiny signals drifted across the double fluorescent traces on the circular screen, to be captured, measured and plotted with uncanny accuracy. The fact that we operated the equipment in conditions of high secrecy, with shaded windows and locked doors, added to the excitement.

Another pleasant surprise awaited me and the other navigators. An ingenious mechanical device, known as the Air Position Indicator, was now in general use. By combining the input of the compass and the air speed indicator, this gadget kept a continuous record of all courses and speeds flown. Instead of laboriously plotting these values as lines on a chart, with the aid of protractor, dividers and calculator, one merely read off the required air position in latitude and longitude from counters on this benignly-winking instrument. It also allowed the pilot the operational freedom of deviating from his given speeds and courses if need be, without driving his poor navigator into extremes of frustration and protest. All this, along with hints that a further revolutionary radar navigational aid was now in use on the squadrons, gave the impression that improving the navigators' lot was something extremely high on the boffins' list of priorities.

The first stage of our crew flying training consisted of hour after hour of circuits and bumps, touch and go landings, overshoots and under-shoots, single-engined landings and general handling. Since this was carried out within sight of the airfield, I was excused most of this tedious business, and spent the time sweating it out in the navigation trainer. Keith found the robust Wellington easier to handle than he had thought, and soon overcame the initial misgivings, common to all the pilots, when first comparing the size and height of it with anything he had flown previously.

I joined the rest of the crew for the first of our cross-country navigation trips. We staggered up to a height of 16,000 feet, and were introduced to flying confined by the twin umbilicals of intercom and oxygen. On route we had a simulated engine fire, followed by a practice parachute drill. After landing and taxying back to dispersal the instructor called for a practice ditching drill, which had us scrambling awkwardly and perspiringly through the upper escape hatches and out onto the wings. Even at this early stage, aspects of operational flying were being brought home to us.

Then came the morning when it was decided that we were now sufficiently proficient as a crew to be allowed into the air without an instructor. We took off for an hour of local flying, feeling like young lovers on their first unchaperoned outing together, absolutely revelling in the unaccustomed freedom. Denis asked if we could overfly his home in the Midlands, some forty miles away, and Keith agreed. I sat in the perspex nose map-reading, puffing away at a cigarette and listening to the radio dance music which Les had fed into the intercom. I couldn't think of anywhere I would rather be: the war seemed a thousand miles away. Eventually Denis was able excitedly to identify his home amidst the sprawl of streets and houses below us, and called on Keith to do a low-level beat-up. Keith declined, with a two-syllabled negative, and we made our way back to the circuit at Moreton in the Marsh. It was here that George spotted something we had all missed. The mushroom-like growth of tents all around the town had disappeared. The Americans had pulled out, taking with them all their equipment, down to the last duckboard. Nothing remained but the scarred and rutted fields to give evidence of the recent trans-Atlantic migration to this part of rural England. Our three American friends were set for their Real Big Deal. Next morning the BBC announced the D-Day landings in Normandy.

The course proceeded, and a propitious spell of clear weather allowed us to complete the required number of bombing exercises on an inland range near Oxford. This was Ken's department, operating from the nose and using the Mark 14 Bombsight, as currently used on the squadrons. The 25 lb practice bombs we dropped generated a puff of smoke on impact, which could be plotted from two ground quadrant huts, and the bombing error determined. The results varied. On one detail, an excellent error of twenty yards was followed by one of two thousand yards plus, as the bomb left the bomb-bay spinning violently.

The latter incident was greeted with hilarity by Denis, who had watched it from the rear turret. There had grown a bit of more or less friendly needle between him and Ken, and they didn't miss an opportunity of ribbing each other. It had started when Denis accused Ken of being decidedly overpaid. He could accept that the pilot got a higher rate of pay than he did because of his skill and responsibility, and the navigator because of his hard work, but not the bomb-aimer, who seemed to do very little.

'I don't get paid for what I do,' protested Ken, 'I'm paid for what I know.' Later, Ken had spotted in the rear gunner's logbook that during training he had scored zero hits when firing live rounds at the drogue target.

'That must mean this crew has the blindest crummiest gunner on the course,' claimed Ken.

'Shouldn't think so,' retorted Denis, who wasn't as ingenuous as he sometimes appeared. 'With you as our bomb-aimer it would be too much of a coincidence!' Advantage Denis.

There were also flying exercises designed to put the gunners through their paces. A Hurricane fighter from a nearby base would carry out simulated attacks on us from the rear, which the gunners had to counter while the pilot carried out the standard evasive procedure – a wildly diving-turning-climbing manoeuvre known as the Corkscrew. A cine camera incorporated in the turret enabled an assessment to be made of the effectiveness of their return fire. Both our gunners entered into the spirit of the game with great enthusiasm, and usually did well.

One morning towards the end of the course we reported to the crewroom, where it was possible to detect if not a wave, at least a ripple of excitement. Three crews had been detailed to carry out Nickel exercises that evening, and Keith was pleased to inform us that ours was one of them. Although not considered an operational trip, a Nickel, as we well knew, was as near as we would get yet awhile. It was the code name for a flight over enemy-occupied territory for the purpose of dropping leaflets, carried in special containers in the Wellington's bomb-bay. Such missions were nowadays allotted to crews training at the OTUs, with the dual purpose of providing a morale booster for the recipients and valuable pre-operational training for the aircrews concerned. Keith had acquired a copy of the particular leaflet we would be dropping. It was a four page sheet titled '*Le Courrier de L'Air, Apporte par Avion,*' which incorporated a message from General de Gaulle and photos of the French Resistance aiding Allied troops in Normandy.

That afternoon we were given the full operational-type briefing treatment, as though we were about to lead a bombing assault on Berlin itself, instead of dropping innocuous reading matter in the vicinity of Le Mans in occupied France. All the specialist officers stood up and said their pieces, and the met man offered us reasonable weather. The Chief Instructor explained that although we had been routed to avoid trouble as far as possible, our target was only fifty miles behind the invasion beaches, and we could expect some opposition. It was enough to whet the appetite of our young gunners, who for the first time would be sitting behind loaded guns.

The crew bus took us out to the aircraft in sufficient time to carry out our preflight checks in daylight. With ground power plugged in, I was able to check my Gee box and instruments, whilst Ken tested his bomb-bay circuits and stores. Denis rotated his turret within its limits, and George inspected the long belts of ammunition feeding into it. Up front Les was busy with his wireless, and ensuring the correct colours of the day were loaded in the Very pistol. Keith was slowly making his way from nose to tail with his external check list in his hand. Everything checkable was checked thoroughly, and nothing was amiss.

We sat on the grass with a last cigarette, talking nonchalantly of other things, as though the coming flight was the last thing on our minds. Then just before the time came to climb aboard, Keith decided the occasion called for a word or two from him.

'Let's take this whole thing seriously tonight. There's a lot we can learn from it. A word to you two gunners. I expect you to cover every inch of sky, until your eyes are hanging out like organ stops. And I don't want any chatter on the intercom unless you have anything important to say – yes, I do mean you Denis.'

As it turned out, the trip was something of an anti-climax. After leaving the English coast soon after nightfall a layer of cloud appeared below us, and persisted throughout. We saw nothing whatever of France, and nothing of the war; not a fleeting sight of a fighter, nor a search light, nor even a solitary burst of flak. We navigated to a calculated point upwind of our target and released our load. The black night was suddenly made bright by our exploding photoflash, displaying below us a vast white sea of cloud. I'm quite sure that the citizens of Le Mans did not awake next morning to find their streets littered with our pamphlets. We were flying at 18,000 feet, with no knowledge of the winds at lower levels which would be affecting them; and there was a fair amount of guesswork in the calculation of our release point. How, for instance, do you determine the forward travel or the terminal velocity of a four page leaflet? They would however be scattered far and wide over north west France, and we could still feel we had done our little bit for the war effort.

The cloud had disappeared again by the time we regained the English coast, and though the country was effectively blacked out there were things to see. An occasional bright white light flashing its Morse characteristic – a navigational beacon whose secret location was listed on my flimsy; the amber runway lighting of a night-flying aerodrome; the sweep of a masked car headlight, or the crimson glow from the footplate of a passing train.

We landed back at base as the eastern sky was lightening. We were tired, but morale was high. There was a cross-wind component on the runway, and Keith's landing was probably the worst one he had made with us. As we taxied away, Denis's voice came from the rear.

'Time of landing, skipper? Do we take the first bounce or the last one?'

Looking back on the trip, I was quite happy with our crew performance. Keith, the most important member, had impressed with his calm and considered approach to the business, and continued to inspire confidence. The two gunners were bursting with youthful zest and enthusiasm, which the long hours of cramped vigilance did not seem to dampen. Les was quietly efficient. There was only one question mark, and that lay against Ken's name. During this trip he had been detailed as assistant navigator, with the responsibility of obtaining and plotting the Gee fixes – a job for which he had received adequate instruction on the ground. After take-off, the first three fixes he had passed me were either misread or misplotted, causing me considerable navigational consternation. After the third one I had lost my equanimity, and testily banished him from the navigation table whilst I did the job myself. He went without demur, as though glad to be away from the responsibility. And that was another thing: once in the air, Ken seemed to undergo a complete personality charge, becoming quite different from the sophisticated fellow we knew on the ground. It seemed to me that his self-confidence evaporated as the aircraft took off, to be restored as soon as we touched down again. It was strange, especially considering the age gap between Ken and the rest of us.

During the final week of the course we were given a day off, and decided to catch a train to nearby Cheltenham. In the course of our wanderings we passed a photographer's shop, and decided to go inside to have a crew photograph taken. We posed in the stylised manner of the time, with Keith smiling benignly and the rest of his grinning brood arranged around him. In spite of the uniforms, we looked on the resultant photo like a group of end-of-the-pier theatricals, but it served its purpose of showing the folks back home what a nice bunch of boys we were flying with.

On final completion of the OTU course we were told we could have a week's leave, then we should report back as a crew to the No 4 Group Aircrew Training School at Acaster Malbis, near York. This information told us two significant things. Firstly, we would eventually be operating with No 4 Group of Bomber Command, whose squadrons were based exclusively in the East Yorkshire area, as distinct from the more usually associated bomber territory of Lincolnshire and East Anglia. Secondly, the group was equipped entirely with Halifaxes, the bomber which always seemed to take second billing to the Lancaster. I was happy about the first fact, since I would be stationed nearer home: not so sure about the second.

It was one of our bemedalled pilot instructors who put the matter of aircraft type in perspective:

'OK, so the Lancs get all the glory and the fancy targets and the pictures in the papers. They have the range and the bomb load, and I wouldn't deny them any credit due. But don't forget the latest Hali has better speed and better rate of climb, and is a hell of a lot tougher. I once did a crash landing in a Hali, and climbed out of it. If I'd done it in a Lanc we would have finished up in tiny pieces. When I'm due my second tour, there's no question which one I'll be choosing.'

If he considered it part of his job to sell the Halifax to us, he succeeded.

We had our leave, and reported back to our new unit. This proved to be a non-flying unit, pleasantly situated on the banks of the Ouse. For the first time we were billeted together as a crew, in a section of a long wooden hut. On the first evening we made our way to the city of York, and inevitably ended up at Betty's Bar, the acknowledged rendezvous of all the aircrew stationed at the dozen airfields within range of the city. The large downstairs lounge bar presented a scene of great animation and noise. Around every table were spread volatile groups in air force blue, officers, NCOs and Waafs, and girls in summer dresses. A hundred conversations were in progress, in every accent of the English-speaking world. We managed to find ourselves a table as one of the crews moved out, and we settled down for a few beers.

Our main topic of conversation was the leave from which we had just returned.

Keith had spent a week in London, staying at the Union Jack Club with his friend Bill. His main impressions had been of the current flying bomb attacks on the city, but he also recalled the great variety of allied uniforms on view and the large numbers of 'Piccadilly flak', as the Americans called the West End prostitutes. The latter two items were related in his mind, as it seemed the girls could recognise every uniform at immediate sight. He himself had been accosted – 'you looking for a good time, Aussie?' – at a range of more than fifty yards.

Ken had spent his leave at his parents' home up north, where his wife was living temporarily. He said he had been nowhere and seen no-one, but had still managed to augment his supply of have-you-heard-this-one stories.

Les had devoted his attentions to his girlfriend of long standing back home and to a cheap second-hand motor bike he had acquired. He had managed to scrounge enough petrol coupons to return on the bike, and had duly arrived back at camp in a haze of blue smoke. He was confident that his acquisition would greatly enhance his quality of life when we settled on a squadron.

The two gunners had spent their leave as any eighteen-year-old with a pound or two in his pocket would be expected to, a round of pubs, cinemas and dance-halls of his home town. George was debating in his mind the pros and cons of getting engaged in wartime, something which was greeted with derision rather than encouragement by his friend Denis, confirming once again that their association was an attraction of opposites.

My own leave had proved to be something of an anti-climax. At home, I found myself alone for most of the day. My young sister was away at school, and my father was either working or employed on Home Guard duties. Even my mother was helping the war effort by working part-time at a local factory turning out radio parts. From her description of the work she did, she could quite conceivably have been employed in assembling components of the Gee box.

I called at the homes of my friends, all of whom were now away in the forces, to learn news of them. One of my best friends, I learned sadly, had lost a leg in the D-Day landings. In town, I met one or two of my former school acquaintances, on leave like myself, and encountered some of the many metamorphoses that the war produced. The smart young army officer to whom I flung a dutiful salute turned out to be a person I vaguely remembered as an inky-fingered schoolboy in a junior form; and the fellow form mate, who had been ragged unmercifully when he had turned up at school with his hair permed, now appeared in the guise of a tough-looking Royal Marine Commando. When the time came for me to say my goodbyes and return to camp I wasn't really sorry; I seemed to have lost touch with things at home.

We finished the round of beers and decided to explore the city, and search out other drinking places. We were on a crew binge, and unless one ducked out on a round there were at least the six mandatory pints to be drunk by each of us before the night was through. We handed over our seats and table to another crew who had just arrived in the crowded bar. They were from a squadron on a twenty-four hour stand-down, and obviously about to make the most of it.

We walked the streets of this historic city, until attracted by the noise from a riverside pub. Once inside, it appeared for the moment that we had been transported to a bar on the Marseille waterfront. It seemed to be crammed exclusively with Frenchmen – mainly dressed in the dark uniforms of the Free French Air Force, but with a handful of naval ratings in their distinctive pom-pom caps, and a few girls. We had found the watering hole of the Free French squadron which was based a few miles outside York. The place was jam-packed, noisy with Gallic music and reeking of pungent French tobacco. Spoken English was nowhere evident, a point taken by Denis when he put in his order to the barman: 'Garçon, six pints de mild, si vous plait.' In due course we stumbled out of the blackout into a city centre dance hall, which had the appearance of being as classy as its name, the De Grey Rooms. The supply of local girls had been augmented by civil servants evacuated from London, and though scores of airmen had now drifted in from the pubs there was no shortage of dancing partners.

We caught the late transport back to camp, after an enjoyable night. We decided that if this represented the ambience of life in No. 4 Group, we were more than happy to be joining it.

The course at Acaster Malbis offered a good example of the thoroughness of aircrew training at this stage of the war. It served a dual purpose. It filled in the gap between two flying courses, the end of the Operational Training Unit and the beginning of the Heavy Conversion Unit, which seldom coincided due to the unpredictability of flying schedules. Its main purpose however was to acquaint aircrews with the facts of life of current operational flying – imparting information which was not to be found in the training manuals, nor published in the newspapers.

We learned at least part of the fascinating and ever-changing story of radio and radar developments and their countermeasures. The Gee system, for example, which had so impressed me at OTU, was now frequently unusable over Germany since it was subjected to enemy jamming. Our boffins, however, had come up with another revolutionary navigational aid, known as H2S. This was an airborne radar transmitter and receiver, entirely independent of ground stations. It produced on a circular screen, positioned alongside the navigator's table, an outline map of the ground over which the aircraft was flying, irrespective of cloud or darkness. Water areas, which reflected none of the radar signals, showed up black on the screen: towns, on the other hand, gave maximum returns and showed up as luminous blotches in the approximate shape of the built-up areas. It was even possible to carry out bombing attacks on towns so displayed without sight of the ground, and the equipment could not be jammed by the enemy. Yet now, as if to emphasise what a cat and mouse business it all was, there were rumours that the Germans had night-fighters equipped to home onto the bombers' H2S transmissions in the darkness. If this was so, it would cause serious restrictions on its use operationally.

Bomber Command carried out its night attacks using individually navigated aircraft, flying in a concentrated stream. The idea was to get as many bombers through the target in as short a time as possible to overwhelm the defences. To help confuse the enemy detection radar, all the bombers dropped bundles of metallised strips, code-named Window, which made it difficult to detect individual aircraft in the stream. Certain bombers carried jamming transmitters: Mandrel, to distort the enemy radar frequencies, and Tinsel, to interfere with communication channels. Radio frequencies used by the Luftwaffe night-fighters and their controllers might be swamped with loud engine noise, or even have fake instructions passed to their pilots by a German speaking RAF crewman. Some bombers carried detection devices, Fishpond and Monica, capable of giving warning of other aircraft in the immediate vicinity. As the story unfolded, it seemed that the Germans were way behind in the deception stakes. How then, I wondered, did their night fighters maintain their impressive record of kills against the bomber stream?

In answer to this, enemy night-fighter techniques were explained to us in some detail. In spite of all the countermeasures, ground radar controllers were usually able to direct their charges to the bomber stream. The twin-crewed fighters carried short-range airborne interception radar which enabled them to home onto their targets – particularly those bombers on the outer fringes of the stream, and the stragglers. The normal curve of pursuit was from the rear, and with their 30mm cannon the fighters could open fire beyond the effective range of the bombers' defensive fire. The Luftwaffe was also currently enjoying some success with twin-engined Junkers 88s and Messerschmitt 110s fitted with upward-firing cannon. If they were able to approach the bomber undetected, they could position themselves in the blind spot directly beneath him and rake the unprotected underbelly in their own good time. The bombers' petrol tanks, fitted inside the wings, were particularly vulnerable to this mode of attack, which the Germans code-named Jazz Music – thus proving that their code names were every bit as esoteric as ours. Again it was impressed upon us that, luck apart, survival was geared to crew alertness, constant vigilance and decisive evasive action.

We learned too about the Command's Pathfinder Force, and its target marking techniques. How a target could be detected and marked on the ground with a variegated supply of brilliantly-coloured pyrotechnics, or, in the event of cloud cover, by sky-marker parachute flares, onto which the Main Force bomb-aimers aimed their loads. How the Oboe equipment, which measured transmissions from two ground stations, could ensure accurate marking even in adverse conditions. And how overall control of the bombing could be carried out by the Master Bomber, whose unenviable job it was to circle the target area for the duration of the attack, issuing instructions on a pre-chosen radio frequency.

The whole course was undemanding, in that we were not expected to take notes or pass exams, but I'm sure we all found it extremely interesting and informative.

Our next posting, the last one before we joined a squadron, took us on a journey of exactly five miles. We were consigned to the Halifax Heavy Conversion Unit at Rufforth, a flying station situated a few miles west of York. We said our goodbyes to Bill Strachan and his crewmen Cyril, Ed, Johnny and Arthur, with whom we had become friendly. They were going to a similar unit, but on a different station, and it was unlikely that we would meet again.

We made the short journey by truck, with Les tailing us on his motor bike. We had barely unloaded our kit outside the Sergeants' Mess at Rufforth when we were approached by a young sergeant, smartly turned out in his best blue.

'Excuse me,' he greeted us. 'Are you Flight Sergeant Anderson's crew?'

'We are.'

'My name's Dick Mundy. I've been assigned as your flight engineer. Pleased to meet you.'

We introduced ourselves, and shook hands all round. He looked to be about twenty years old, a Londoner from his accent, and a fledgling aircrew from the newness of his stripes and brevet. 'I've been waiting all morning to meet you,' he said. 'I was curious to see what sort of blokes I was joining.'

'What do you think now you've seen us?' asked Keith.

'Well, I was expecting most of you to be older than you seem to be.'

'Sorry to disappoint you,' grinned Keith. 'Maybe we'll all look a lot older in six months time.'

Our new crew member had already organised accommodation for us in one of the huts, so we were soon settled in. After lunch in the Mess, we wandered down to the dispersals to take a close look at our new aircraft type. By its very nature, its size and destructive potential, a heavy bomber is a sinister and awesome sight, even when in repose on the airfield hardstanding. I stood with Keith in front of the Mark 3 Halifax, eyeing its huge hundred-foot wingspan set with four powerful-looking radial engines, and its long cavernous bomb-bay. Keith had that reflective look which I had seen before, when he had taken his first close look at a Wellington, and I knew just what he was thinking. How will I lift this heavy-looking monster off the ground with a full load of bombs, and how the hell will I land it from the dizzy height of that cockpit way up there? He was subconsciously flexing the fingers of his right hand: 'I expect I'll get used to handling four throttles, like I got used to handling two on the Wimpey. It seems a million years since those carefree single-engined days on the old Harvard.'

We climbed aboard to inspect our various crew positions. I moved forward along the upward-sloping metal tunnel, clambered over the two main spars to the crew cabin, then squeezed my way down the steps into the nose compartment. The wireless cabin was a small alcove on the port side, where Les would sit at his set with the rudder pedals and the soles of Keith's flying boots directly above his head. The navigation table was further forward, where I would sit facing the port fuselage, in an area which could be completely enclosed by canvas curtains. An array of instrument panels and radar units were grouped around on metal brackets, forming what almost seemed like a protective cocoon. In the floor directly beneath my bench-type seat was fitted the upward lifting emergency forward escape hatch, which was reassuring. Further forward, the floor was padded to allow the bomb-aimer to lie prone as he operated the bombsight in the perspex nose. Altogether it seemed a well designed setup, and the whole aircraft gave a general impression of reassuring solidity.

The course progressed on similar lines to that recently completed at Moreton in the Marsh. Most of the work fell on Keith, as the early days were taken up with circuit flying, accompanied by a screen pilot. It did not take him long to master the intricacies of four-engined flying, and to strike up a working relationship with his new flight engineer.

Dick appeared to be an efficient young man, keen to be assimilated into the crew, and to impress us with his technical know-how. He had been a mechanic in civilian life, and had just completed his flight engineer's course, which did not involve very much actual flying. He seemed to have been brainwashed into believing he was the only member of the crew with any sort of technical knowledge. He was however already beginning to revise this idea, as he confided to me.

'I must admit our skipper has surprised me. They told us that when we got into a crew we'd find that the pilot was just a glorified driver of airframes, who would know as much about engines as we do about navigation. From what I've seen so far, he knows every bit as much as I do'

I smiled to myself. It was my experience that all pilots had a perfectly sound grasp of technical matters pertaining to the type of aircraft they flew, and Keith moreover had been studying engineering to degree level at university. He was hardly likely to be upstaged by our engineer, no matter how seriously the young sprog took his job.

The latter part of our conversion course was taken up by more navigation exercises, using the new H2S equipment. This was supposed to be operated by the bomb-aimer, sitting alongside me at the navigation table, but Ken again demonstrated that with the best will in the world he was just not cut out for the job. The illuminated blotches on the screen, which represented built-up areas on the ground, had to be tied in with towns as marked on the map, and could be a tricky business. Time and again, as a result of misidentification of towns, I was fed inaccurate fixes, with chaotic results to the navigation. Something had to be done. Duff fixes whilst flying over England was one thing: their consequences when we came to fly in a bomber stream over Germany I hardly dared to contemplate.

Keith, Ken and I, as the crew navigation team, got together to discuss the matter dispassionately. As a result, we decided on a change of crew responsibilities. Whenever possible, Ken would fly sitting alongside the pilot, where he was normally positioned for take-offs and landings, and Keith would allow him practice at handling the aircraft. In other words, he would act as an assistant pilot instead of a second navigator, except of course when he was engaged in his bombing duties. I myself would take over full responsibility for the operation of the navigational radar. If it appeared that I was being over-officious, or that I was impugning his capabilities, the thing was done quite amicably. It demonstrated again

Ken's strange lack of assertiveness in matters relating to his role in the air.

Our last flying trip was a Command night Bullseye exercise – a cross country with a single-run practice bomb attack on a coastal bombing range. The next day, at the flight office, we found that our posting notice to our operational station had arrived. We were to proceed in three days time as a replacement crew to No 158 Squadron at Lissett, the largest squadron in 4 Group.

Nobody was quite sure where Lissett was situated. We knew that some of the airfields in the Group were way out in the wilds, miles from the nearest decent sized town. I delved into my nav bag for the quarter inch map of Northern England. There it was, clearly marked. Near the coast, alongside the Hull to Bridlington road, and no more than six miles from the popular east coast holiday resort. If we had been given our own choice of the dozen 4 Group squadrons, this is the location we would undoubtedly have chosen.

On the last night our crew held an end-of-course party in the bar of the local village pub. We had been at Rufforth less than two months, but in that time had established a friendly relationship with several of the Waafs with whom we had come in contact. This was almost entirely due to the efforts of Denis. The combination of his unfailing good humour, ingenuous chatter and wholesome schoolboy image never failed to charm them, or set their maternal instincts going. He had issued a general invitation to our party, and to our surprise half a dozen of the girls turned up to give us a send-off.

The party went well, as the drinks flowed, and tongues were loosened. George was to be heard earnestly quizzing a young Waaf on the feminine views of early engagements and wartime marriages. The pretty brunette from the parachute packing section was looking at Keith like he was the answer to any maiden's prayer, whilst Denis circulated and spilled his beer over all and sundry. Ken picked out a few tunes on the worn piano, including a silly catchy song of the period called *Mairzy Doats and Dozy Doats*. Strange to relate, of all the memorable songs the war produced, this was the one which in future years never failed to evoke for me the most nostalgic memories of these wartime days.

During the course of the evening, Mary and Babs, the two Waafs from the MT Section who drove the aircrew transports, called for order. They gave Andy's crew their best wishes for the future, and called on Denis to accept a good luck token on the crew's behalf. This proved to be a hand-made cloth doll in the form of a smiling airman, complete with blue uniform, shiny buttons and cap, and no doubt modelled on Denis himself.

Denis of course was tickled pink by all this. He christened it there and then 'Herman the Airman', with a finger dipped in his beer glass. He appointed it official crew mascot, with honorary rank of sergeant since it would be flying on all our ops in the rear turret, with Denis as its guardian. He called on all present to take up their glasses and drink a toast:

'To Herman the Airman, and his successful first tour.'

We all cheered loudly, and drained our glasses, with the few locals at the bar looking on tolerantly. In the alcoholic glow now suffusing us, I'm sure we all saw ourselves in the true mould of Errol Flynn and his intrepid comrades of the Dawn Patrol, tossing off a toast before leaping into the air to confront the enemy. There followed a whole series of light-hearted toasts from all of us round the table; and of no great interest to anyone other than possibly a psychologist. We drank to 'Butch' Harris of Bomber Command, who was not unpopular with his aircrews in spite of his ruthless image; to Mae West, whose upper structure had been immortalised in the naming of the RAF's life jacket; to the Waaf, who had recruited the country's prettiest girls; to Vera Lynn, who put into song what we all felt; and even to Joe Stalin, whose Red Army was currently taking the pressure off us in Europe. And finally to Andy, who had got himself the best crew in 4 Group – and by this time we fully believed it!

We ended the evening with a sing-song. The sentimental songs of the day were followed by the old air force songs, whose words were picked up sooner or later by every airman with a bit of service in. And some of the newer songs:

> 'They say there's a Halifax leaving the Ruhr,
> Bound for old Blighty's shore,
> Heavily laden with petrified men,
> Prostrate and prone on the floor . . .'

It was long after closing time when the patient landlord finally got us off the premises, and we steered an unsteady course through the blackout towards camp. Our guests were safely conveyed back to the Waaf site, goodbyes were said, and Denis's promises to write acknowledged.

There would be outsize hangovers for the crew next morning, but general satisfaction that we were leaving on a high note. The thought was there that our send-off from the Waafs had a certain significance. Rufforth, and units exactly like it, turned out crews for the squadrons like meat from a mincer. Nameless faces came and went, with nothing to distinguish them from their predecessors or successors. Yet the girls had picked on us for special treatment. The inference was that Andy's crew were seen to be a little bit out of the ordinary, a little bit more special. We had acquired not only the final training and the extra crew member but added goodwill and an accredited good luck token.

Now we were ready for anything.

7

First Op

T he train which, in effect, was taking us to our own particular part of the war, was in no great hurry to do so. The branch line from York took us over the gentle curves and undulations of the Yorkshire Wolds, and through a series of small market towns and village halts, with a stop at each one. This quiet and peaceful region had known many invaders throughout its long history. Vikings and Romans, Saxons and Normans, all had left their mark. Now it seemed that it had been invaded once more. Young men and women dressed in air force blue had come to build their settlements of corrugated iron and plastered brick, and to lay great swathes of concrete over the flat farmlands.

Even on this cloudy and chilly November morning the East Riding countryside looked attractive, with its trim meadows and neat hedgerows and tree-sheltered farmsteads: a tribute to a thousand years of good husbandry.

I was sitting by the window of our compartment, with the responsibility of seeing that we did not overshoot our destination. The train began to slow down again as we approached another small station, which did not seem to have any supporting village or habitations in its vicinity. The platform came into view, with the name, Burton Agnes, clearly displayed. This was the name on the crew travel warrant which I carried. This was where our operational career, like that of countless others before us and after us, was set to begin.

We climbed out and stood huddled on the platform, with our greatcoat collars turned up about our ears, waiting for Les to retrieve his motor bike from the luggage van. Overhead, two Halifaxes droned by, flying at circuit height. Two yellow diagonal bands on their tail fins stood out against the matt black of their bodies. This, presumably, was the identification marking carried by the aircraft of our new squadron.

An airman in a stained leather jerkin suddenly materialised. 'Are you the crew for Lissett, chiefie?' he addressed Keith. 'I have your transport outside.'

We loaded our kitbags and manhandled the motor bike into the back of the three-tonner, and I climbed up alongside the driver. We moved off, along a narrow winding country lane.

'How far to the airfield?' I asked.

'Oh, about five miles to the main site, but it's a dispersed camp and the domestic sites are scattered all over the place. I'll give you a tip. Get yourself organised with a pushbike as soon as you can.'

'What's it like here?'

The question was purely rhetorical. One could hardly be asking the real questions. How do the crews react on a unit like this where the possibility of death or injury is ever present? Is there a spirit of devil-may-care like the films portrayed, or is it one of constant anxiety and suppressed fear? Do many people crack up, or opt out? Are we well looked after by our superiors? Are our aircraft well serviced? And how long does it take for a sprog crew to become assimilated into a squadron?

The driver had given my question due thought. 'Oh, it's not bad, I suppose. The grub's OK, and there isn't much bullshit.' It was the answer I could have expected. No self-respecting airman would dream of expressing more satisfaction with his lot than that.

We eventually reached the camp, and stopped to report in at the guardroom. The main site, a hotchpotch of red brick and grey pre-fabrication, was separated from the village of Lissett by a small copse. The ancient stone church, with its apron of sloping gravestones and fringe of old cottages seemed to emphasise the transience of its wartime neighbour. There was no village pub or even a shop in view. Across the main road, as our driver pointed out, was the site containing the Officers', Sergeants' and Airmens' Messes, large rounded structures of corrugated iron. The airfield itself consisted of three intersecting concrete runways, with associated taxiways and dispersal pens, imposed on the grassland adjacent to the main road.

The living quarters were situated in various sites round the periphery of the aerodrome, and to one of these we were now driven. A rutted path led from the country lane to a group of Nissen huts huddled round a brick ablutions block. A line of bare elm trees helped break the force of the strong easterly wind, which brought to our noses the tang of woodsmoke. We unloaded our kit outside the small picket post, from which emerged the airman who was in charge of the site.

'How many of you are there? Seven? I'll put you all together in hut number three. It's the best we have available. Follow me, please.'

If this was the best available accommodation, then the worst must have been absolutely horrific. The hut was dark and gloomy, containing just eight iron bedsteads and adjacent bedside lockers. A cast-iron stove in the centre had spewed cold ashes onto the flagstones beneath, and a deposit of dust and fluff was visible under each bed. Metal brackets attached to the walls showed where wooden shelving had once been fitted. We gazed around, in some dismay. 'My God,' said Ken. 'Has 'Butch' Harris inspected this place lately? I've kept ferrets in better conditions than this.'

The airman was apologetic.

'I'm sorry about the shelves. They've been broken off and used for firewood. We ran out of fuel once, and the aircrews were burning everything they could get their hands on. One crew found a telegraph pole and brought it back to burn. And I would advise you to make sure your coke ration is kept locked up in the hut when you are not here, otherwise the other huts will pinch it.'

We each selected a bed, and began to unpack our kit. The airman left, and returned bearing a pile of clean sheets.

'I should have mentioned that if you want breakfast in the mornings a crew coach calls at the site at 0730, to take you to the Sergeants' Mess. It's a long walk if you miss it.' He made to leave again, and paused at the door. 'I'm sorry the hut isn't very tidy, but they've only just finished carrying the kit away.'

He left, and we pondered his last remark. 'Does that mean we're sleeping in dead mens' beds?' asked Dick.

No-one knew. And really, did it make any difference if we were?

Les had been out foraging for firewood, and very soon he had the coke stove burning. With the chill taken out of the air, the beds made up and our kit stowed, the hut took on a slightly more cheerful aspect.

'Home sweet home,' said Denis. 'It isn't the Ritz, but it's home.'

Later we left, to make our way to the Sergeants' Mess for tea. It was indeed a long walk, especially with a gale force wind from the North Sea in our faces.

I entered the crowded Mess dining room, and queued at the servery. As I sat down with my plate of sausage and chips, I felt a hearty clap on the back. Turning round, I was delighted to be confronted with my friend Cyril's smiling face. He and his crew and my own crew had defied all the odds by being posted to the same squadron; their conversion course had finished before ours, and they had arrived here a week previously. What a tonic it was to see their familiar faces amongst all these strangers.

Keith too was delighted to meet up again with Bill, his fellow pilot and compatriot. Our two crews spent the evening together, gently imbibing at the bar. I sat and talked with Cyril. It was traditional that members of a bomber crew worked, lived and drank together, but how nice it was to be able to talk shop with a fellow tradesman for a change.

Later in the evening the Tannoy came to life with a brief announcement that owing to the strong cross-winds all flying for the night was cancelled. Within minutes the bar had filled up with aircrew NCOs, and we moved with our drinks into the anteroom. The atmosphere was pleasantly relaxed as we sprawled in our easy chairs. A blazing log fire in the large brick fireplace cast a cosy glow, and at the far end of the room the piano was being quietly played by a New Zealand warrant officer.

Periodically I found myself carefully taking stock of my surroundings. The company was becoming noisy and boisterous as the beer flowed freely, but then that was normal in any Sergeants' Mess of the period. Looking around, there was really nothing to convey that the pressures of operational flying were much greater than those to which we were accustomed. It was certainly impossible to pick out any individual and say to oneself: 'This fellow is sweating on his first op' or 'This one is near the end of his tour, and it shows.' If I was subconsciously looking for signs of a hand that shook enough to spill the beer, or a facial twitch of noticeable proportions, then I was unsuccessful. I found it quite reassuring.

The voices around grew louder, and I unashamedly listened in to interesting snatches of conversation, as the babel ebbed and flowed.

It was obviously all shop talk:

'. . . And the skipper said sod this for a lark, it's getting bloody dangerous – I'm climbing another thousand feet . . .'

'. . . She's had three boyfriends in six months, and every one gets the chop . . .'

'. . . So I figured that with two flight commanders flying it must be an easy target . . .'

Or nearly all shop talk:

'. . . And she said this doesn't mean I don't love my husband and I said of course not . . .'

What a fascinating story, I thought, could be woven around every one of them.

We remained talking long after the bar had closed. When we finally wended our way back to our billets we had great difficulty in finding them. After all, even if we had been sober, one Nissen hut is very much like another in the blackout.

Next morning we collected our arrival chits and commenced the rounds, performing the dual function of booking ourselves in at each section and acquainting ourselves with the general layout of the station. The final call was to our individual aircrew sections.

The Navigation Leader was in his office, busily engaged in assessing logs and charts handed in after the last operation. I introduced myself, with the diffidence of a new boy meeting his headmaster, but his friendly manner soon put me at ease. It was always my experience that the shared profession of navigation provided a kind of freemasonry, quite irrespective of rank or nationality. He told me there were some thirty navigators on the strength, ranging from sprogs like myself to veterans on the tail end of their tour. A tour consisted of thirty completed ops. We would not be put on the ops crew list until we had performed some local flying exercises, and familiarised ourselves with the squadron procedures and equipment. It was current squadron policy to recommend for commissioning all pilots and navigators after their successful completion of ten trips, unless they had in some way blotted their copy books. We shook hands, and I left with the happy feeling of already belonging.

Early the following morning we took off on the first of our training flights. I sat in the nose with a map, familiarising myself with the local terrain. To the north-east jutted the rocky promontory of Flamborough Head, from where the gently curving sandy coastline extended southwards as far as distant Spurn Point and the mouth of the Humber. Our airfield lay some two miles from the coast, and the same distance away was the long ribbon of concrete which represented the Carnaby emergency landing strip. Nearly two miles in length, and the width of three ordinary runways, it was one of three Bomber Command havens for crippled bombers. It seemed to me to be a very handy thing to have right on your doorstep.

We flew low over the sea, and our gunners had some firing practice at a flame float dropped from the aircraft. For the last half hour Keith had Ken in the copilot's seat to handle the controls, where he seemed quite happy. It was reassuring for the rest of us to know that if anything unfortunate happened to Keith, there was someone else capable of keeping us in the air.

We landed back at base, and as we taxied back to the aircraft dispersal it soon became apparent that ops were in the offing. The whole place, so peaceful when we had taken off an hour previously, was now like a disturbed ant hill. Overalled ground crews swarmed on wing and fuselage, attaching umbilicals from the petrol bowsers, replacing engine cowlings, polishing turrets. Officers in cars and airmen on bicycles sped along the perimeters. Tractors towing bomb trolleys and trucks carrying long shiny belts of ammunition converged on the aircraft. There was a sense of purpose behind the whole orchestration which was quite stunning.

Our crew as yet had no part to play in this scene. We were mere bystanders throughout the afternoon, amidst the urgent comings and goings of the aircrews as they prepared for the night. We were playing cards in our hut in the early evening when a sudden staccato burst from across the airfield heralded the first engine start-up. There followed the gradual build-up of engine noise, until it became a loud sustained reverberation. Finally came the crescendo as the first take-off power was applied, and the first heavily-laden Halifax lumbered into the air. We abandoned our game, as we counted seventeen more. We had slept for many hours before they returned, unheard.

The next week or two was a period of some frustration for us, as we waited for our crew to be included in the operational battle order. Especially so since Bill and his crew had happily got their first trip under their belts. It was equally frustrating for our met man, who could offer good weather at Lissett, and good weather over Germany, but seldom the two together. Surely the stresses of flying on ops would be no greater than the strain of this interminable waiting.

When our name did finally appear on the board, there was still concern and indecision about the weather. Three times the Tannoy announced a postponement of briefing times. Then, in the early evening, the final decision was made: navigation briefing for pilots, navigators and bomb-aimers at midnight, main briefing an hour later, first take-off at 0230. That meant another wait, but not long enough to think of getting any sleep in.

Keith and I walked over to the Sergeants' Mess, with three hours to kill before reporting in. The atmosphere there was in sharp contrast to that of my previous evening visit. The bar was empty, and the airman behind the counter had only bothered to remove one of the hatches, for the sale of cigarettes. Most of the chairs in the anteroom were occupied by sprawling figures, wearing aircrew sweaters under their battledress and fur-lined flying boots. We found a couple of easy chairs, and I lay back with my eyes closed. From the radio, permanently tuned to the BBC's forces' programme, came the muted strains of *Jealousy*. No-one was attempting to make conversation. Perversely, the thought of an early night in bed with the warm glow of the stove and good book suddenly seemed very appealing, now that it was not available.

Keith had been pondering the forthcoming trip. 'What a god-awful time to be taking off, after all this waiting. At least, we'll be landing in daylight.'

Andy's crew and ground crew aboard 'N-NAN' – a brand new Halifax Mk VI just delivered to 158 Squadron.

The crew (*left to right*): Les Lamb (wireless operator), George Tuohy (mid-upper gunner), Denis Till (rear gunner), Keith Anderson (pilot), Len Cooper (bomb-aimer), Dick Mundy (engineer), Harry Lomas (navigator). In front row Sgt Smith and two of his ground crew.

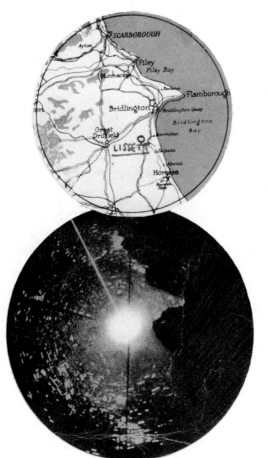

H2S navigational aid, showing map of the area and the screen presentation.

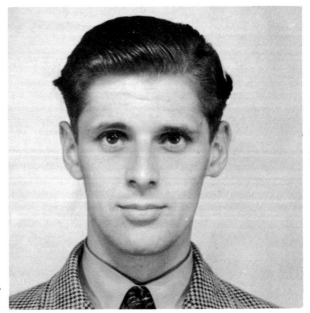

The author's 'escape photograph'. This was carried on operations for use in a faked passport.

LE COURRIER DE L'AIR

PORTE PAR AVION   LONDRES, LE 20 JUILLET 1944

onneur aux Forces Françaises de l'Intérieur

ne se passe pas un jour sans que les Forces ançaises de l'Intérieur n'aient l'honneur un communiqué.

ce soit par le communiqué du Quartier al Suprême allié ou par les communications par les milieux français autorisés de Londres, ations Unies sont tenues au courant de la e que n'ont jamais cessé de livrer les patriotes ls combattant l'envahisseur sur le sol natal. Allemands et les traîtres ont cherché, mais en à flétrir du nom de " terrorisme " les actes eux et habilement conçus des Français pérant sous les ordres du général Koenig, nt l'ennemi là où les coups portent le plus. guerre lasse, les Allemands menacent d'exécomme francs-tireurs tous les soldats des qui tomberaient sous leur coupe.
rs alliés veillent.

ceux de nos lecteurs qui n'auraient pas ssance de l'avertissement donné aux Allepar le général Eisenhower, Commandant ne des Forces Expéditionnaires alliées, nous iuisons le texte de ce document qui ne pas à équivoque :

e Commandant Suprême des forces expédiires alliées possède aujourd'hui la preuve le que les forces allemandes d'occupation ance, se conformant aux déclarations faites uin 1944 par le Commandant-en-Chef des s allemandes de l'Ouest, traitent les membres roupes de résistance français comme des tireurs.

F.F.I. font partie des F.E.A.

n conséquence, le Commandant Suprême e :

Les Forces Françaises de l'Intérieur cont une force combattante placée sous le andement du général Koenig; elles forment une intégrante des forces expéditionnaires alliées;

les F.F.I. ont pris ouvertement les armes l'ennemi et ont reçu ordre de conduire leurs ons en conformité avec les lois de la guerre ; oortent un insigne distinctif et le général ower les considère comme une armée placée on commandement ;

dans ces conditions les représailles exercées les groupes de résistance constituent une on flagrante des lois de la guerre auxquelles lemands sont tenus de se soumettre. De mes ne peuvent que fortifier la détermination ations Unies de mener rapidement la guerre fin victorieuse, afin que justice soit rendue ;

le Commandant Suprême est résolu que ffort soit mis en œuvre pour découvrir et r les auteurs des atrocités commises contre embres des forces armées placées sous son andement. Des mesures ont déjà été prises te fin. Les coupables seront livrés sans à la justice."

Le général Koenig, Commandant des F.F.I., en conférence avec le général Montgomery et M. Coulet, Commissaire de la France libérée, au Q.G. britannique en Normandie

Soldats des F.F.I. à Caen

F 75

Allies' leaflet dropped over Le Mans, 1944.

'One of our bridges is missing.' Picture taken during daylight attack on the Rhine bridges at Cologne, 2 March 1945.

The attack on Wangerooge Island, 25 April 1945. This was the last target of the war for the author.

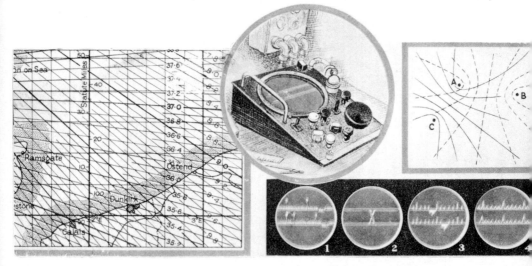

Bomber Command's primary navigational aid – the Gee System.

Opposite: Photograph of the
author wearing the short-lived
'Aircrew One' rank badges.

The end of *Lili Marlene*.

Reunion with Australian wartime skipper. (*Left to right*) Keith Anderson, Helene Anderson, the author, Joan Lomas.

Reunion with George Tuohy (*left*) our mid-upper gunner, at the Squadron reunion.

'I only hope it's a short trip,' I said. 'I can hardly keep my eyes open now.'

'I've seen the crew chief. He says they're loading mixed bombs and incendiaries, and a normal fuel load. To the ground crew that means the Ruhr.'

Eventually the time came for us to report to the main briefing room, the largest assembly point on the station, situated in the Operations Block. Here some two dozen trestle tables and benches were arranged, facing the briefing platform. The large wall chart before us was hidden behind a curtain, in front of which stood the Station Navigation Officer at his lectern. On the stroke of midnight he signalled to the service policeman at the door, who went out, locking the door behind him.

'Captains please answer for your crews as I call the roll,' he said. This formality completed, he walked to the wall chart and with a dramatic sweep opened the curtain. Our route was revealed, marked by a long red ribbon. The target was not very far into Germany, but it was situated in the large patch on the map marked in red, which I knew represented the heavily defended industrial Ruhr. There was little reaction from the other crews.

> 'Well gentlemen, it's the Happy Valley again. Your target tonight is the
> large railway marshalling yards at Duisberg, Germany's biggest inland
> port, situated at the confluence of the rivers Rhine and Ruhr . . .'

There wasn't time for any speculation on the trip or the target. There was a busy hour ahead of me – drawing in the route on my plotting chart, marking danger areas, and calculating courses and times for each leg on my flight plan. The met man was on hand to supply us with estimated winds for each region and height band. His forecast weather was of broken layers of cloud over the continent, which we should clear at our planned flying height of 20,000 feet. He implied that conditions were marginal, and the met people were doing us a favour by letting us go.

I was the last to finish flight planning, distracted by a peculiar ritual going on up front. One of the officer navigators, a tall lugubrious Canadian, was on his feet with arm raised in mock benediction, amidst the sound of loud catcalls from the audience.

'Sit down, Sammy, you silly sod,' yelled some-one, with unconscious alliteration. 'We don't want to know.'

This was Flying Officer Samuels, a well-known squadron character. His party piece, apparently, was to stand up at the end of nav briefing to give his estimate of squadron losses for the night, having given due

97

consideration to the crew list, the weather outlook and the location of the target. Ignoring the calls, he now began to stab a finger around the room.

'Sammy says tonight one crew meets the Grim Reaper. Just the one. But it might be you, or you, or you!'

I did not know what to make of this macabre humour, though most of the others seemed to find it amusing. Sammy's skipper, another Canadian, was sitting at the next table, and he leaned over to address us:

'Take no notice. We're near the end of our tour, and the guy's going flak happy.' He no doubt meant to be reassuring, but completely spoiled the effect by adding: 'You'd be surprised how often he gets it right.'

Further distraction and discussion was avoided by the arrival *en masse* of the rest of the crew members, who crammed themselves on the benches by their crew tables. Moments later we were called to attention as the briefing team entered the room, headed by the Station Commander, Group Captain Sawyer, and our Squadron Commander, Wing Commander Dobson. It was my first sight of our top brass. Both were experienced Halifax captains, well beribboned and, it seemed, well respected.

The main briefing followed the normal format, with each of the specialist officers having the floor in turn. The weather was still the talking point. It was considered unlikely that we would be able to see the ground over the continent, so we could expect the Pathfinders to be marking our aiming point with red sky markers, usually the least accurate method.

The Station Commander wished us all a good trip, and the briefing ended. As I was gathering up my charts and equipment into my nav bag, a good-looking young Canadian flying officer pilot came to our table to shake hands with Keith, and wish him good luck. Like us, he and his crew were on their first trip tonight. We appreciated the gesture, and reciprocated heartily.

As we all trooped out towards the locker room, where we would don our flying kit, Mae West and parachute harness, there came a sudden call from the briefing room. It was the Station Navigation Officer:

'Sorry chaps, but there's been an alteration to the route. All navigators are to return for further briefing. The rest of the crews are to proceed to their aircraft, and start engines at the briefed times, even if the navigators are not aboard.'

Back to the drawing boards went twenty cursing navigators. The change in the route was not drastic, nor was the reason for it explained to us, but it involved a lot of work in a hurry. Our time on target, which we were expected to achieve within one minute either side, was unchanged, but the new route involved changing all our recently calculated times at each turning point, and take-off time itself.

The noise of eighty Bristol Hercules engines ripped the night air as we sped from the briefing room in the waiting transports, to be dropped off individually at our aircraft. The ground crew lads helped me aboard K-King, bracing themselves against the slipstream as they handed up my nav bag and parachute pack. At least the cold air helped dispel the sweat I had generated over the last half hour. Keith was already taxying before I had settled in my take-off position. After kicking my heels for over eighteen hours, I was off on my first op with my flight plan incomplete, my equipment unchecked and my brain a jumble of conflicting figures.

The delay involving the navigators meant the earlier take-offs were already running behind schedule. A long queue of Halifaxes had built up near the take-off point. Anxiously I checked my watch as the minutes ticked by, and the urgency was in my voice as I called up on intercom:

'Nav to skipper. Take-off time in one minute. How are we doing?'

'No chance, nav. You'll have to relax. There are four, maybe five, in front of us still. We'll have to turn the taps on after take-off and hope for the best. Everybody's in the same boat.'

We gradually moved forward, until eventually getting the green light from the runway controller's caravan, signifying permission to line up and take-off. Keith's heavy breathing into his microphone showed the effort he was putting into his taxying. This was the first time he had been called upon to move a fully bombed-up Halifax, and he was finding it no easy task. One wrong burst of throttle could result in a wheel leaving the narrow tarmac perimeter, sinking up to the axle in the soft grass, and blocking the traffic for the rest of the night.

Finally we rumbled down the runway, seven minutes behind schedule. Sitting as I was in the mid-section of the aircraft, I was extremely conscious of the four tons of high explosive in the bomb-bay directly beneath me. I found myself tightly holding my breath and positively willing us into the air, until the rumblings and bouncings eased into smooth flight. Keith already had our first course set on his compass repeater, and I could sense the turn almost before the wheels had retracted into their nacelles. By the time I had scrambled forward and settled in at the navigation table in the nose, we had reached our intermediate height of 5,000 feet and levelled out. After much juggling with the power settings, Keith and Dick were able to boost our speed by 15 mph, which would eventually be sufficient to make up the time we had lost.

I had been well indoctrinated during my training in the responsibilities of a navigator in the Main Force of Bomber Command. My aim was twofold. First, to keep the aircraft at all times as close as humanly possible to the pencilled track lines on my chart; and secondly, to maintain planned times of arrival at each turning point. This achieved, our position near the centre of the bomber stream would be ensured. And this undoubtedly was the safest place to be: just like ships in a convoy, where the more valuable the cargo carried, the nearer the centre of the convoy they were positioned. I always took my job seriously, and anything which detracted from these aims, such as wrong fixes or late take-offs, tended to make me excessively tetchy, as no doubt Ken would testify.

It was a pitch black night, and since we were flying between layers of cloud we could see nothing of the ground or the stars, and certainly nothing of our companions. As we crossed the English coast near Brighton, it was hard to visualise that we were but one of six hundred being channelled to the same target. A few minutes later, when our estimated position was at the French coast near Dieppe, I passed our new north-easterly course to the pilot, with instructions to commence climbing to bombing height. It was at this moment that we hit a sudden gust of turbulence; it felt as if our wings were fluttering, and my stomach fluttered with them.

'It's alright,' came Keith's calm voice, 'we're hitting slipstreams from other aircraft. Looks like we're on track, navigator.'

I was relieved to hear it. My imagination had begun to stray from its bounds. Looking out into the black void, I had begun to wonder whether some dreadful miscalculation on my part had sent us ploughing a lonely furrow in a totally wrong direction – inevitably to be picked off by our enemies in due course.

For the next hour or so I was completely engrossed in the navigation, so much so that although I could sense a rising tension, I was far too busy to have any great fears about our safety. The Gee signals on the set at my side were now subject to jamming by the Germans, and the two green fluorescent lines on the screen were covered with what looked exactly like grass. However, I found that with patience and some manipulation, it was occasionally possible to detect and measure the required signals amongst all this mush, and to thus obtain a quick lucky fix. All was quiet on the intercom, and I wondered how the others were feeling, especially our young gunners, who had nothing to relieve the monotony of staring into the black night.

It was Keith's voice which eventually broke the silence: 'Flak up ahead. It's predicted stuff, well below us. Nothing to worry about.'

100

I parted the curtains and glanced through the perspex nose, where Ken was lying as he set up the required data on his bombsight. It was my first sighting of flak. It showed up as twinkling yellow pinpricks in the sky, which looked completely innocuous, but it didn't take much imagination to appreciate that each pinprick generated an area of flying shrapnel which would penetrate anything in its path.

The sight was enough to bring home to me very forcibly that flying for us was no longer the friendly business to which we had become accustomed. Hitherto, everything had been geared to the safety of the aircraft and crew. At the first hint of danger we could call on a whole variety of people concerned with our welfare – controllers, radio direction finders, coastguards, rescue teams and others. Now, everybody was trying to kill us.

I passed on to the skipper the information that, on my latest calculations, we would need a further 10 mph increase in airspeed to reach our target on the exact planned time. He replied that he was not prepared to comply, as we were already making inroads on our reserve fuel, which was a good enough reason. I also announced that we were now flying over Germany itself.

The latter was of academic interest to everyone except Denis, who had previously asked me to let him know when we crossed the border. He was carrying in his turret, apart from Herman the Airman, two or three empty bottles which he had acquired. These were not there for the same purpose as the one carried up front for the possible use of the pilot. Denis had heard from somewhere or other that an empty bottle, dropped from a great height, produced the sound of loud banshee wailing which was quite terrifying to anyone on the ground. Though the rest of us ridiculed the idea, he thought this would be well worth the effort involved. No wonder, as I told him later, the Germans called us the *terrorflieger*!

We turned onto the last course for the target.

'Only five minutes to go, bomb-aimer,' I called. 'Can you see anything ahead? The sky-markers should be burning.'

'Not a thing,' said Ken. 'Just solid cloud below us.'

Keith, as briefed, now switched the VHF onto intercom, to pick up any last minute instructions from the Master Bomber, the airborne controller who would have been orbiting the target area since the attack began. Immediately our ears were assailed by a loud high-pitched whine, above which several crew-members tried to make themselves heard at once. Keith's voice was the loudest:

'Wireless op, what's the matter with this bloody VHF? Check it.'

From the nose: 'I can see a sort of red glow in the cloud tops ahead. I'll take us towards it. Left, left, . . . steady.'

101

From the pilot, loudly: 'You'll have to shout louder, bomb-aimer. I can barely hear you.'

From the tail: 'There's a Hali closing on us from the port.' Then loudly: '*Watch it*, George!'

From the mid-upper turret: 'Got it, Den. It's just below us. My God. Two more. One, starboard level – '

From the pilot, shouting: '*Cut the bloody cackle, gunners*! We're supposed to be on a bombing run. There's millions of Halis around. Carry on, bomb-aimer.'

From the nose, faintly: 'Bomb doors open, master switch on. I can see red markers burning in the cloud tops. Left, left, . . . steady.'

Although Ken was shouting into his microphone, his voice was becoming hard to decipher amid the all-pervading screeching and howling. Suddenly, it occurred to me that this was no ordinary radio interference. The Germans had detected the Master Bomber's frequency, and were successfully jamming it. Not a word of his broadcast had got through to us. They were using exactly the same tactics as we tried to use against their defences.

Then, as from a great distance, came the welcome shout: 'Bombs gone, bomb doors closed.' At this moment of bomb release, I was supposed to enter in my navigation log various readings from my instrument panel, but the general confusion and noise pounding my ears had completely destroyed my concentration. Pencil poised, I gazed at the panel and tried to focus my mind. Indicated airspeed – 168 mph; true course – 047 degrees; indicated altitude – 20,100 feet; time –; time? I was looking at my watch, where the time was clearly displayed. The relative positions of the two fingers registered in my mind. Unfortunately, my brain seemed unable to convert this into an actual time which I could enter in my log. It was a strange feeling, until I realised what was happening. The combined effects of stress, fatigue, loud noise and maybe oxygen lack, had momentarily blacked out my reasoning processes. I pressed my oxygen mask tightly to my face and took several deep gulps. This did the trick. My watch now registered a time of 0629 – two minutes late on planned time. At this moment Keith switched off the VHF and the dreadful cacophony ceased. It was the feeling you get in the dentist's chair when he finally switches off his drill.

We flew on after bomb release for thirty seconds, until our target photograph had been taken. The gunners were closely monitoring other bombers visible on either side of us. It looked frightening, but we were all on a similar course and the risk of collision was not great at this moment. The dangerous bit came a minute or two later, when we all had to make a ninety degree turn to the left to start the homeward trek. We had just got into the turn when there came a roar of engines and a huge black shadow swept over us, almost taking our mid upper turret with it. We could almost hear George's teeth chattering with shock as he reported it.

'That was another Halifax, skipper. It missed us by inches.' And if George said inches, then he meant inches.

Once on a westerly heading, we soon regained our composure, and our spirits were rising by the minute. We went into a slow descent which took us into cloud, and though we picked up a bit of ice we were effectively screened from anything the enemy could do to frighten us. When we eventually broke cloud we were over the North Sea.

Keith was not for relaxing yet: 'Keep your eyes skinned, everybody. We're not home yet. And the intercom discipline near the target was diabolical. It's something we shall have to talk about later.'

Grey dawn was breaking as we neared the English coast, and for the first time our companions were fully revealed. The bomber stream, so concentrated at the target, was now well scattered, with some aircraft mere dots in the far distance. Our immediate neighbours were Halifaxes from other squadrons of the group. George knew all the identification markings, and gave us a commentary.

'This one on the port beam is a Frenchman from Elvington; see the red trellis on his tail, and the cross of Lorraine. The one beyond it is from Shiny Ten Squadron at Melbourne. The one on the starboard side with the yellow horizontal bars is from the Aussie squadron at Driffield. Look Denis, the mid-upper is giving us two fingers – cheeky devil!'

'That's alright,' said Denis. 'I gave it to him first.'

We reached Lissett in full daylight. The cloud had disappeared, and the visibility was good. The air traffic controllers were stacking the aircraft at 500 feet intervals, awaiting their turn to land, and since we were one of the last crews back I knew we had a long wait.

I tried to recall objectively my feelings at the target, when we had been called upon for the first time to drop live bombs. I had previously sometimes wondered whether I would experience any feelings of compunction about the devastation, any feelings of compassion for the recipients on the ground. The answer was an emphatic no. We had all been conditioned by our experiences of the bombing of our own country. I recalled my own impressions of Manchester's Christmas blitz; the sight of the shopping centre in flames, the rows of shabby terraced houses ripped apart by high explosives. As far as we were concerned, the enemy had sown the wind, and was now reaping the whirlwind, until such time as they cried 'enough'. I assumed that with typical German efficiency their children would have long since been evacuated from their industrial centres, and their civilians confined in their deep shelters. No, my instincts had been entirely those of self preservation, and that of my comrades.

Finally back in the Operations Block, we sat at a table whilst the Intelligence Officer conducted our crew debrief. We looked tired and hollow-eyed, with faces still creased from the pressure of our oxygen masks, but we felt happy as we sipped the hot sweet tea. We had done our first trip. We had coped. We were operational.

In all honesty, there was precious little to report, and I could not feel that our efforts had greatly furthered the cause. We had seen nothing except cloud, had not been attacked, and had bombed dimly-seen sky markers, whose accuracy was an unknown factor. The officer summed it up: 'I think that all that can be claimed on the night is that a considerable weight of explosive was dropped on Germany in the general area of Duisburg.'

Denis happened to mention to him the business with the bottles. 'Pity the poor Germans,' was his comment. 'The Russians advancing from the east; the Allies from the west. Now Anderson's crew come up with the ultimate weapon – the whistling bottles! The end is in sight.'

None of the other crews had anything untoward to report, apart from a few icing problems. It came as a shock, therefore, when we heard that one of the squadron aircraft had failed to return. Sammy had guessed right again. The missing crew had been on their first trip, like us. They were nearly all Canadians – and captained by the young flying officer who had come over to shake Keith's hand and wish us luck.

We handed in our parachute packs and survival kits, then walked to the mess for the traditional post-ops meal – bacon, beans and fried egg. We were tired but content. Yet, we all felt a sense of anti-climax. We had braced ourselves for tonight, over a long period. We had psychologically adjusted ourselves to cope if necessary with relentless fighter attacks, massed searchlights or horrendous flak. We had experienced nothing like it; just the mere nuisance of radar jamming and radio interference. The fear we had felt had been the fear of colliding with our fellow travellers, not the enemy. In a peculiar sense we felt cheated – we just hadn't been put to the test.

As Denis expressed it: 'Only twenty-nine to go. If this is all there is to it, what's all the fuss been about?'

8

SPIRIT OF CHRISTMAS '44

As Christmas approached, the weather really clamped. For days the cloudbase seemed to rise no higher than the treetops, and the rain came steadily down. In the dispersals, the Halifaxes stood silent, the rainwater dripping from their canvas covers to form large iridescent puddles on the oily tarmac. Elsewhere, the airmen moved around shrouded in their rubber capes, which kept them dry at the expense of permanently soaked trouser bottoms. On the domestic sites, the pathways were trodden into squelching quagmires, and the tin huts were running with condensation. The only thing to cheer us was a persistent rumour that if the weather didn't improve rapidly there might be a general stand-down over Christmas, enabling most of us to get home for a day or two. In anticipation of this happy event, Les offered to drop me right on my doorstep on his way home by motorbike. I responded by mapping out a route, to help overcome the wartime inconvenience of generally unsignposted roads and towns.

Although the flying had been scrubbed, there was plenty to do for everyone. The hardworking ground crews had the pressure taken off them, and were able to catch up on routine servicing jobs. For the aircrews there were more mundane tasks – assessing logs, utilising the various ground trainers, or browsing through training manuals and intelligence reports. 'Tee Emm', the humourously presented training memorandum incorporating the clottish mishaps of Pilot Officer Percy Prune, was in demand at this time.

My own particular hideaway at quiet times like this was the well-organised Station Intelligence Library in the Ops Block, where one was always assured of an interesting hour. This was where the target photographs of the latest operation were pinned up, along with the official assessment of its success. As expected, our own target photograph of Duisburg showed only the markers glowing in the clouds. One item which I found interesting was a backplot of a recent raid, showing on a large-scale map the position of every bomber in the stream at one particular instant. The extent of the scatter, due to the fact that at night each aircraft was navigated individually, was quite an eye-opener. Here also was displayed the crew photographs of those recently reported shot down or missing. Since individual names were note widely known on the squadron, this was usually the only means of identifying faces which would no longer be seen around the Messes.

On a day of inactivity it was announced that all aircrews were to assemble in the briefing room after lunch. The word got round that some line shooter from group had been sent to bore us by pontificating on 'Escape and Evasion'. The news was not well received. Most people had been expecting a midday stand-down, with options of a trip into Brid or a card school in the Mess. I had the feeling that this captive audience, well sprinkled with irreverent colonials, would be venting their disapproval on the lecturer, whoever he was.

In fact, the man waiting to be introduced to us by the Squadron Commander surprisingly turned out to be a cheerful cheeky-faced young flight sergeant engineer. Below his brevet he wore the ribbon of the Military Medal – a most unusual decoration for an airman. But then, he was an unusual fellow.

The CO called the room to order.

'May I introduce Flight Sergeant Harry Simister, a former member of this squadron. He had the misfortune of having to bale out of a blazing Halifax over Berlin in the summer of 1943. Today he is back here to give us the benefit of his experiences.'

Flight engineers, as a breed, are generally acknowledged to be self-reliant and resourceful types, and this fellow was certainly no exception. After landing safely near a wood, the story went, he buried his parachute and holed up for a day. He then decided that come what may he was going to try to make his way home. With the aid of a stolen bicycle he found his way to two of the Baltic ports, in a vain attempt to board a neutral ship. Undeterred, he then decided to pedal his way westwards towards occupied Holland. To help him on his way he had a tiny compass and a map of Europe from his escape kit, a saddlebag filled with raw vegetables dug up from the fields, and a single German phrase in his vocabulary – *'Heil Hitler'*.

In a story which was modestly understated, told in a broad northern accent, he gave us a delightfully comical account of his progress. Notwithstanding the hazards of patrolling policemen, hostile farm dogs and inquisitive Hitler Youths, along with the general inconveniences of thunderstorms, punctured tyres and persistent diarrhoea, he finally succeeded in crossing the Dutch border. Here he fortunately met up with Dutch patriots, who passed him along the line until he eventually found himself in Switzerland, where he could have sat out the war. Instead, he 'escaped' back into France, and joined forces with the Maquis, until finally liberated by the American invasion of southern France. He made it all sound as jolly as a minor initiative test set by a scoutmaster to keep his pack amused.

After his talk, he asked if there were any questions we would like to put to him.

'Yes,' said our squadron commander. 'I'm interested in the morale factor. When was yours at its lowest? What would you say was the worst moment of your whole escapade?'

He gave the question due consideration.

'I think, sir, the time I discovered I had the screaming 'abdabs, and nothing to wipe my arse on except a cabbage leaf.'

It was a good punchline for a well told story, and brought the house down. Our CO's final word – that successful escape or evasion demanded the twin requisites of great determination and sheer guts – was entirely superfluous.

The following morning, on reporting to the flight office, our skipper was informed that we had been permanently allotted one of the squadron aircraft, M-Mike, for our crew use. This would be the Halifax we would use for ops, subject to serviceability, for the rest of our tour. We were pleased about this. For the first time we now had a proprietary interest in a particular aircraft. Every aircraft had its own idiosyncrasies – things like a particular tendency to swing on take-off, or an unexplainable lack of signal strength on the radar. Now we could attempt to sort them out, or at least learn to live with them. We would also now have our own ground crew, which would enable us to form a closer working relationship with those on whom we would rely so much.

Keith and the engineer announced their intention of walking down to the dispersals to inspect our new charge and meet the ground crew. The rest of us decided to tag along.

The Naafi van had just preceded us, so we caught the ground crew chief, Sergeant Smith, and two of his fitters on their morning tea break. They were sitting in their tiny wooden shack, a shelter from the rain and icy winds from the North Sea. The door bore a plate saying 'No Hawkers, No Circulars,' and the chalked inscription 'Ubendum, Wemendum'.

We all introduced ourselves, and shook hands.

'Well,' said the sergeant, 'you've got yourself a decent kite – as good as any on the station. I'd say. She's done well over fifty ops, without too much trouble. The last aircrew did a full tour on her.'

We were glad to hear it. We had heard the theory propounded in some quarters that sprog crews were usually lumbered with the aircraft the senior crews wanted rid of: those prone to things like engine oil leaks or mag drops, bomb hang-ups or gun stoppages.

After a few minutes of technical discussion, we crossed the dispersal to inspect our new charge. Halifax Mark 3, serial no. MZ366, Callsign M-Mike, had a dark and weathered look. The first thing we noted was the insignia painted on the port side of the nose. Above the stencilled rows of bombs, signifying the number of ops flown, was the painting of a leggy semi-nude blonde in a provocative pose, and the name *Lili Marlene*.

'Hmm,' mused Keith. 'Whoever thought of naming his aircraft after a German whore?'

'It's not very patriotic, is it?' said Denis. 'Probably unlucky too. We don't we change it? How about *Betty Grable*?'

'Don't be a clot,' said Ken. 'The aircraft's M-Mike. The name's supposed to begin with an M.'

'Alright. How about *Miss Betty Grable*?'

Keith intervened: 'We won't worry about the name. We'll take the chief's word that she's a real classy lady. If she's done over fifty ops I'd hardly call her unlucky.'

'Speaking of luck,' said Sergeant Smith, 'just take a look at F-Freddie in the other dispersal.'

We did. It was called *Friday the Thirteenth*. Its nose was adorned with various bad luck symbols, along with a painted representation of the Grim Reaper, and the printed warning: 'As ye sow, so shall ye reap.'

'Would you believe,' he said, 'that this has flown more ops than any other Halifax in Bomber Command – nearly a hundred? The crews fight to fly in her, so you can't tell me that aircrews are as superstitious as everybody says they are.'

I wouldn't quite agree with his conclusion. In my experience, aircrews, like most people engaged in dangerous jobs, were an exceptionally superstitious lot. Few crews went on ops without a talisman of some sort – as witness our own Herman the Airman. Either that, or they carried out some peculiar ritual before take-off, such as kicking the tyres or urinating on the tail wheel. In the case of *Friday the Thirteenth*, some brave individual had in the first place defied the fates by plastering his aircraft with signs of ill omen – and had got away with it. Thereafter, by a form of inverted superstition, it had become established as a lucky aircraft. And that was the reason it was in such demand.

Our hopes of a stand-down over Christmas soon faded. The great pall of cloud suddenly lifted, then disappeared, and flying was on again. Within a few hours, half the squadron crews were on their way to bomb the railway yards at Cologne. Our crew were not involved, but Sammy, the squadron Cassandra, and his Canadian crew took part in what was the final trip of their tour of ops. Sammy apparently stood up and confidently predicted no squadron losses, and was right again. After debriefing for the last time, he and his crew disappeared into the night bearing the bottles of Canadian rye whiskey they had been stockpiling in their flying lockers for just this occasion. Ops briefings would never be quite the same again.

Over on the continent, von Runstedt's offensive from the Ardennes was going on, aided by the poor weather which had grounded the air forces. Now the weather had improved, there would be no shortage of urgent targets for the attention of Bomber Command.

In the early morning darkness of Christmas Eve we were called from our beds to be briefed for a daylight operation. All of us who trooped into the briefing room were expecting a tactical target in support of the army, who were manoeuvring to halt the German advance. The red ribbon on the map however was seen to extend once more into the heart of the Ruhr. It was a measure of the changed balance of the war that what would have once been considered a near suicidal daylight mission now evinced only a few whistles of surprise. For myself, however, I had not yet acquired such sang-froid. I remember thinking that if this was to be the start of our Christmas flying programme, then Bomber Command were not doing us any festive favours.

'Your target today, gentlemen, is one you can approach with a certain amount of relish. It is the former civil aerodrome at Essen-Mulheim, which now houses units of the Luftwaffe's day and night fighters . . . It's a hornets' nest, and they'll be out to sting you, and I don't have to tell you about the strength of the Ruhr flak defences . . . You will fly in loose formation behind three leaders . . . Over two hundred heavies engaged . . . Ideal weather conditions . . . And the good news is that from five degrees east you will be escorted by long range Spitfires . . .'

The other significant feature of the briefing was the met man's contribution. An intense anti-cyclone now prevailed over western Europe. In addition to near cloudless skies, the winds at all heights would be so light and variable they could for all practical purposes be ignored. This was as unusual as the weather was unseasonable. For the navigator, preparing the flight plan involved the resolving of several triangles of velocity incorporating track, wind and course. With zero wind to consider today, these triangles now became straight lines. For this reason, and the fact that today we would be playing follow-my-leader, flight planning took up only a fraction of the normal time. We reached *Lili Marlene* with half an hour to spare before take-off, a nice change from the situation on our previous trip.

The armourers had just finished winching the bombs into the cavernous bomb-bay, and the train of trolleys was just being towed away. Sixteen 500 pounders nestled in sinister array. On one of them, someone had chalked 'Compliments of the Season' on its rough cast-iron casing.

Although all of us in the crew tried to appear cool and nonchalant, there was an undeniable air of excitement. Today we would be on our mettle. This would be our baptism of fire. After today, we would be operational with the best of them. The feeling must have communicated itself to our ground crew, who fussed around us like broody hens. One of the fitters climbed onto the upper fuselage and vigorously polished the mid-upper turret with a large yellow duster. I heard him say to George, who was inside: 'A gunner once told me he had given his pilot evasive action against a fighter, then found it was a dead fly on the perspex!'

Just before midday the three leading aircraft took off, manned by three of the most experienced crews, and as briefed proceeded to orbit Flamborough Head. Periodically they fired off red Very cartridges, so that the rest of the force could take off in turn, identify the leaders, then take up position behind them. When the whole squadron was airborne, they set a southerly course down the coast, on the first leg to the Naze. Another Halifax eased alongside, positioning itself about forty yards away on our starboard beam, and we received a cheery wave from Bill in the pilot's seat.

As we passed the Humber estuary, we were joined by the formations from the other Yorkshire based Halifax squadrons, who aligned themselves ahead of us. None of the crews attempted the close formation flying favoured by the Americans, which always looked so good on the news reels. There wasn't really any point. Whatever formation they adopted, they were outgunned by the fighters: better to have a bit of elbow room to carry out evasive manoeuvres if necessary. At the Naze we rendezvoused with a force of Lancasters, and as if by divine right they eased themselves into the leading position of the formation as we turned eastwards.

We flew over the continent at our bombing height of 19,000 feet.

Since I did not have to remain glued to my navigation table on this trip, I plugged into the oxygen wander lead and moved forward the few paces into the nose. I was curious to see what was going on outside, especially in view of the exceptionally good visibility. As we flew directly above the area of ground fighting, I looked down and soon saw evidence of it. Amidst the dull green and brown patchwork was an isolated village, with every building on its single street either smoking or blazing furiously. Soon afterwards a flak battery fired a salvo, and I saw the shell bursts way below us; I felt it was more in the nature of a token two-fingered salute than anything else.

We carried on our easterly heading. Flying conditions were smooth, except for the occasional fluttering as we caught the slip-stream of one of the leading aircraft. Soon it was time to start Windowing. As each Halifax dispensed its loose bundles of silver foil, they were blown back, then dropped like a million raindrops twinkling in the sunlight.

By now we were approaching the border of Germany itself, with flak bursts beginning to speckle the sky. But where was the Luftwaffe? Where were their Me 109s and the even more formidable Fw 190s and their reputedly uncatchable new jets? Surely they must start their onslaught before we started to lay our bombs. Surely we would not be allowed to violate their lair unmolested.

The answer was way above our heads. We had long since passed our fighter escort rendezvous, but as yet had seen nothing of them. Way up in the blue upper atmosphere however there were appearing entwining patterns of white vapour trails, indicating interceptions and combats way beyond our ken. The Spitfire boys were containing them, without a doubt. The debt we owed them from Battle of Britain days was still accruing.

We reached our last turning point to the north of the target, and the whole formation wheeled to the right. There was a perceptible closing of ranks, as though involuntarily huddling together for comfort. The really heavy flak started, and I found it both alarming and fascinating. Each burst manifested itself as a flash of flame amidst a suddenly expanding puff of oily black smoke, which due to aircraft movement seemed to be rushing past at 200 mph. The loud crump of the explosion could be heard above the noise of the engines.

We steadied on course, in the slipstream of our three leaders, who were in loose formation about a hundred yards ahead. It was the engineer's job to dispense the bundles of Window through the flare chute at fixed intervals. I called up Dick to remind him that he should now be doubling the rate of dispatch until we had passed the target. I had the feeling we would need all the help we could get; this was the most heavily defended area in Europe.

Ken was in the nose by this time. I noticed that instead of lying prone on the floor he was huddled over his bombsight, and I knew just how he felt. With the vast Ruhr complex coming up, and already opening up on us with its big guns, it was an instinctive thing to make oneself as small a target as possible. It was his excited voice which broke the silence.

'I can see the target markers going down, skipper. Way ahead. Must be twenty miles away.'

Keith acknowledged, and switched on the VHF. This time, the broadcast was coming through loud and clear.

'Chugboat from King Cole. Aim at the centre of the reds. They're bang on target.' It was a very correct English voice, calm and unhurried.

'Left, left, steady,' came the voice of our bomb-aimer, as he took an extended line of sight from the bombsight.

The Master Bomber was jollying us along: 'Chugboat from King Cole. The bombing is excellent, and concentrated. Keep it going. Keep the kettle boiling.'

I saw more of the cherry-red markers cascading on the target ahead. Shortly afterwards King Cole was on the air again. 'The back-up reds have fallen short. Bomb-aimers – overshoot by three seconds. I repeat. All Chugboat aircraft overshoot back-up reds by three seconds.'

I could spare only a few moments' appreciation of this prompt and efficient control of the bombing. There was far too much going on to occupy my mind. Below us, Germany's industrial heartland appeared as a conglomerate of towns and factories, railways and waterways. Although there was some industrial haze, the red markers ahead were burning brilliantly on the ground, and smoke was rising steeply from the bombing. But what concerned me most was the ominous closeness of the black shell-bursts appearing amongst the aircraft ahead. Whatever method of gun-laying they were using, they seemed to have got our height assessed down to the last yard.

One of the Halifaxes ahead was slowly losing height, with a whisp of smoke trailing from its port inner engine. Suddenly, the whole wing erupted into yellow flames, sweeping back almost to the tailplane. This was more than an engine fire, which, with luck, could be contained – this was a ruptured main petrol tank. It could only be a matter of seconds before the whole wing burned off, then the crippled bomber would spin to earth like a falling sycamore seed. I found myself desperately willing the crew to bale out before it was too late. It dropped suddenly from my view, leaving a spiral of smoke. Keith held it in sight for a little longer. Then his steady voice came through on inter-com: 'Halifax ahead going down in flames. Log the position and time, navigator. No parachutes sighted.'

By this time, the adrenaline was really flowing, bringing to my mind an added awareness. My emotions were a wild mixture of apprehension, excitement and curiosity. At the same time, the sight of the formation advancing remorselessly and unswervingly amidst the exploding shells prompted another feeling, an unexpected one. It was a warm glow, hard to define. Call it pride, *esprit de corps*, comradeship, or a combination of them all. It did not last long, because it was replaced by a sudden painful thought. If anything was to happen to us in the next vital minutes, my parents would be receiving the dreaded telegram – the one that began 'Deeply regret to inform you . . .' – on Christmas Eve, of all times!

I quickly put the thought out of mind. An active imagination was the very least of the qualities required for operational flying. Too often, I was discovering, one's mind strayed to those repressed fears, those mental taboos, like the dread of being frizzled in a sudden fireball or having a face ripped away by flying shrapnel. The answer was to focus the mind completely on the job in hand, whether it was calculating a wind or flying a steady course or merely searching a segment of sky.

As Ken guided us towards the bomb release point, we were heading straight for what looked like a thick curtain of black cloud, into which the Halifaxes ahead of us were entering and completely disappearing from sight. It was the smoke from the intense barrage of flak, and there was no way round it. We were far too close to our release point to even think of evasive action. We would just have to plough a way through it.

Now a moment of high drama. The VHF had remained silent for some time. Now the voice of the Master Bomber came through clearly.

'King Cole to Deputy. I'm on fire, and going down. Take over. I repeat. Take over.'

The voice was exactly the same as it had been before, cool and unhurried, without the slightest trace of panic. The tone was such that he could have been merely announcing that he was about to break off for a coffee or a cigarette. So much so, it took a few seconds for the reality to register in my mind. This, then, was how it could sometimes happen. The calm acceptance that the odds against survival had been stacked too high; the dedication which demanded the handing over of the task, with what might well be the last earthly utterance. The final evocation of the simple words used in so many citations – devotion to duty.

There was a silence. Every member of every crew must have been holding his breath, as we were. Then came the acknowledgement from the stand-by Pathfinder crew.

'King Cole from Deputy. Taking over. Taking over. Good Luck!' A further pause. The show goes on. 'Chugboat aircraft carry on over-shooting markers by three seconds.'

There was no time to look below for the stricken aircraft. We were almost there, and in the thick of it. The crump of an exploding shell, and fear as the aircraft lurches violently. Are we hit? The bomb-aimer is continuing his patter.

'Steady . . . steady . . . steady. Bombs gone. Bomb doors closed.'

A moment of intense relief as we sense the bombs leaving the aircraft – always a psychological moment this. Then the long agonising wait. Due to the bombs' forward travel, we still have nearly two miles to go before we are directly overhead the target and our vertical photo-graph is taken. More than half a minute of straight and level flight, when we are at our most vulnerable. A shattering explosion, sounding way above the noise of our engines. This time we are hit, for sure. The unmistakeable sound of shrapnel biting into the metal fuselage. I look backwards in alarm. Are we still under control? All I can see of Keith from the nose are his feet, but they are still reassuringly firmly set on the rudder pedals. Anybody hurt? The intercom stays silent. Any damage in the nose? No holes apparent.

There are still about fifteen seconds to go, and I can't resist moving forward to another quick look at the target.

What a marvellous prang! The centre of the aerodrome, with its runways, is completely obliterated by smoke and dust and flames, and the remorseless spread of the bombing has reached the outer peri-meter. Not a single bomb seems to have gone astray. Now we are overhead, and I can see the sudden shock waves of what must be our own bombs exploding.

That's it. Our photo is taken, and it's nose down and away. Still no sign of the Luftwaffe, and every second now is taking us further from the flak. Nobody wants to hang about, and already the formation is beginning to spread out.

A startled exclamation from Keith breaks the silence: 'Good God. Somebody's taken a packet. Take a look, starboard beam.'

It is Z-Zombie, one of the three leaders we have been following for the last three hours. Now it is lagging, and we are overtaking it. There is a gaping hole in the crew cabin, directly behind the pilot's seat, almost big enough to drive a car through. The metal fuselage around it has been rolled back like an old sardine tin. Miraculously, the pilot is still in his position, and all four engines are running; it is descending, but still under control. We recognise it as Flight Lieutenant Jack Watson's Halifax, and it is soon obvious that he is attempting to get his crippled aircraft home. The wonder is that he has survived an explosion at such close proximity.

Soon we have left behind us the smoking skies of Germany, and the fears and uncertainties with it. The natural resilience of youth takes over. Now is the time for a cigarette and a bite of chocolate, and a joke or two.

The formation is now well scattered, and when we finally cross the coast south of Dunkirk, one of our number overflies the port itself, some ten miles off track. It is, as we have been warned, a place not yet cleared of Germans, and the careless fellow is pursued by persistent light flak, close enough to frighten him. An hour ago we would have sympathised, but it is a measure of our present mood that we find it quite hilarious, and we are in full accord with Denis's stricture: 'Serves the silly bugger right for cutting corners, and trying to jump the queue for the stack.'

The sea crossing was uneventful, and we finally landed at base without too much waiting. We taxied to our dispersal, where Smithy was waiting to marshal us in. He looked quite concerned.

'I suppose you know you have been hit,' he shouted up to Keith. 'Anybody hurt?'

'We had a pretty good idea,' answered Keith. 'We're all OK.'

Smithy had spotted, in particular, a four inch gash in the nose – directly in line with where the navigator's head would be positioned! The shrapnel, as we later discover, had penetrated the tough dur-alumin skin like so much tissue paper; fortunately, its further progress had been halted by one of the large component boxes of the Gee equipment, fitted to the interior.

After the engines had been shut down, Smithy carried out an external inspection of his charge, with a keen eye. There were plenty of other holes, but nothing vital had been hit, and patching it up would present no major problems. Some of us poked around, trying without success to retrieve any fragments of German shrapnel as souvenirs, until the crew transport arrived to take us to debriefing.

Here, as successive crews arrived to put in their reports, it was soon apparent that today's attack had been highly effective. It also proved, to anyone who might have doubted it, that Bomber Command could provide very accurate high level bombing – given a visual sighting of the target, reasonable visibility and no fighter harassment on the bomb run.

Although more than half of them suffered some form of flak damage, no squadron aircraft were lost, and casualties were minimal. As the crews sat round the tables, nursing their hot drinks, they had that eager animation of those with a good story to tell. Strange how in the telling, events which had been quite hair-raising at the time now took on a comical or even bizarre aspect.

Pride of place went to the crew of Z-Zombie, whose crippled aircraft had made a safe landing on the emergency strip at neighbouring Carnaby. Over the target an anti-aircraft shell had scored a direct hit without exploding. In its path from floor to roof it had hit a bank of compressed oxygen cylinders, situated behind the pilot, which had themselves exploded – with the spectacular results we had observed. The only injuries among the crew, after the initial shock, were two cases of frostbite and one of concussion. We were all agreed that getting the battered Halifax home had been a tremendous feat of airmanship, well worth the gong which no doubt would be forthcoming.

In lighter vein was the story of my friend Dai Johnson, a volatile Welshman and fellow navigator. On the bomb run, he had suffered the shock of being suddenly drenched with anti-freeze when a shell fragment pierced the floor near his foot and burst open the glycol tank above his head. But even this could not be claimed as the ultimate in close shaves. One of the flight engineers was proudly showing off the Mae West he had been wearing on the bomb run; it had been slashed open by a flying fragment, without his receiving even a scratch.

It was only after returning for our post-flight bacon and egg to the Sergeants' Mess, festooned with paper chains and holly, that I was reminded that today was indeed Christmas Eve. The events of the day had put thoughts of the festive season completely out of mind. It had been anything but a Christmassy sort of day; anything but a spirit of goodwill had prevailed. The four tons of bombs we had dropped on the Germans ourselves had been matched in sheer ill will by the amount of high explosive they had flung up at us. At least, we had been given a purely military target – an active Luftwaffe fighter base, whose destruction could only bring beneficial results, as far as we were concerned. I remembered my feelings of indignation at the untimeliness of the Luftwaffe's Christmas blitz on my native city, four long years ago. Even today's weather had been ridiculously unseasonable: whoever heard of a Christmas with clear blue skies and spring-like sunshine?

There was a party, with dancing, laid on in the Mess that evening. There were plenty of girls in attendance, including a coachload of nurses collected from all the local hospitals. Normally, I would have had a few beers and joined whole-heartedly in the fun. All the girls seemed to be enjoying themselves – accepting spilt drinks, clumsy dancing and noisy choruses in good spirit. But somehow, I just couldn't seem to get in the mood.

After the excitements of the day, some sort of reaction had set in. Now I felt jaded and withdrawn. On the dance floor, the usual light conversation wouldn't come. My mind was suffering some kind of time warp; it was having trouble in adjusting to the contrast between what was happening now, and what had been happening earlier. 'This is ridiculous,' it was saying. 'Barely six hours ago you were high over the Ruhr, in mortal fear of your aircraft blowing apart. Just look at you now – dancing around and trying to make humorous small talk.' It was no better at the crowded bar. While those around me were noisily rendering *I'm Dreaming of a White Christmas*, my thoughts were dwelling on King Cole's last call, and a burning Halifax breaking up. And what was wrong with the beer tonight? It just wasn't performing its usual function of overcoming inhibitions and blotting out unwanted images.

Looking around the crowded anteroom, the others didn't seem at all inhibited, so the fault must lie with me. Maybe this mental switch-off was something you acquired with experience. After all, I was new to this whole operational business.

Really, it was a good party, but it wasn't a Christmas party. There was nothing of the usual Christmas magic: how could there be? Christmas 1944, I decided, was a write-off.

I had enough sense to see that in my present state I was no use to myself or anyone else. I finished my drink and quietly slipped out of the door, on my way to an early bed. Outside, as though to emphasise that this was not really a season of goodwill, I passed two gunners who had gone to settle some half-drunken argument. In the bright moonlight, they were quietly pummelling each other.

I slept soundly that night, undisturbed by the other crew members as they drifted back to the hut one by one.

'Merry Christmas, everybody.' It was Denis's voice which awakened me. 'It's Christmas Day, and we've been given a twenty-four hour stand-down. We've overslept, but there's breakfast in bed for those who want it.'

The sun was shining brightly through the window. I felt fit and refreshed.

Breakfast materialised in the shape of a wedge of the tinned fruit cake received from Keith's folks in Australia, and a sip of lukewarm coffee from yesterday's flask. We washed and shaved in leisurely fashion, and polished our best blue buttons, prior to walking to the Sergeants' Mess for our Christmas Dinner.

The Mess bar was already open, if indeed it had ever closed overnight, and the cheery sound of carol singing blared from the radio in the anteroom. Soon the Group Captain and his retinue arrived for the customary courtesy drink, and this period, under the influence of traditional Sergeants' Mess hospitality, extended itself until such time as everyone was suitably lubricated.

Then it was time for the aircrew sergeants and other senior NCOs to troop out for the time-honoured ritual of serving the airmens' Christmas dinner. There was a genuinely good relationship between the aircrews and the ground staff on the station. For our part, we appreciated the dedicated work that went into the servicing of our aircraft, and the generally supportive attitude of all the other trades-men and women. The ground crews turned out in all weathers at any time of day or night, and nothing was ever too much trouble for them; few aircrews celebrated the end of a tour without a thank-you party for those who had helped them achieve it.

In the Airmens' Mess, the dinners were served willingly, if inex-pertly, amid much good-humoured banter. Thumbs were in the soup, beer glasses filled to overflowing, and the occasional dropped plate was greeted by mighty cheers. Giggling Waafs were caught under the mistletoe. It was all very convivial.

Later, we sat down for our own dinner in the Sergeants' Mess, and were served in similar fashion by the officers. Most crews had at least one officer in their number, and there were no great rank barriers between the sergeants and the junior officers. Afterwards, I stretched out in a chair by the log fire, replete and relaxed.

The lunch-time beer, followed by unusually rich fare amid hearty good fellowship, had induced a mood of happy and optimistic contemplation. Christmas seemed to have caught up with me at last.

I gazed at the large Christmas tree in the corner, and noticed for the first time that it had been laboriously decorated with silver metallised strips – the self-same Window which we dropped from the bombers. In a funny sort of way, such pragmatism seemed to my mind to symbolise the necessary ambivalence when called upon to celebrate the season of goodwill in times like these. Yesterday, the war had been waged strenuously, and tomorrow no doubt would be the same. But today, the spirit of goodwill towards men had taken over. The Germans had been allowed some respite from the bombing. Doubtless, even in their battered cities, they would like us be singing *Silent Night*, wishing their families were together, and drinking a toast to better Christmases to come. I remembered reading about the opposing soldiers in World War One who had celebrated this festive season by kicking a football together in No Man's Land, and I understood how they had felt.

This was the sixth Christmas of the war, and of necessity many of its traditional aspects had disappeared. This did not mean that its significance was any the less, nor that it could just be written off for the duration. This year there was another factor. There was not the slightest doubt in any of our minds that this was to be the last Christmas of the war – at least as far as the war in Europe was concerned. Next Christmas would hopefully be one of peace and understanding, of home and family. A real Christmas.

And things were now going well enough for us to believe that almost all of us would be around to celebrate it.

9

THE LONGEST NIGHT

I sensed an unusual lightness and brightness, even before I was consciously awake. My eyes slowly focused, not on the accustomed grey metal corrugations of our Nissen hut, but on a glossy wall dazzlingly white with morning sunlight. Even the blankets under my chin were white, instead of the usual drab brown. I thought I must be in the middle of a dream.

'How are you feeling this morning?'

The voice belonged to a medical orderly in a long white coat, who was standing at my bedside, holding a cup of tea.

'I feel fine,' I said, and meant it. I had had a long undisturbed sleep, and felt wonderfully refreshed.

'Good,' said the orderly, 'I'll bring you some breakfast. The MO will be round to see you shortly. Here's a cuppa to be going on with.'

I sat up, and looked round the little ward; only one of the other six beds was occupied. I remembered, it held a young airman with whom I had chatted last night, after first being bedded here in Station Sick Quarters. He had suffered a painful tumble from the wing of a Halifax on which he had been working. He seemed to be still asleep.

The Medical Officer arrived some time later. He took my temperature, and felt my pulse.

'Has your headache gone?'

'Yes, completely.'

'Any other symptons? Dizziness? Nausea?'

'No. Nothing at all. I'm fine.' It all seemed a lot of fuss over nothing.

'Good. You can be discharged. You understand, we had to put you under observation for twelve hours – a standard precaution for all cases of anoxia.'

Anoxia. Or, as we called it, oxygen lack. A confusing and insidious malady, as I had discovered to my cost last night. Something which could give you a lift like a skinful of booze, then suddenly drop you with an enormous hangover. Something which could put the mind into a state of regression. Something which, in the end, could put you into a sleep

120

from which you wouldn't wake up. Even now, though we had talked about the events last night after we had landed, my mind found it difficult to put things into sequence . . .

We had taken off at dusk, on our seventh op. We were still only in the first week of the new year, but had already rattled up four trips since Boxing Day; at this rate, if our luck held, fingers crossed, we could finish our tour within three months. As navigator, and implied crew statistician and mathematician, I had already worked out that on current loss figures the odds of a successful completion were better than evens once we had done ten trips. We were well on our way.

Our target for tonight was the railway complex at Hanover, a city reputed to be well served by its defences. Situated halfway between the Ruhr and Berlin, it was to be our deepest penetration into Germany. Maybe that was why the route was unexpectedly direct, virtually a straight line eastwards across the North Sea and Holland to a point north of Hanover, instead of the usual doglegs. The other unusual feature concerned our height. Normally we flew at an intermediate height for an hour or two, only climbing to high altitude when we were well over the continent. Tonight we were briefed to ascend to 20,000 feet as soon as we set course, and to maintain that height to the target. The reason for this, it was explained, was the forecast of large cumulo-nimbus clouds over the sea, with tops up to 18,000 feet. There was a bit of a groan when this part of the flight plan was announced. True, none of us relished the thought of ploughing our bombed-up Halifaxes through active thunderstorms, but it meant being constricted by our oxygen leads for many long hours, with an outside air temperature of -40 C. There was also the point, raised by one of the more experienced crews, that our flying so high so early on the route meant that we would be appearing on the German early warning radar screens that much sooner.

We set off on a course of 095 degrees across the North Sea. When we levelled out at 20,000 feet, the forecast thunderclouds were already visible ahead, their tops reflecting the last light from the west. I switched on the H2S, with the idea of obtaining an accurate fix when we crossed the Dutch Coast in due course. I spent several minutes attempting to tune it in, without much success. I was not particularly worried: in fact, I was suffused with a pleasant feeling of well-being which was quite unusual at this outbound stage of a trip. I abandoned the set, and began to draw lines on my chart, undeterred by the slight headache I was developing. I turned up my table light in an effort to dispel the black spots which kept appearing on the chart. All that happened was that they now appeared in bright colours. It was at this time that I heard the captain's voice; it sounded a long distance away, as though he was calling from the far end of a long tunnel.

'Hallo, nav. You haven't passed me your estimate for the Dutch coast yet.'

'Why not?' I replied, after due deliberation.

'That's what I'm asking you.'

There was a pause. This was getting beyond me.

'Are you alright, navigator?' There was a note of urgency in Keith's voice.

'Course I'm alright. Are you alright, skipper? Are you alright, Denis? Are you alright . . .'

Keith interrupted, loudly: 'Bomb-aimer, go take a look at him, quickly. Check his oxygen.'

Ken moved to the navigation position. By the time he got there, I was slumped over my table, completely unconscious. The rubber tube from my oxygen mask had a broken bakelite connector, and was dangling freely; the aircraft supply tube had dropped to the floor, from where it was discharging my vital oxygen supply into the air. How long I had been in this unfortunate situation was anybody's guess.

I was happily unaware of the ensuing period of panic as Ken and Les together struggled to fit me with the spare mask and helmet, always carried in the engineer's bag, and to reconnect me to the oxygen flow. When their efforts were rewarded by my return to some sort of consciousness, I was aware that a discussion was going on regarding our next course of action.

'Can you take over the navigation, bomb-aimer, until the navigator recovers?' Keith asked.

Poor Ken found himself in something of a predicament. Having long since been banned by me from the navigation table, his confidence, never very apparent in the air, was particularly low in navigational matters. In addition, he was now gazing with some dismay at my log and chart. The North Sea area of the chart was criss-crossed with a maze of meaningless lines. And on the log, every column was filled with a pencilled '095' with the figures growing progressively larger and more indistinct, until the whole page was a mass of childish scribble. It was the strange doodle of a mind regressing towards infancy, in effect.

'I can't make head or tail of this log and chart, skipper,' said Ken. 'They are both just a scrawl. I think we'll have to abort this trip.'

I sat at my table taking large breaths of oxygen, with the new mask, which was poorly fitting, cupped to my face. I knew vaguely what was going on, but I wanted no part of it. My recent mood of well-being had been replaced by feelings of acute depression, and my headache had now reached migraine intensity.

'How are you feeling, navigator?' asked Keith. 'What do you think?'
'I think we should go home,' I said.

Keith paused only for a few seconds. Way ahead, he could see searchlights sweeping the skies at the enemy coast.

'Right. We're going back. I'm not prepared to go stooging over Germany with a crook navigator. I'll be descending and turning left till we're clear of traffic, then I'll turn onto reciprocal course. I'll try to avoid any cloud build-ups. Keep your eyes peeled, gunners.'

Halfway through our turn there came a muffled cry from our mid-upper gunner as a large black shadow crossed our path. There were still hazards involved, even in an early return. There were also important details to be considered. A wireless message to base, telling them we were returning early with a U/S (unserviceable) navigator; the disposal of our bomb load; the checking of our identification transmitter; and the placing of a crew member in the astrodome to fire off the identification colours in the event of being intercepted by our own night-fighters.

We levelled out when well below oxygen height, and Ken duly jettisoned our bombs in the middle of the North Sea. Denis hazarded the thought that all was not wasted – we might have hit an unsuspecting U-Boat! By this time I had recovered sufficiently to take a Gee fix, and pass a corrected course for Lissett. To tell the truth, I was now feeling so much brighter that I began to have second thoughts about our action in turning back. Had we done the right thing? What in fact was the recognised course of action in this eventuality? Certainly it was some-thing which had never been considered or mentioned in training. Was the official policy press-on-regardless, or live-to-fight-another-day? When I thought of tonight's wasted effort I began to feel guilty. Surely I should have had the sense to check my oxygen connection; surely I should have recognised the symptoms of oxygen lack. As it was, the war effort had lost out on a thousand gallons of fuel and a full bomb load, my skipper had had additional responsibilities thrust upon him, and my crew had missed out on another trip towards their required thirty.

We landed back at base without further incident, after being airborne for over three hours. A crew coach awaited us at dispersal, along with an ambulance and the Medical Officer. The coach driver had a message for Keith:

'The captain of the aircraft to report immediately to the Squadron Commander in the Ops Room.' He made it sound ominously like a summons to the headmaster's study for a thrashing. For my part, although I protested that there was now nothing wrong with me apart from a headache, I was instructed by the MO to climb aboard the ambulance, and to spend the night at Station Sick Quarters.

And that was where I now found myself, feeling a good deal better than I thought I ought to be, and with last night's events rapidly receding from my mind. I was more concerned now with news of Keith's later encounter with the CO, and reports on the raid we had missed.

As it happened, I did not have long to wait. I was dressing, prior to reporting in at the squadron, when Keith walked into the ward. He had come to check on my availability, as he was expecting our crew to be operating again later in the day.

His news was startling. Last night the squadron had suffered its worst casualties since our arrival. As we had half expected, the direct routing and the early climb had given the Luftwaffe ample warning, and sufficient time to have their fighters up in strength. They may even have been able to predict the target. From the Dutch coast to the target crews had reported interceptions and combats, whilst the flak in the Hanover area had been accurate and heavy. In addition to our early return, one of our squadron Halifaxes had crash-landed in East Anglia, very severely damaged but brilliantly handled by its pilot, Flight Lieutenant McLennan. By all accounts, when outbound to the target, it had been hit on its under-belly by a Lancaster desperately evading an attacking Junkers 88. The Lanc had plunged to earth, but the Hali had demonstrated yet again its robustness by making it back to England. The really bad news was that three other Lissett aircraft had failed to return – their fate unknown. Keith named the missing captains, and I tried to picture the faces of the crew members. One of the navigators concerned I remembered well – I had borrowed five cigarettes from him at briefing. Sadly, that was a debt that would never be repaid.

Keith went on to describe his interview with the squadron CO:

'To be quite honest, I'm not quite sure whether you would describe it as a fatherly chat or a gentle bollicking, or both. I told him what had happened, and the decision I had made. He told me what he thought I should have done. First of all, fix you up with the spare helmet and mask. Then plug you in to a portable oxygen bottle, set to 100% oxygen, until you were well enough to carry on with your job. In the meantime, the bomb-aimer should have taken over the navigation. I explained that the log and chart were all screwed up; he said we could have flown using just the flight plan for a spell, hoping you could sort things out later.'

'Sounds reasonable enough, I suppose,' I conceded. 'But it's easy to come up with answers with hindsight.'

Keith resumed:

'I was beginning to feel a bit of a bludger by this time. Anyway, I felt better about it later on, when the crews got back. He came up to me and said: 'It looks like you made the right decision after all, Andy. By the sound of things, it wasn't a night to be swanning around off track.' When you come to think about it, he has to keep a sharp eye on crews who have aborted a trip. After all, there must be cases on record of crews returning early with all sorts of stories about illnesses or equipment failure, when the truth was that they didn't fancy going near the target.'

It was a point I hadn't considered before. Anyway, that was all now behind us. We walked the half mile from Sick Quarters to the B Flight office, to find that we were indeed on the night's battle order. A spare navigator had been nominated to stand by to take my place, but I was able to confirm my availability. On the crew room notice board my navigation log from the previous night had been pinned up, as a warning and an example of the insidious effects of oxygen lack.

There was barely time for a cup of tea and a bun at the Naafi van before we had to report for navigation briefing. Lessons had been learned from the ill-fated Hanover trip. Tonight's route consisted of no less than twenty-two different legs zig-zagging across the continent, and we would not be climbing to bombing height of 18,000 feet until we were close to the present front line of the ground fighting. In accordance with Bomber Command's current policy of dislocating Germany's rail system, we were given the task tonight of destroying the railway complex at a place called Hanau. This was an industrial town to the east of Frankfurt, with large marshalling yards, and, as we were told quite irrelevantly, the birthplace of the brothers Grimm. Of more concern to us, it was situated away from the red-shaded areas on the map which denoted known heavy flak concentrations.

We took off in the late afternoon, flying once again in *Lili Marlene* – patched up good as new after her peppering over the Ruhr on Christmas Eve. It was her sixtieth operation, and our second attempt at our seventh. On the face of it, this seemed to be one of our easier trips; and that is the way it turned out, as uneventful as any of us could have wished. The weather was standard for these winter nights – clear upper skies, with almost continual cloud below, which cut out the searchlights and made the flak sporadic. Once or twice the gunners reported tracer fire in the distance, showing that there were fighters in the offing, but we were not troubled. The red and green target markers were burning above the cloud tops, and attracted us like moths to a lantern. Ken aimed at the centre of the cluster, as instructed. Aiming at drifting skymarkers was the least accurate method of bombing, but tonight they were reasonably well concentrated, and hopefully the bombs would not be too scattered.

The homeward route was circuitous, and involved both climbing and descending legs until reaching the Dutch coast. Thereafter it was a long gradual descent, and since it was B Flight's turn to get back earliest, Keith let the airspeed build up beyond our briefed speed. As a result, of the twenty-one squadron aircraft involved, we were the second one home, and were given permission by radio to land immediately. Considering that the last crew back would spend about half an hour circling in the stack above the airfield, we appreciated our good fortune. This had been a good trip for us in all respects, and made up for the previous night's wasted effort. Soon we would be clutching our steaming mugs of coffee and drawing deeply on our cigarettes, as the patient debriefers entered up our reports. Come to think of it, it was a Saturday night, and there was still time for a drink in the Mess bar afterwards.

Les and I hurriedly packed our gear and moved rearwards from the nose, crawling past Ken in the co-pilot's seat, to take up our landing positions. I looked out of the side window in passing; I could see the twin yellow lines of the runway lights, and the red pundit beacon flashing its Morse identification signal, but upper cloud now obscured the stars and the night was inky black. George was just climbing from his mid-upper turret to join Les and me in our normal landing position, the padded rest bench between the two main spars, aft of the crew cabin. The rest of the crew were in their usual positions.

I was not plugged in on intercom, so could not follow the landing patter between the pilot and engineer, but I could sense what was going on. There was the usual jolt as the heavy undercarriage was lowered on the down-wind leg, and I could feel we were doing a fairly tight circuit. The engine note changed as power was adjusted for the landing approach, and I heard the creaking sound of the flaps lowering. Subconsciously I awaited the final cut-off of engine noise, and the moments of nothingness until the squeal of the tyres on the runway. They never came. I sensed a sudden yawing motion, followed by the sound of take-off power quickly applied. We must be going round again. In confirmation, George, who was sitting next to me on intercom, gave a semi-circular motion of his hand to indicate we were overshooting. There followed the sound of the undercarriage being retracted, and the thud as the wheels locked into their housing. I remember thinking that we would not be very popular with the crews waiting in the queue behind us, nor with the Air Traffic Controllers, whose rapid-landing pattern would now become that much more complicated.

Shortly afterwards, with full power on the engines and a speed of about 150 mph, we hit the ground!

The initial impact hurled the three of us against the forward bulkhead. We lay there unconscious, in a tangled heap of limbs . . .

There was no means of measuring time, but it was probably within a minute that I regained my senses. My first impression was of the uncanny stillness and quietness surrounding us. The compartment was lit up with the glow of the fire which engulfed the whole of the cockpit ahead of us. Acrid smoke was seeping down the length of the fuselage, rapidly reducing visibility. I saw that Les had already staggered to his feet, and was attempting to place the folding ladder up to the escape hatch in the roof immediately above us. George, on the floor beneath me, was just beginning to stir, his face a black mask of blood.

Shocked and dazed, without a word being said, the three of us managed to climb painfully up the ladder, and clamber through the hatch onto the top of the fuselage. We looked around. We were situated near the edge of a ploughed field, whose frozen furrows were illuminated by the ever-increasing flames ahead. All that remained of *Lili Marlene* was the central fuselage section and tail unit; behind us lay a trail of smaller fires where we had shed our wings, wheels, fuel tanks and engines in our headlong career over farmland and hedgerows. Incredibly, our path had taken us clear of the large trees and other obstructions which, had we hit them, would have folded the fuselage like a concertina.

As we slid one by one to the ground, Keith suddenly appeared before us out of the smoke. He held a handkerchief to try to stem the flow from a badly gashed forehead. As he saw the three of us on our feet, his face was transformed with a look of intense relief.

'Thank God you're OK. I thought you'd all bought it.'

'What's happened to the rest of the crew?' I asked.

'Dick and I made it out of the pilot's escape hatch before the fire really took hold, but he looks crook. He's collapsed over by that hedge. I don't know what's happened to Ken.'

At that moment there came a sudden cry for help from the rear. It was Denis's voice. 'Someone help me,' he shouted. 'I'm trapped in the turret.'

We rushed round the tail of the aircraft. The rear turret appeared buckled, but intact. Denis must have just come round after a severe buffeting; his blooded face was visible behind the four .303 Brownings, encased in a cage of gunmetal and perspex.

'How am I to get out?' he cried. 'The turret won't rotate, and the rear doors are jammed.'

'Don't worry, Denis,' I called. 'There are four of us here. We'll get you out in no time.' I wasn't sure how we were going to do it. It would take a sledgehammer to break a way through the perspex, and the way the fire was creeping backwards we had only a few minutes available. The spread of the fire astonished me. I realised that it had started from broken petrol lines, and its progress down the fuselage had been assisted by such combustibles as oxygen and hydraulic oil lines. What I had not realised before was that the metal alloy of the airframe itself would burn upon reaching a certain temperature. That was what had now happened. *Lili Marlene*'s fuselage was now like a burning torch with the flames spreading down the handle. Soon they would be among the long belts of ammunition feeding the turrets. I didn't want to be around when that happened.

Denis appeared to find our presence reassuring. 'If you'll give me a hand,' he said, 'I'm going to try to climb out through the clear vision panel. It's my only chance.'

I looked at the small open panel between the guns, not much bigger than a shoe box, and metaphorically shook my head. Not a chance, I thought. He will be lucky even to get his head through it. We should be looking for something to smash the perspex casing. We're wasting time. Soon he'll be roasting before our eyes. We must do something *now*!

I was wrong. After some rapid contortive effort inside the turret, Denis managed to shed his electrically-heated flying overall and his battledress top. Moments later his tousled head shot through the open panel like a jack-in-the-box. Four pairs of hands gripped his hair, head and shoulders in a concerted heave. He became jammed tight, and shouted in pain. This time I said it, as the panic rose in me: 'We're wasting time!'

I was wrong again, and never so happy to be so. I had heard it said that if a man can get his head through an aperture, he can get the rest of his body through it. Now I believe it. By pushing with his feet, and with a gigantic contortion of his shoulders, Denis suddenly popped out of his turret. It happened so unexpectedly that his wiry body eluded our grasp, and dropped heavily to the ground. He lay there gasping with relief and exertion. We helped him to his feet, and prepared to move away from the heat. Then suddenly remembering, he returned to the turret, put his arm through the open panel and retrieved our lucky mascot, Herman the Airman, from its customary stowage by the guns.

As we moved away from the tail, there came a loud bang from the aircraft and a Very cartridge shot up into the air, exploded in its pistol by the heat. For a short time the whole scene was illuminated by an eerie green light. By the glow we could see a figure lying prone on the ground, several yards in front of the burning nose section. We knew this must be Ken, the only crew member still unaccounted for.

We rushed over to him. He was lying face downwards in the ridged earth, unconscious and breathing harshly. Although his face seemed unmarked, blood was seeping from the leather flaps of his flying helmet. From his position in relation to the aircraft, it appeared that he had been flung out on its final deceleration. He was obviously seriously injured.

Our first concern was to get him away from the burning aircraft. The heat was now intense. A muffled explosion from inside the fuselage sent a huge tongue of flame and a shower of sparks skywards. That must have been the oxygen bottles going up. We carried him as best we could to the verge of the field where Dick was lying, and settled him down on the ground.

There was now sufficient illumination to take stock of our surroundings. Some two hundred yards beyond the aircraft we could make out a row of cottages, bordering what appeared to be the main street of a village. Another few seconds of headlong travel and we would have undoubtedly ploughed into them, with horrific consequences. A few figures had now appeared on the edge of the glow, and a broad Yorkshire voice called out: 'Are there any bombs on board?'

'No,' I shouted, 'but keep well clear. There'll be ammunition exploding soon. Where is this place?'

'North Frodingham. Can we help you?'

'Yes,' I said. 'Ring up the aerodrome at Lissett, and tell them where we are. Tell them we need an ambulance urgently.'

'No need. It's on its way.' The uniformed figure approached us rapidly. 'I saw the fire from the Control Tower, and followed the glow in my car. I've alerted the ambulance. It should arrive any minute.' It was a voice of calmness and authority. In the glow I recognised Wing Commander Dobson, our squadron CO.

He seemed to take in the scene without need of explanation. His first action was to peel off his greatcoat and lay it on the wet earth alongside Ken's unconscious body. He bade us assist in gently lifting him onto it. It was the coat I had admired when I had seen it at briefing – brand new, thick piled and expensive looking. Now it lay plastered in mud, with blood oozing onto it. It was a simple spontaneous gesture I would remember for the rest of my life. He said:

'We shall need two stretchers when the ambulance arrives. In the meantime, those of you who can walk make your way towards that group of people over there. They are standing outside the village pub. You can wait inside until we can get you to Sick Quarters.'

The landlord of the Blue Post had but recently called time, and was engaged in washing up the glasses when a departed customer had rushed in with the news that there was a burning bomber in the field behind the pub. The few remaining customers, mainly elderly farm-workers, had hurried out to see what assistance they could render. These were the figures we had first seen and warned in the glow of the fire. Now they gazed with avid interest as we entered the bar room, and our startling appearance was reflected in their faces. All five of us had heavily blood-stained faces, as a result of scalp abrasions; both my knees had swollen to twice their normal size, so that I was unable to walk unaided; some of our clothing was badly stained and torn; and altogether we brought into the bar the all-pervading smell of smoke and scorching. Whatever the landlord's wife thought about our sudden intrusion, she soon came up with the traditional English antidote to shock – hot sweet tea. We sat drinking it on the wooden benches in front of the dying embers, and none of us spoke. Our minds were numbed. One or two curious villagers poked a face round the door, but none of them knew what to say to us.

The ambulance and the MO soon arrived. Ken and Dick were brought by stretcher and laid in the ambulance. Ken was still uncon-scious, but Dick was able to talk, though in pain. The MO decided that these two should be taken immediately to the nearest hospital at Driffield, whilst the rest of us awaited another ambulance to take us to Sick Quarters on camp.

We had to wait quite a long time, sufficient in fact for me to smoke three cigarettes in rapid succession, and add feelings of acute nausea to my other aches and pains. When we finally climbed aboard, I could see that *Lili Marlene* was still burning, with an occasional popping of exploding bullets from the tail. Squadron aircraft were still droning overhead. Some crews were widening their normal circuits to overfly the fire and take a good look at it. No doubt there would be speculation as to who were the unlucky crew involved in the crash. Smithy would have long since learned that his pride and joy would not be returning.

So it came about that the ambulance conveyed me and my crewmates to the isolated Sick Quarters site from which I had walked away only twelve hours previously. The young airman to whom I had said cheerio was still there, his face a picture when I hobbled into the ward. They needn't have changed the sheets I thought wryly, as I claimed my old bed.

The Chief Medical Officer and his staff spent an hour or so treating our injuries. None of us were seriously hurt. Once we had been cleaned up, stitched, bandaged, pyjamaed and bedded, we had undergone a complete transformation.

In spite of the sedation we had received, sleep would not come to ease our discomfort. The events of the night were running endlessly through our minds, and there were questions which we wanted answering. First and foremost, what had caused the crash?

Keith in particular was concerned with this question, and he could not really come up with an answer. His recollection was of a slight drift away from the runway at a late stage of the landing approach. Since the runway length would not safely permit a delayed touchdown point, he had decided to overshoot and go round again. To this end he had applied overshoot power, and brought up the undercarriage. At this crucial point the number four engine had unaccountably cut out. He and the engineer had quickly carried out the necessary drill, done dozens of times in practice, and the engine was satisfactorily feathered. By this time we had left the runway lights behind us, and the night was particularly dark. Everything seemed under control. A quick glance at the altimeter showed a height of 400 feet above the ground – just about the height expected at this stage. The next moment we had hit the ground. Keith was under the impression momentarily, that we had been involved in a mid-air collision.

The second question concerned Ken. How come that two men sitting side by side, as had been Keith and Ken in the two pilots' seats, should fare so differently? Keith had been stunned when his head shot forward, but had recovered in time to unfasten his safety belt and escape through the upper hatch. Ken however, as far as we could determine, had been flung from the aircraft with great force when we had finally come to rest. Even Dick, who must have been rattled around like a pea in a whistle, without benefit of safety straps, had managed to climb out of the hatch successfully. They were questions I could not answer. They returned time and time again to my mind, which was a kaleidoscope of constantly changing images. It dwelt on the condition of our two crewmates, about whom there was no news forthcoming. I thought about my parents, and only hoped they had not been informed about the accident; it would only add to their worries. I suppose that it was one of the symptoms of shock that as I tried to sleep I was plagued by feelings of deep uneasiness. It was some psychological factor to do with the awesome contrast between the roar of the engines and the sudden transition to the silence of the burning fuselage. The ache from my legs was enough to ensure a night of discomfort, no matter how I tossed and turned. I prayed for the dawn, on what was the longest night of my life.

Eventually daylight filtered into the ward, and I gazed at it reflected on the glossy white walls, as I had on the previous morning. It served to brighten my spirits. Soon, breakfast was served at our bedsides, and conversation resumed.

Les was the only one of us allowed out of bed. After the breakfast trays had been cleared, he called into the adjacent office to seek news of our two crewmates. The room was empty, but there was a typewritten sheet of paper lying on the desk. He glanced at it, then brought it out to show us, without a word.

It was a list of our crew names, with the addresses of our next of kin. Against the name of the five of us was the typewritten letter 'I'. Against Dick's name were the letters 'S.I'. Against Ken's name was the letter 'K'. That was how we learned that Ken was dead.

The news came as a great shock, not lessened by the fact that it was something half expected. My first reaction, quite irrational, was to recall the day at Moreton in the Marsh when we had gathered in the hangar for the ritual of crewing up. It had been at my instigation that Ken had been approached; it had been my suggestion to grab someone of a more mature age. Thus it followed that had I kept my mouth shut, Ken would still be alive. I realised at once that this was mere sophistry. In times of war, men died every day by nature of the job they were called upon to do. Who could say that Ken would have survived even thus far with another crew?

It had been obvious to me for some time that Ken did not enjoy his flying. Maybe enjoy is not the right word. The rest of us, I'm sure, looked upon flying as a worthwhile job which gave fulfilment to our youthful exuberance and liking for excitement. We felt that although little more than boys ourselves, we gained maturity by being seen to do a man's job. It was a job which gave a degree of satisfaction rather than enjoyment. Ken, being so much older, did not feel this to the same extent. He was also the only one of us married, which must have put added stresses upon him. In spite of this, he had never tried to avoid his commitment, and had never been less than a good crew member. He had done what he had to do, to the best of his ability, and without complaint.

And that is an epitaph I for one would be glad to settle for.

10

Third Time Unlucky

O ur accident brought forth various ramifications, not least of which was the unexpected amount of sympathy and general goodwill which was directed our way over the next few weeks.

We were held in Sick Quarters for about a week, in the care of the friendly medical staff. We had plenty of visitors, mainly members of Bill's crew, who came to chat and share the cosy warmth of the ward. Cyril told me they had seen our aircraft burning brightly on the ground while waiting their turn to land, without knowing which crew was involved. Their view had been that such was the conflagration nobody could possibly have got out of it. They were very pleased to have been proved wrong.

The news about Dick was that he was recovering well in hospital, and though he would remain there for some time he was expecting to resume flying with us eventually. One of his fellow engineers had been to visit him. He reported that Dick was bedbound, with his lower abdomen encased in what looked like a wicker basket stuffed with cotton wool; he was quite perky, and sent word to us that his wedding tackle was intact.

We had been looking forward to sick leave as soon as the MO discharged us. We were in good heart. We had absorbed the shock of losing our crewmate: on an operational flying station, one soon learned not to dwell on these things. Our hopes of a quick getaway were dashed however. We were informed that there would be a formal board of enquiry into our accident, and we would have to remain on camp until it was completed. An investigating officer would be arriving from nearby Leconfield to conduct the enquiry. We didn't like the sound of that at all. Bureaucratic processes in the services tended to be long drawn-out affairs; we didn't feel that we could contribute any more information than we had already given anyway.

The officer from Leconfield proved to be a friendly Australian pilot from the Halifax squadron there, and hailed from Sydney, like Keith. He was at great pains to assure us that he was entirely sympathetic towards us, and that he was not here to conduct any form of inquisition. His brief was to collect information in the form of statements from all the crew, and any reports, diagrams and photographs as appropriate. He came to see us in the ward, and handed cigarettes around; later, he and Keith reminisced about carefree days swimming at Bondi and surfing at Manly. His task took him only a few days. He called to say goodbye, bringing the typewritten statement for us to sign, and provided each of us with a photograph of the heap of ashes and portion of tailplane which was all that remained of *Lili Marlene*. None of us ever heard anything further about the enquiry. Presumably there were no lessons to be learned from the accident, and the details were filed away and forgotten. Aircraft write-offs in Bomber Command were unfortunately too frequent to warrant a great deal of time and trouble in their investigation.

Soon afterwards we were granted fourteen days sick leave. I limped down to Pay Accounts to collect my pay. I was pleased to discover that after more than a year in the rank of sergeant I had now received automatic promotion to flight sergeant; I could put up a crown above the three strips on my sleeves, and my pay had gone up to sixteen shillings and sixpence per day. In addition to some back pay, and the four shillings ration allowance for each day's leave, I now also qualified for the Nuffield Allowance. This little-known increment, payable only to operational aircrew while on leave, and paid out of the pocket of Lord Nuffield, the Morris Motors magnate, amounted to five shillings a day. It was much appreciated by the recipients. It paid for a night's accommodation at a serviceman's club, or the cost of a night's beer. I would be starting my leave more affluent than I had ever been before.

Afterwards I popped into the Navigation Section. I had lost all my navigators' equipment in the crash, except the watch I wore on my wrist, and decided to draw replacement gear while I had an hour to spare. The officer concerned went through the motions of striking off all the items on my loan card, from plastic ruler to bubble sextant.

'I suppose you lost your navigation watch as well,' he said.

'No,' I replied. 'That was on my wrist.'

He looked up at me. 'Are you quite sure you didn't have it pinned to your table like some navigators do, and lost it in the panic?'

'Quite sure,' I replied unwittingly.

I could have kicked myself all the way to the door. I can only think that the accident had dulled my wits.

I had invited Keith to spend his leave with me at home, and we travelled together by train. Our appearance was calculated to inspire considerate treatment and sympathetic murmurings on the way –

Keith with his pilots' wings standing out against the dark blue Australian uniform, and a large white bandage over his forehead, and me with my walking stick and limp. A party of army girls took it upon themselves to carry our kit for us when we changed trains, and found seats for us on our connection. We modestly forbore to shoot a line about our flying experiences, though possibly there were occasions when the limp was more pronounced than need be, and the bandage was adjusted to a more heroic angle. At Manchester, where we boarded a bus on the final stage of the journey, the conductress looked quite pained when I proffered the fares. 'Nay,' she said, in the broadest of Lancashire accents, 'I'm taking no money off you brave lads.' She didn't. In fact, a few minutes later she pushed a handful of silver into my hand. 'We've had a whip round upstairs. Have a drink on us when you get home. And happy landings.'

It was a similar story later in the week, when we called for a drink in the local pubs – the drink arrived either on the house or paid for by a customer. At the local dance hall we held court at the bar, with sympathetic girls in attendance. There were other aircrew sergeants present, but none could boast a wounded skipper in tow – and an Australian to boot. We seemed to be riding on a constant crest of solicitude and well-wishings, which we accepted as an unexpected perk of the job.

Other repercussions of our accident offered less gratification. Not least was the effect on our families.

I had tried to shield my parents from worry by writing nothing about our operational flying. I wrote home in general terms, and since I had been so long in training I hoped they would assume that I was still flying around England on harmless cross-country exercises, which I had sometimes described in detail. I was pleased that they had received no official notification of our crash to alarm them, though of course this was nullified by the shock of Keith and I arriving home in a damaged condition. I told them about the accident, and they were obviously concerned. We still did not talk about our missions over Germany, and they did not ask; I think they thought that the more they knew, the more they would worry. It was beginning to get through to me that the dangers of our job were far more keenly felt by our close family than they were on the squadron itself.

Both my parents and young sister were quite taken with Keith, the quiet Australian with the polite manners and fascinating accent. My mother fussed and mothered him, and provided one particular item of light relief. She prepared one day a succulent pie for dinner, which we had half consumed before Keith and I discovered that it was in fact a rabbit pie. Keith's embarrassment was obvious as he found himself unable to complete the meal. I explained to mother that rabbits were considered to be vermin by Australians, and that it was like serving an Englishman with a cooked rat. Didn't she know that? 'Everybody knows there are plenty of rabbits in Australia,' she said, with feminine logic. 'I assumed that rabbit pie would be the national dish.' It probably wasn't quite as funny as it seemed to me at the time.

As for my twelve-year-old sister Barbara, one glance at this glamorous young visitor was quite sufficient to relegate Nelson Eddy to second place in her affections.

The day arrived when we had arranged to meet the other three crewmembers and travel together by train to visit Ken's family. He had been buried in his local cemetery, and none of us of course had been able to attend the funeral. It had been a unanimous decision that we should go to offer our condolences, and perhaps ease their sorrow a little by our expressions of esteem for our former crewmate. We knew that Ken had been very close to his parents, and that he and his wife had lived with them since their marriage. It promised to be an emotional meeting, one to which we were not looking forward.

After a two hour train journey, followed by a long wander through the streets of the town, we eventually reached the address we had been searching for. We grouped ourselves round the front door of the semi-detached house, and rang the bell. There was no immediate response, and I had a feeling of relief; if there was nobody at home we would have to send our condolences by letter. Keith rang again, and this time the door opened. The man who appeared was obviously Ken's father. He stared at us for a moment or two, then a look of recognition dawned on his face.

'Come in, lads,' he said. He was quite composed. It wasn't going to be so bad, after all. He led us to the parlour, at the back of the house. The room was stuffy and gloomy, with the curtains partly drawn. My eyes were drawn to a large framed photograph of Ken, sporting his brand new bomb-aimers' brevet and sergeants' stripes, over the mantelpiece. In a chair by the fireside sat Ken's mother. She looked very old and haggard.

'It's the lads from Ken's crew, mother,' said her husband.

There was no response. She just looked at us hard and long.

'Good of you to come and see us,' continued her husband. 'I'm afraid you've missed Ken's wife. She has gone to stay with her own family in Scotland.'

There was an uncomfortable silence. Ken's mother continued to stare at us, and there was not the slightest look of welcome in her gaze. I got a horrible feeling that we had miscalculated the effect of our visit. Keith started to express a few stumbling words of sympathy. Suddenly Ken's mother spoke. Her tone was harsh.

'Just look. Hardly a scratch amongst you. All of you here, without a scratch. And yet my lad is buried in that graveyard out there. Why? Just tell me why it had to be him?' There was no answer. It was a question which would never be answered. Now she was crying bitterly, and her husband tried in vain to comfort her. 'I begged him not to go flying. He didn't have to go flying. And now he's dead. They sent an officer to his funeral. He had mud on his shoes. An officer with mud on his shoes – that's all they thought about my son.' Her body was now racked with sobbing, and her voice was hysterical.

The rest of us were silent as her husband tried again to soothe her. Further words from us were pointless. It was plain to see that our visit had come far too soon after the event.

'I'm sorry lads,' he said. 'My wife just hasn't come to terms with it yet. Ken was her only child, and she thought the world of him. I appreciate your visit. I think it would be best if you went now.'

He led us to the front door. Here we did manage to voice a few words of sympathy in turn. There were tears in his eyes as he shook hands with each of us.

'Thank you for coming, lads. It can't have been an easy time for you. I'm sorry you had to meet us like this.'

It was a relief to all of us when the front door closed behind us, and we set off on the long journey home. The whole scene had taken about five minutes to unfold. I wondered whether my own mother would have reacted in a similar manner under the same circumstances. I thought not. I hoped not.

We split up at the railway station, to return to our respective homes. As Keith and I stood on the platform awaiting our train, we gazed wryly at the wartime poster on the wall opposite: 'Is your journey really necessary?'

I supposed that Ken's mother would eventually come to terms with her son's death, but I doubted that she would ever be the same woman. She was as much a casualty of war as those sustained on the battlefield. Today's events had reinforced my view that in Bomber Command's war it was the families at home who bore the brunt. On the squadrons we had the excitement and the satisfaction and the comradeship to sustain us; our families had nothing but constant anxiety and occasional heart-break. I knew that bad news was always conveyed by telegram, delivered inappropriately by cheerfully whistling youths in pill-box hats riding post office bicycles. I had enough imagination to realise that the mere

137

sight of one of them in the locality must bring a chilling fear to every wife and parent with a loved one on active service.

This question of family concern was further extended after our leave ended, and we returned to Lissett. In my mail pigeon-hole in the Mess I found an air-letter from Australia awaiting me. It was from Keith's father, and was in effect an impassioned appeal for news about Keith. His parents had received a cable to say that their son had been injured while engaged in air operations. There were no other details, and to their worried minds it could mean anything from a sprained ankle to a broken spine. Keith's letters home, like my own, apparently contained no details of his operational flying, and they were desperate for information. Ironically, he added that he had sent an identical letter to the bomb-aimer of the crew.

I wasted no time in sending off an airmail letter containing as many details as I thought would pass the censor. I emphasised that all the crew held Keith in high esteem, both as a captain and a friend, and that the accident had occurred as a result of unfortunate circumstances. As regards his injury, his only souvenir of it would be a scar partly hidden by his hairline. I hoped it would help allay their anxieties, which, with their son operating 12,000 miles from home, must be even greater than those of my own family.

The day after our return, we received a cursory medical check and were regraded as fit for flying duties. As a crew without a bomb-aimer or an engineer, the prospects of an early appearance on the battle order seemed fairly remote. Far more likely that we would be joining the faceless fringe of 'spare bods' who hung around at briefings ready to step in as replacements for crewmen sick or incapacitated. It was a prospect none of us relished: nobody liked the idea of flying ops with a bunch of strangers.

That evening we were confined to our billets by the weather. The airfield was under a carpet of snow, and all day the snow ploughs had been trying to keep the runways and perimeters clear. All available aircrews, officers and NCOs alike, had been volunteered into assisting with spades and brooms. Tonight we rested on our beds, luxuriating in the heat blasted out by the stove. Our coke supplies had accumulated during our leave, and we had stuffed the stove so that its cast-iron casing glowed red hot. By this glow, the two empty beds stacked with folded blankets gave us a mute reminder of our absent crewmates.

We were talking over the latest items of news. On the brighter side, Dick was now out of hospital, and was expecting to be rejoining us in three weeks time. And *Friday the Thirteenth* had finally made it – the first Halifax to achieve the magic total of one hundred ops. It was a plane much in demand. The flight commander's crew were the present sitting tenants, so there was little chance of our gaining it as a replacement for *Lili Marlene*.

On the less bright side, three squadron crews had been lost during our leave – two of them having Aussie skippers. One of them was believed to have been involved in a midair collision, so there was little hope of survival for them.

The other item concerned us all, since it involved a new system of scoring a tour of ops. Originally a tour consisted of thirty completed ops, followed by a rest tour of at least six months, and a second tour of twenty more trips. Then a refinement had been introduced whereby a Germany trip earned four points, while a target in occupied territory rated only three: a total of 120 points was required. Few argued with the principle involved – that in terms of sweat and stress a flog to Berlin and back was worth far more than, say, a quickie to a flying-bomb site near the channel coast. Now the requirement had been upped to 144 points, equivalent to another six German targets. We decided that this was a pretty poor show, especially when one considered the large number of new crews currently being churned out by the training units. We ourselves were so far removed from the end of our tour that the question was merely of speculative interest; but to a crew sweating it out on their final trips we felt it would prove a very considerable imposition. We expected better of 'Butch' Harris.

Further discussion on the subject was arrested by a knock on the hut door, and the entry of a snow-capped figure in a warrant officers' uniform. He brushed the snow from his greatcoat, and greeted us in an accent unmistakably from the heart of the Black Country.

'I've come to introduce myself. The name's Len Cooper. I'm your new bomb-aimer.'

We gazed at him with interest, and surprise. He seemed incredibly old – thirty-five if he was a day. He had taken off his hat; his narrow forehead, with its receding hairline, and the grin on his jowled face, gave him the look of a friendly old hamster. When the introductions had been completed, he sat down near the stove and lit up a battered old pipe. There was something reassuringly solid and avuncular about him – an impression which was not dispelled when he began to talk to us about himself. He had already completed a tour of ops on Halifaxes, and after a rest period spent working in a clothing stores, was about to start his second tour with us. He seemed quite happy at the prospect. 'You miss the excitement of squadron life, once you're away from it. Anyway, ops today are a piece of cake compared with the old days, it seems to me.'

139

When asked by Denis what he thought about the new points scoring system, he dismissed it airily.

'Shouldn't worry about that, son. The war will be over before then. You'll see. Where are you from, by the way? Sutton Coldfield? I thought you weren't a million miles from Brum.' His easy manner and air of unflapability charmed me. A mature second tour crewmate was just what we wanted at this stage. If not exactly a father figure, we seemed at least to have acquired a favourite uncle figure.

The weather improved, and we carried out a couple of training flights with Old Len, as we had soon come to know him, and a borrowed engineer. The following day, instead of the expected night training detail we were due for, we found ourselves booked for ops that night. The word soon filtered through that all aircraft were being fitted with long-range fuel tanks, which meant a very deep penetration into Germany. Before briefing we made our way to dispersals to view our allotted aircraft, Q-Queenie, in daylight.

The extra petrol was carried in three rectangular tanks, with associated fuel lines, fitted in the forward section of the bomb-bay, and occupying about a third of its space. The remaining bomb stations were filled with 500 pounders and incendiary cannisters. The thought struck me that there would be no future in a crash landing with this installation directly beneath us.

I felt that our trip tonight would take us somewhere in support of the Russians, who were now making spectacular advances on the Eastern Front, and I was right. The target was announced as Chemnitz, a large town in eastern Germany near the Czechoslovakian border, and an important communications centre currently full of retreating German forces. The Russian implications of the trip were brought home to us after the main briefing. In addition to the normal issue of the plastic-cased evasion kit containing maps, emergency food, compass and currency, we were each presented with a bib to wear in the event of finding ourselves in the proximity of the Russian army. The bib bore a large Union Jack motif, and an inscription in Russian reading: 'I am English.' This of course provided a certain amount of derisory comment.

'It's no use to me – I'm an Aussie, not a Pom.'

'Do we know if any of these Russkies can read?'

'I'll need no Union Jack. They'll hear me miles away shouting 'Joe for King!'

Our crew were in a subdued mood as we drove out to the aircraft. Our engineer for the night, a young sergeant who had only recently joined the squadron, was understandably quiet. Keith too was quietly contemplative, and I thought I knew what was in his mind. Our latest

140

two trips had resulted in an early return and an aircraft write-off. What could go wrong tonight? My own mind was dwelling uneasily on the length of tonight's trip, a marathon nine hours. My secret irrational fear had always been that one night I would find myself unable to cope with my navigational responsibilities due to sheer fatigue and mental inertia. I would find myself far into a hostile land – hopelessly and irrevocably lost, and my befuddled brain unable to act. Tonight, I knew, the fatigue factor would be at its maximum. Should I take the amphetamine tablets always made available to us? George and Denis always took them on long trips to keep themselves alert. I was reluctant to do so: after all, they were a drug. Maybe I should hold on and see how I felt later in the trip. I remembered that tonight we had Old Len with us, on the first trip of his second tour. He could operate the H2S. That would be a good help. I looked across at him. He was sitting puffing away at his old pipe, and looking completely unconcerned. A morale booster in himself.

We took off soon after dark, and the early part of the trip was uneventful. The weather was good, with just occasional patches of cloud below. We crossed the French coast near Boulogne, and turned due east; as usual at turning points we caught a flutter of slipstreams. Tonight's attack was to be by far the heaviest Chemnitz had received.

Since D-Day a new Gee chain had been established with transmitters on French soil, which provided extended cover over the continent. Tonight the signals were coming through unjammed, and our new bomb-aimer seated by my side was having no difficulty in fixing our position.

Keith's voice broke a long silence:

'Looks like the Rhine coming up ahead, navigator.'

'Roger,' I acknowledged.

'What's that town about twenty miles to starboard, nav?' This time the voice was George's.

'Koblenz,' I said, shortly. I tried to discourage distracting questions like that.

'Someone's off track, and being coned by searchlights over there. Looks like he's having a hard time.'

'Keep your eyes off the searchlights,' said Keith. 'You'll ruin your night vision. There's bound to be fighters around tonight.'

All was quiet again as we droned on over the Bavarian uplands. The trip was going well. I felt I was pacing myself nicely – I had no feeling of tiredness yet.

It was the engineer who next broke the silence: 'Permission to transfer fuel from bomb-bay tanks, skipper.'

'Carry on, engineer. Don't even think about lighting a crafty cigarette, anyone, for the next half hour.'

It was a straight-forward operation. Some of our main petrol tanks in the wings would by now be almost empty. The time had come to top them up by pumping fuel from the overload tanks in the bomb-bay.

When things start to go wrong in the air, very often something is sensed long before the trouble actually manifests itself. Maybe it was something to do with the strong smell of petrol which became apparent even with my mask tightly fastened over my face, or perhaps it was the sound of voices raised in the pilots' compartment above my head. Whatever it was, I was half expecting the call from the captain. When it came, on intercom, his voice sounded quite normal; under the circumstances, that represented a supreme example of self control:

'Captain to crew. We have an emergency. The engineer has just managed to lose us 700 gallons of fuel. It's been vented into the slipstream instead of into the tanks. We're going to need a rethink, and quickly.'

He waited a moment or two, to let us digest this startling news. Then:

'Navigator, I want to know how long to go to the target. Also, I want to know if we can reach England if we turn round now. The engineer is working out a new endurance figure, then we'll think about our options.'

Knowing Keith as I did, his calm reaction didn't surprise me. Other pilots, I'm sure, might well have reacted by seizing the unfortunate engineer by the throat and beating his head against the fuselage in a frenzy of rage and frustration. Especially in view of the misfortunes which had bedevilled us of late. The fact remained, as Keith well appreciated, that we would still require an important contribution from him, inexperienced and prone to mistakes though he be. The recriminations could come later.

One fact was plain. We were still an hour's flying from our target, and with our overload fuel apparently dissipated, we had no chance whatever of reaching Chemnitz and then getting back to home territory. Two alternatives were briefly considered: pressing on to bomb, then either carrying on eastwards in search of an airfield in Russian-occupied territory, or looking for a landing ground in Allied-held France. Both were rejected as being completely impracticable in darkness. Our only option was to turn around and head for the nearest airfield available in England. My quick calculation showed that we could reach Manston – that haven for fuel-starved bombers on the Kent coast – within three hours if we flew direct. Had we sufficient fuel? With all of us figuratively breathing down his neck, our chastened engineer came up with his computed endurance figure. About three and a half hours. Keith was in the turn before the figure had registered with the rest of us. 'It's an early return,' he said. 'Again.'

It might have been the only viable option, but it certainly wasn't an easy one. Now we were on our own, a lone target for the enemy radar or prowling fighters. We had to fly, in a headwind, on a straight course to save time and at an economical cruising speed to conserve fuel. We also had to try to avoid flying over defended areas like large towns and industrial areas. At the end of it, if we got back safely, there was bound to be an inquest on our second unscheduled early return. And at the back of our minds was the gnawing thought that after another dodgy trip we would once again have scored no points towards the completion of our tour.

Old Len called up soon after we had turned about: 'What about our bombs, skipper? Do you want me to jettison?'

'Can you see anything ahead worth bombing?'

'Not really. It's black as pitch below.'

Nobody, thankfully, came up with a suggestion that we should carry out a solo attack on one of the towns marked on my chart. We had all taken good note of the fate of the bomber who had strayed alone over Koblenz. I had a better idea.

'Hang on a minute, bomb-aimer. I'll see if there's anything suitable showing up on H2S.'

I quickly tuned in the set. There were no large town returns on the screen, but a few miles ahead appeared a small intensely bright blotch – exactly the strong ground return provided by a factory complex. I suggested that we should carry out a blind bombing run on it, and this in fact is what we did. At a late stage the bomb-aimer took over visually, as he thought he could detect its dark outline below, alongside some sort of waterway. He thought it might be a power station, and away went our bombs. Whatever it was, there must be people today still wondering why their part of rural Germany was singled out for attack by a lone bomber.

The next three hours seemed interminable. Once we were back within Gee range I was obtaining regular fixes, and just could not believe how slowly these plotted positions were moving westwards along my chart. The intercom was silent, except that occasionally someone would switch on as though to speak, then switch off as though he had changed his mind; it added to the tension running the length of the aircraft like an electric charge. Apart from myself and Les, who was maintaining a wireless watch, every pair of eyes was straining into the darkness. I would not describe it as fear which held us. Fear implies a positive emotion

143

which arises suddenly to numb the mind and paralyse the actions: it was more a constant nagging anxiety which over a period can be just as stressful.

Our two gunners in particular were uncharacteristically edgy. Once or twice they developed a feeling that we were being stalked, and asked Keith to weave the aircraft when some dark shape seemed to be materialising behind us. Nothing developed. When eventually I was able to announce that we had crossed into Belgium there was an appreciable easing of tension.

A minute later, Denis suddenly shouted; 'Corkscrew port - GO!'

Within the instant Keith had flung the aircraft into a stomach-churning diving turn, which glued me to my seat and sent my equipment flying from my table. Before the manoeuvre had time to develop, George's voice broke in loudly: 'It's OK. It's a Yank.' We eased into level flight, and breathed again. Both gunners had identified the aircraft which had tailed us and then broken away above us as an American Black Widow night-fighter – its distinctive twin tail booms unmistakeable in plan view. He must have homed onto us with his detection radar, satisfied himself we were friendly, then carried on his way. It must have been pretty obvious to him that we were not hostile – our size and our four engine exhausts would have indicated so – but we had no such indication about him. He had pushed his luck coming in so close. Another fraction of a second and both gunners would have opened up, and could hardly have missed.

Suitably chastened, we proceeded with renewed vigilance. While still flying over the continent Keith was able to contact Manston on VHF, to tell them we were short of fuel and to request a landing. It was oddly reassuring to hear the English voice coming across the water, requesting our remaining endurance, in a matter-of-fact tone. We passed on our engineer's revised figure of forty minutes, and there was a short pause.

'Roger, Luxsoap Queenie. Regret we have a runway obstruction at this time. Can you accept a diversion to Woodbridge?'

'Standby,' called Keith. 'Can we make it, nav?'

'Yes,' I said. 'It'll take about twenty minutes.'

Since we were approaching from the east, there was not a great difference in distance involved. Woodbridge was the middle one of the three east coast emergency landing grounds, situated near the Suffolk coast, offering the same facilities as Manston and Carnaby. We called up our acceptance of the diversion, and I passed a course to the pilot.

Our destination was lit up like a Christmas tree, and visible many miles away. A vertical searchlight beam pierced the night sky, to attract like moths those aircraft limping homewards across the North Sea. A profusion of white, red and green lights marked the approach, runway and taxiways. It was so conspicuous I wondered why the Luftwaffe weren't in attendance.

We called them up at twenty miles range, and were given permission to carry out a direct approach from east to west under radio control. The runway was 4,000 yards long, the longest in the country, and we were going to need it. As we prepared to land, we discovered our mechanical problems were not yet over. For some reason we had lost all our pneumatic pressure, which meant that we would be unable to apply brakes for the wheels after landing. If Keith had reacted with a string of wild Australian oaths at this final turning of the screw, who would have blamed him? To be attempting his first night landing for weeks, his first since the crash, on a strange airfield, after a long exhausting but abortive flight, and now with this further complication – we could only marvel at his equanimity. It was a measure of our confidence in him that we took up our landing positions with feelings of sympathy rather than any apprehension for our safety.

He made an excellent landing right at the earliest touchdown point, cut all engines as soon as possible, and we gradually came to a halt just before the end of the runway. A large towing vehicle was there to hook up to our tailwheel and take us off the runway to the parking area. This was an airfield fully geared to handling emergencies, quite impressively so. Fire tenders and ambulances were at the ready, and had we ended up blocking the runway, a large bulldozer was available to shovel us off. Administered by the RAF, it was situated near the American bases in East Anglia, and busily catered for the USAAF by day and Bomber Command by night. As we drove to Operations in the crew coach we could see plenty of evidence of crashed and shot-up previous customers. We passed a Fortress which even in the darkness we could see to have a horribly mangled tail unit; they had used hose pipes, we were told, to clean the blood and guts out of the rear turret.

We told our story to a debriefing officer in Operations, while we nursed a cup of tea and a tot of rum. Later we had a hot meal, and were then bedded down in the adjacent diversion huts. Other diverted aircraft landed throughout the early morning hours, but I heard none of them. I had soon fallen into an exhausted sleep.

Next morning, our brakes repaired, we flew back to Lissett. Our story was told again in full. As a result, the unfortunate engineer was held entirely responsible for our failure to carry out the operation as briefed. He was interviewed by the Engineering Leader, found to have unacceptable gaps in his knowledge of the job, and immediately removed from flying duties.

For the rest of us there was a surprisingly sympathetic hearing, prompted no doubt by our recent misfortunes. Keith was commended for generally making the right decisions. The final verdict came as a pleasant surprise. In view of our efforts in not wasting our bomb load, the expected annotation in the flight authorisation book of 'D.N.C.O.' – 'Duty Not Carried Out' – would be replaced by 'D.C.O. – Alternative Target.' That meant we scored full points for the trip.

Welcome and unexpected as this was, we only hoped future points would not be so hard earned. One of us expressed the wish that the law of averages would operate to bring an end to our current run of bad luck.

Old Len, philosophising from behind his pipe, put things into perspective as he saw them.

'Bad luck? You don't talk about bad luck when you get back without a scratch. That's good luck. Same as there's no such thing as a bad landing when you can walk away from it. Bad luck in this game is when you don't come back. Until that happens, count your blessings.'

11

NIGHT OF THE BANDITS

I t was the second time within a week that we had been called upon to attack this particular objective. We had no complaints about that – it was not a target that caused us any great anxiety. It had a lot of the features we liked to see in a target: it was well clear of the big guns of the Ruhr and other industrial areas, not too deep inside Germany, of obvious military significance, compact in size, and, as far as we knew, not particularly well defended. It was in fact one of the synthetic oil plants, at a place called Kamen, where the resourceful Germans produced petroleum products, of which they were desperately short, from coal, of which they had an abundance.

The fact that this was a second visit proved, without our being actually told so, that the first one had failed to achieve any sort of results. This surprised none of us who had taken part in it. It had been a complete shambles. To start with, although it had been flown in daylight, the cloud had been solid throughout; that meant that the visual sighting essential on so small a target had not been forthcoming. Something, too, must have gone wrong with the Pathfinders' target markers – either they had not gone down at the right time or they had fallen out of sight below the cloud. There had been heavy jamming of the radio channel on which the Master Bomber had been trying desperately to bring some sort of control. In the end, we had heard his exasperated voice telling crews to drop their bombs on their best navigational aid. Since we had flown in K-King, which was not fitted with H2S, we had bombed on the evidence of our last Gee fix; since we were operating at extreme Gee range, that could have meant an error of five miles or more. It had been like throwing darts at a dartboard blindfolded.

In view of all this, it was difficult to see why we were expected to do better tonight, when the weather forecast again gave cloud cover over Germany, and sky marking would probably have to be employed. Presumably there would be sufficiently large numbers of bombers involved to give a percentage chance of some bombs destroying the target.

For tonight's trip we welcomed back Dick, recently returned from sick leave. We had done seven ops without him, flying with spare engineers, and we were glad to have him back. He seemed none the worse for his long layoff. We told him about the spare engineer who had accidentally pumped away all our overload fuel on the way to Chemnitz, and he thought it quite hilarious. This was our fourteenth op, having completed the supposedly unlucky thirteenth a few days previously with a completely incident-free trip to Cologne. Denis had missed one of our trips, having gone sick with a severe cold, so tonight was his thirteenth. We told him how lucky he was to get such a soft target for it.

The trip went according to plan. We crossed the Rhine north of the Ruhr, and came back south of it, without undue trouble. The only incident of note was that our imperturbable new bomb-aimer became at least slightly perturbed as we turned towards the target. He happened to be in the nose, looking out, when another Halifax whistled by us in the nearest of near misses. The traffic congestion which was a feature of the current massed raids was something to which he was not yet accustomed. As expected, the target was obscured by cloud, but the skymarkers were burning and seemed nicely concentrated.

We crossed the English coast inbound at Orfordness, well pleased with ourselves. This was the point where the tensions of the night quickly faded from the mind, and the general relaxation manifested in several ways – a gulp of hot coffee, a bite on a chocolate bar, chatter on the intercom. Like Denis's comment from the rear: 'Did somebody say something about unlucky thirteen?' It was now standard practice to switch on navigation lights to cut down the risk of collisions, as the Main Force began to fan out towards their various bases. Luftwaffe forays over England were now a thing of the past; they now seemed fully committed to the defence of the Fatherland. Keith lost no time in switching on, and other aircrafts' red and green wingtip lights soon began to twinkle around us.

Minutes later, Denis called up to announce that he could see anti-aircraft fire coming up from the ground some miles behind us.

'Are you sure?' asked Keith, in the half-jocular tone one often unconsciously used when conversing with our rear gunner. 'We're a long way from the Ruhr, you know.'

'Course I'm bloody sure,' said Denis indignantly. 'D'you think I don't know flak when I see it?'

'Probably someone crossing the coast off track, or too low,' I said, 'and they're getting a reminder. These pongos are a trigger-happy lot.'

As we proceeded across Norfolk, George in the mid-upper turret was the next to call up:

'Aircraft behind us, without lights. Can you see it, Denis?'

'I can see something, vaguely. Our tail light's on, and it's ruined my night vision.'

'Does it look like another Hali?' asked Keith.

'Hard to say,' said George. 'It looks a bit small. Could be a Mosquito.'

'Keep your eyes on it, and call out if it closes.'

Suddenly the cabin was lit up as a brilliant stream of tracer shot by on either side of us. Simultaneously, a shout from one of the gunners superimposed itself above the rattle of machine-gun fire – 'CORK-SCREW PORT – GO!' The aircraft within the moment seemed to be standing on its nose as we hurtled earthwards. Almost before the shrill call from the turret had registered, the intercom went dead.

The sudden fear hit me with the impact of an unexpected physical blow. This is it, I thought. We have been raked by cannon shells. The controls have been shot away, and the other crewmen killed. Soon we'll hit the ground. The instinct for self-preservation told me I should be grabbing my parachute pack, folding my seat, lifting the trapdoor of the downward escape hatch and leaping out into the darkness. I made a desperate effort, but could do nothing. The G forces had me pinned inexorably to my seat; I could even feel the flesh on my face pulling downwards. Though I could manage feeble movements of my limbs, I was effectually as helpless as a fly on a flypaper. I was going to die.

My reactions were not what I might have expected. Having accepted that it was physically impossible to escape, I felt no urgent need for despairing frenzied effort. The end would be sudden and painless, and the fear was suddenly expunged. There came no flashbacks of my past life. All I was conscious of was a feeling of resignation, and intense sadness that all was going to end like this.

Under such circumstances, time itself becomes immeasurable. I will never know just how long it was before I sensed an easing of our downwards plunge, a relaxation of gravity's hold on me. I was able to move in my seat, to appreciate that the engine note seemed back to normal, and to discover that my unplugged intercom lead was lying on the floor. I bent down, and plugged it into its socket. I was in time to hear Keith calling for a full crew intercom check from rear turret to nose, and to answer in my turn. My feelings could be likened to those of a condemned man whose reprieve arrives as he stands on the scaffold. My first thought was that I would never be unhappy again as long as I lived.

As we flew homeward at low level, I was able to get the full story. Our attacker had tailed us, lined himself up, then suddenly closed and opened fire. By some miracle he seemed to have missed. His tracer shells had sprayed each side of us, but slightly below, and as far as we could tell we were undamaged. As he broke away our gunners identified him as a single-seater fighter, almost certainly a Messerschmitt 109, and both of them got in a burst. Keith meantime had commenced evasive action, instinctively switching off our external lights. Having forced the aircraft into a sudden violent dive, he had decided to continue the twisting descent until we had lost several thousand feet, and were likely to have thrown off our pursuer. It was just my misfortune that my intercom plug had been torn from its socket at this time, for Keith had found time to reassure the rest of the crew that everything was under control.

It soon became apparent that the attack upon us was not an isolated incident but part of concerted effort by Luftwaffe units. A large number of their fighters, presumably fitted with long-range fuel tanks, had infiltrated the returning bomber stream. They had held their fire until the bombers had become easy prey over England, with their external lights on and their crews off guard. We were soon to learn how their audacious plan would cause unprecedented chaos, as they pursued their largely unsuspecting quarry throughout eastern England this night.

We must have been one of the very first bombers to be attacked, and in one sense we were lucky – at least we realised the danger which now existed. Others were not so fortunate. Many were still flying unsuspectingly with all lights on, as they made their complacent passage to their home airfields. From our low level position we could see them above and behind us. The cloud had now disappeared, and a bright moon was shining.

Our gunners reported their first sight of a bomber shot down as we neared The Wash. Over on our right appeared a sustained burst of tracer fire from behind, a dull red glow as the bomber's wing tanks caught fire, and the final flash as it hit the ground. From here to the Humber we saw four more shot down, in almost identical fashion. None of the stricken bombers returned fire; in fact, one of them was blindly firing off the colours of the day as he was hit – obviously under the impression that he was being tailed by one of our own fighters. It was a slaughter terrible to see. It was like watching a horror film, where you know the victim is being stalked by his murderer, but you can do nothing to warn him.

Les had broken wireless silence with a message to base after our own attack, so Lissett at least knew about the German infiltration. As we approached we were relieved to note that landings were still taking place, though with restricted lighting – just the twin rows of white lights bordering the main runway. There were now no navigation lights in evidence in the skies. Everybody had got the message at last. We were given permission to join the circuit for landing.

150

Keith and Dick had commenced their pre-landing checks when there came a sudden call on the local frequency, in the familiar tones of the Waaf officer Controller:

'All Luxsoap aircraft from Step-in. Bandits! Dogleg!'

'Sod it!' Keith's voice expressed sheer frustration. 'Another two minutes and we could have been down.'

We all shared his exasperation. The message meant that no Lissett aircraft would be allowed to land because of local enemy intruder activity; instead, we were to leave the area temporarily. I hurriedly crawled back into the nose to work out a course. As we left the circuit, another urgent call came over the air. We all instantly recognised Bill Strachan's Australian voice.

'Step-in from Luxsoap Roger. Require immediate emergency landing. Have been shot up in the circuit, and damaged. Have ambulance ready.'

A slight pause. Then the Controller's steady voice.

'Roger from Step-in. Permission to land. Extreme caution. Ambulance alerted.'

We were stunned into silence. Of all the crews to run into trouble, it had to be Bill's – whose every crew member virtually was an alter ego. Bill was Keith's friend, Cyril was mine; Ed, the wireless op, was Les's longtime mate, and the two gunners had done basic training with ours. Who needed the ambulance, we wondered. As if in answer to our unspoken question, George's quiet voice came on intercom:

'It's old Arthur Tait in the rear turret.' We did not know what had happened, but if someone had become a casualty, it was an odds on bet that the Tail End Charlie would have been involved.

As the airfield gradually receded, Denis reported the runway lights out, but he thought that Bill's aircraft had landed safely. There was sporadic firing going on, and shortly afterwards both gunners reported yet another blazing bomber lighting the sky. It dropped to earth in a flaming arc, about ten miles from the airfield. Both of them were convinced that it was one of our squadron Halifaxes. When was it all going to end?

Fifteen minutes later we had completed our diversionary dogleg and were on our way back to Lissett, which was still in darkness. Again we requested permission to land. The answer was an emphatic negative. The airfield had been under attack, and was closed to all aircraft, as was nearby Carnaby. We were to proceed to our briefed diversion aerodrome, flying as low as possible to avoid enemy radar detection.

'Where is our diversion field, navigator?' asked Keith.

151

'Hawarden, in North Wales,' I replied. 'It'll take us about forty-five minutes; we'll be flying into a headwind.'

'We've had it then,' called Dick. 'I've just revised our fuel endurance, and it's about thirty minutes. We'll have to find somewhere nearer than that to land.'

A short sharp discussion followed. After consulting my map, I thought our best bet was to head north and attempt to get in at one of the 6 Group bomber bases, which lay some forty or fifty miles away. I felt there was a good chance that the intruders would not have penetrated so far north in view of their limited fuel capacity. I couldn't help feeling what a ridiculous situation seemed to have developed. The war was acknowledged to be now in its final phase, with the Germans being crushed on all fronts. Yet here we were, on our own territory, being made to scuttle around like frightened rabbits seeking refuge from the ferrets which had found their way into the warren.

Some twenty minutes later we were in the Tees-side area. Everything was in total darkness, with no sign of any airfield activity. Selecting one of the larger operational bases in the vicinity, Middleton St George, we called them up on their approach frequency, requesting a landing. A Canadian voice responded. The message was that all airfield lighting had been switched off on receipt of an air raid red alert, and the airfield was closed.

I had an uneasy vision of our being shunted from airfield to airfield and each time being denied a landing, until in the end, with fuel tanks almost dry, we would have to take to our parachutes somewhere over this dark countryside. The thought deepened the depression brought on by the events of the last two hours.

Keith too had had enough. The time had come for positive action: we were going to attempt a landing here, come what may. He called up again, explained that our fuel shortage was now critical, and virtually demanded airfield lighting for a quick emergency landing. They could hardly refuse us. We were told to standby, presumably while our request was referred to higher authority; then the voice announced that the runway lights would be switched on, and we were cleared for an immediate landing. Extreme care was required, as enemy activity had been reported locally.

Moments later, the twin bars of light materialised on the ground way out to port, showing that we were handily placed on the downwind leg for landing. Once again we scrambled to our positions. As we did so, another crew were heard on the radio asking for permission to land. From the pilot's accent, there was little doubt that this was a Free French

152

crew from Elvington, who, like us, had fled north in search of a landing ground. They were told to attempt to follow us in.

Keith told George to remain in his turret for landing, to maintain a lookout, and to be ready to use his guns. The moonlight was now exceptionally bright – the Germans had picked the night carefully for their operation. The tension had built up to a nail-biting intensity as we turned for our final approach. It was short and steady, but time seemed to have gone into abeyance. With wheels and flaps down, and committed to landing, this was when we were most vulnerable to attack. And, somehow, each one of us sensed that a sinister presence lurked nearby who could not fail to be drawn by the sudden appearance of the runway lighting.

It was without a doubt the most eagerly-awaited touchdown of our whole flying careers. I found myself quite literally counting every second of the approach, until on intercom I heard the final instruction to the engineer – 'cut engines' – and we slowly sank onto the runway.

We hit the ground with the nerve-grating noise of a spoon scraping an old tin plate. We bounced into the air with a force that bent my chin to my knees, came down again, then veered sharply to the right. I knew we had left the runway, and prayed there were no obstacles in our path. As our wheels dug into the soft grass the port undercarriage collapsed, and we swung violently to the left before coming to rest with the floor tilted crazily. Once more we picked ourselves from the floor and scrambled through the upper escape hatch, with the fear of fire uppermost in our minds. As we dropped onto the grass, and gathered under the upward-sloping wing, the runway lights were suddenly extinguished. By the light of the moon we could see that we had followed a semi-circular path from the runway, as evidenced by the twin ruts in the grass, and in fact our port wing was now jutting out over the runway by about twenty feet.

We were a silent bunch. The shock of landing, the exertions of our rapid exit and the sheer thankfulness at finding ourselves on *terra firma* had left us undisposed to conversation. Then suddenly from the perimeter of the airfield came a rapid 'pom-pom-pom' as light anti-aircraft guns opened up, and a stream of tracer shot up into the skies. A dark shadow sped along the runway at a height of about 200 feet. As it passed almost over our heads it was clearly identifiable as a twin-engined Junkers 88. Only the fact that we had veered off the runway, and were thus out of his line of sight, saved us from a strafing. As the shadow merged into the darkness we could hear the pinging of shrapnel falling to earth on the concrete runway alongside us. It suddenly occurred to us that our shelter under the wing of our stranded aircraft was probably the most dangerous spot on the airfield if the intruder returned for another

153

run. We listened carefully for the sound of approaching engine noise, ready to sprint for our lives. All was quiet. The alerted ground defences had scared him off, we decided. We wondered what had happened to the unlucky French crew who had been hoping to land after us. They must have been told that our damaged Halifax was effectively blocking the runway, and they would have to seek sanctuary elsewhere. Shortly afterwards we heard distant gunfire, and the sound of a muffled explosion: its significance did not become apparent until much later.

After a long wait, the Station Duty Officer and a crew transport arrived to take us to Operations. The station was a Lancaster base, manned by the Royal Canadian Air Force, whose aircraft had not been operating this particular night. Just as well, since we had for the time being put their main runway out of action. One of the Intelligence Officers arrived to debrief us, and took detailed notes of what we had seen and done since midnight, when we had first crossed the English coast and received such an unfriendly reception. We were still telling our story when the startling news came through that the Free French Halifax which was supposed to follow us in had been shot down a few miles from the airfield. First reports indicated that although the bomber had crash-landed, the crew had managed to escape. We hoped it was true. Their fate and ours, it seemed, had hinged on the simple fact of who had called up first, and received first priority for landing.

After the debriefing we were taken to the Sergeants' Mess, where the night cook provided us with a substantial post-flight meal. In the meanwhile, the duty crew were engaged in towing our aircraft away from the main runway. All was now quiet, with the intruders well on their way home. They would all have a long and navigationally demanding sea crossing to contend with, and we wished them all the fuel problems we ourselves had experienced.

This night of surprises was by no means yet over. The meal finished, and relaxing with a mug of excellent Canadian coffee, we received a visitor. He introduced himself as the Station Engineering Officer, and he addressed himself to Keith.

'I understand you guys reported being attacked by an intruder, without being hit. Is that right?'

'That's right.'

'Then I've got news for you. I've just inspected your aircraft, and it looks like a Cat E job.'

He paused, and we looked at him in some surprise. Category E meant the aircraft was too badly damaged to be repaired. As far as we knew we had suffered a burst tyre and a collapsed undercarriage leg – relatively

154

minor damage which would certainly never warrant a write-off. He continued:

> 'The flaps and lower fuselage have been badly serrated by cannon fire. Also cannon shells have exploded by the starboard wing root, making the whole wing structurally unsound. In fact, violent manoeuvring of the aircraft could have torn the whole wing off.'

We looked at each other with startled expressions. I'm sure we were all thinking as I was of the moment after the tracer burst, when Keith had all but stood our aircraft on its nose. That had been easily the most violent manoeuvre any of us had ever experienced.

'Yes,' he went on, 'you've been very lucky. I might add that one tyre was shot to ribbons, and the other one burst on landing. That would account for your gyrations after touchdown.'

There was a stunned silence. 'I'm glad you told us that,' said Keith drily. 'I've kept telling myself my landings are usually better than this one was.'

This latest news put a slightly different slant on things. During our meal we had talked disparagingly of the capability of the German pilot who had visually homed onto our tail-light, closed to his required range, lined up his sights, aimed and fired in his own time – and had still managed to miss us completely! I had advanced my theory that since the Me 109 was not generally used as a night-fighter, the Germans had probably scraped the barrel to mount tonight's offensive – just as trainee crews had been used in the RAF's first thousand bomber attack on Cologne, way back in 1942. Now the fact had been established that he had not missed us, and indeed our survival had been attributable to an error of less than a single degree in the elevation of his guns. There could have been many causes for this; a sudden air pocket, badly harmonized guns, or even a flutter of turbulence from our slipstream. Whatever the reason, it looked like our lucky mascot was still performing valiantly.

We stayed at Middleton St George for what remained of the night, and the following afternoon a squadron Halifax arrived to ferry us back to Lissett. We immediately plied the crew with questions. Naturally the first one concerned Bill and his crew, whom we had left in a state of emergency. It appeared that they had made a good landing despite the attentions of persistent Ju 88. In the exchange of fire, which had continued even after they had landed, it had been their rear gunner who had sustained injury, just as we had anticipated. Arthur Tait had been severely wounded in the chest and leg by cannon fire, and the waiting ambulance had rushed him to hospital.

The other sad news was that the aircraft we had seen to crash near Lissett contained one of the squadron's senior crews. All had died. The irony was that they had completed a normal tour, but under the recently revised scoring system they had been kept back for a further six trips. Having returned from their thirty-first op, they had been shot down in their own airfield's circuit. The captain had been a religious man, and well respected. It was common knowledge on the squadron that before each trip he and his crew held a little prayer session together, after boarding their aircraft. Their tour had proceeded without troubles: now it had ended like this. What could one make of it all?

The other news concerned the activity on the airfield after we had cleared the area. In addition to the attacks on the bombers attempting to land, one at least of the intruders had carried out strafing runs across the base. One such run had been aimed at the Control Tower, on whose flat roof the Station Commander was blazing away with a Bren gun. Recently landed Halifaxes had elevated the machine-guns in their turrets and joined in the mêlée. Clusters of 'butterfly bombs,' small but deadly anti-personnel bombs, had been dropped indiscriminately, without doing much damage. It seemed we had missed a lot of excitement.

Our crew had been so involved in the events of the night, and the Luftwaffe had seemed to carry out their objectives so efficiently, that I was curious to learn as much as I could about the operation. I made several requests for further details from the Intelligence section, over the next few weeks. Apart from the fact that it had been code-named Operation Gisela by the Germans, and was thought to have been a last despairing effort to deal a crippling blow to Bomber Command, little news seemed to be available. It had been estimated that some seventy or eighty fighters had been involved, of which seven had been claimed shot down. I was more interested in our own losses, which must have been heavy on the evidence of what we had seen. On that score, there was no information whatsoever, and nobody was prepared to speculate.

For us, it had been a night to remember. For Bomber Command, it seemed, it had been a night to forget.

12

THE END IN SIGHT

As our tour of operations continued, it gradually became harder to recall to mind the events which went to make it up, or put them in any sort of chronological order. In spite of all the alarms and excitements involved, there was an essential sameness about the operational routine which was quite surprising. The course of each briefing, I found, became indistinguishable from that of the previous one – an hour of hectic calculations, followed by the unchanging exhortations of the specialist briefing officers, and a weather outlook which always seemed to involve the approach or recession of a front or occlusion, and the prospect of extensive cloud cover. The only variation was the position of the pins on the wallchart which guided the long red ribbon to its extremity and back again.

As for the various targets we were allotted, their aiming points were not presented as carefully pinpointed industrial structures, but merely as clusters of highly coloured pyrotechnics dropped by our precursors. Some of the targets, with rolling Germanic names like Recklinghausen, Reisholz and Hemmingstedt, meant nothing to us, though their military significance was spelled out to us. With the cloudy weather presently prevailing, sky marking of targets was usually employed both by day and night; and though there might be a different permutation of colours, one sky marking scene was very much like all the others.

Let me hastily add that this was not the case when conditions were clear and visibility good. My first real sight of a night target presented a truly awesome spectacle, never to be forgotten. We had been sent to bomb the I.G. Farben chemical plant, situated by the Rhine at Ludwigshafen. The bombing was well under way when we got there, and it was like looking down on a brightly floodlit stage from high above the dark auditorium. Centre stage were the markers, cascading their green and red candles of dazzling intensity, putting a shimmering sheen on the rising smoke. The ground was becoming mottled with the dull red glow of fires already taken hold. Blue-white searchlight beams restlessly arcing and probing the skies formed a backdrop, and exploding photoflashes reflected in the river to define the whole scene. High in the black sky bursting shells twinkled like golden fireflies. The stark beauty and intensity of the colour reminded me of a giant fireworks tableau I had witnessed during the Jubilee celebrations. The only thing missing was 'God Save The King' spelt out in letters of fire.

Perhaps another reason for my feeling that life was becoming stereotyped, and day-to-day events indistinguishable from each other, was that no day of the week now had any special significance. We reported in for duty every day of the week, and the day's work depended entirely on the flying programme. This in turn depended on either the weather or the serviceability state of the aircraft. As aircrew, we carried out no extraneous duties like drills or pickets or church parades, which would cause us to make note of the day of the week or date of the month. The eagerly awaited stand-downs were as likely to be announced in the middle of the week as at weekends. We carried out virtually no physical exercises except walking or cycling round the camp. The idea that crews should be kept in a high state of physical fitness had long since been abandoned. It had been found that it was not the trained athletes who coped best with the cramped confinements of the bomber cabins, but rather the types who could happily miss half a night's sleep playing poker in a stuffy bar-room. We flew at all hours of the day and night, which meant correspondingly irregular meals and sleeping hours. No wonder operational crew photographs tended to show young men who looked pale and hollow-eyed behind the grins.

I do not mean to imply from the foregoing that life had become dull. Someone defined ops flying as 95% boredom and 5% terror, which was an exaggeration on both counts. Life can never be dull when every few days people are shooting at you with intent to kill. But it was a period, I found, when I could best recall various incidents by linking them to a sub-title in my mind – a sort of mental shorthand.

There was, for instance, the spell classified in my mind as the 'Land-away Andy Syndrome.'

The sequence started on the night of the intruders, when we managed to land on and off the runway at Middleton St George. After being ferried back to base the following day, we found ourselves that night heading once again for Chemnitz with overload fuel tanks. This time there was no nonsense with the fuel transfer, and we reached and bombed our target. Unfortunately we spent long periods in cloud, where we acquired considerable accretions of ice. To maintain speed,

Keith had to apply increased power to all engines. In consequence, after another long nail-biting return leg, we managed to reach Manston, thankfully free of bandits, with about ten minutes petrol remaining in our tanks.

Two nights later, we were on our way to attack an oil refinery situated near the German border with Denmark. We were flying in N-Nan, a brand new replacement Halifax allotted to us for the rest of our tour. It had flown only a handful of hours, but had already proved itself to be prone to various teething troubles. While still over the North Sea, the port inner engine developed a serious oil leak; eventually the engine had to be shut down to avoid serious damage. With memories of our previous abortive early return still fresh, there was no question of not pressing on to our target. The problem was that we had not yet reached our bombing height, and on three engines our aircraft refused to climb a further inch. Yet again Keith was called upon to make an instant fateful decision. He called on Len to jettison half our bombload. Thereafter, painfully slowly, the altimeter needle began to record a gradual increase in height. We eventually reached our target, clearly identifiable by the yellow illuminating flares which ringed it, still about 2,000 feet below the rest of the stream. We could only keep our fingers crossed that we could avoid the rain of bombs coming down from above. On our return to base, well behind the rest of the squadron, we were instructed to make our three-engined landing at nearby Carnaby. Once again we had failed to make it home.

We flew the same aircraft, with engine repaired, on our next operation – a thousand bomber raid on the Krupps works at Essen, in daylight. Yet again we had to bomb through cloud, so could not see the devastation below wrought by five thousand tons of high explosive. The sheer size of the raid seemed to have overwhelmed the notorious flak defences: there was nothing like the barrage we had experienced on Christmas Eve. The phenomenon we did see was the layer of white cloud over Essen quickly darkening from the effect of the smoke, then rising from the heat below to form what looked like the cap of a giant brown mushroom. On the way home, the aircraft's hydraulic system began to malfunction. For no apparent reason the bomb doors flew open, and defied efforts to close them. When we eventually got back to base and prepared to land, it was found that we had no indication that the undercarriage was locked down. Rather than risk our collapsing onto the runway, Control once again told us to make for the emergency strip at Carnaby. We took up crash positions for the landing: we were becoming inured to this sort of thing. We touched down without mishap, and taxied to the parking area to await our ground crew from Lissett, coming to inspect their troublesome charge.

The ground crew contrived to get N-Nan back on the line in time for our next operation, which my logbook tells me was to a German town called Homberg. My only recollection of it is that on the way home a sudden Australian oath signified further tribulation. By some strange quirk of the hydraulic system, the heavy undercarriage had lowered itself into the locked position, where it remained in spite of all Keith's efforts to raise it again. Flying with wheels down meant a significant increase in fuel consumption, and a reduction in speed; the weather at base was deteriorating, according to the latest group broadcast Les had just picked up. There was only one course of action available. Ruefully I plotted a course for the nearest suitable diversion airfield – our old friend Manston again.

Today had been our nineteenth operation. On eight occasions, through no particular fault of our own, we had failed to get back home; today's effort made it five in a row. Bomber Command had three emergency airfields, and we had patronised them all. If records were kept for this sort of thing, then we must have broken them all.

We did in fact received some sort of a mention in dispatches. The station Intelligence summary contained the following paragraph:

> One last word of congratulation to Flight Sergeant Anderson. Recently, having the misfortune to lose an engine an hour before the target, he jettisoned eight bombs and pressed on to bomb successfully. Since then he has had further troubles, but he and his crew have come up smiling. Let's wish him better luck for the rest of his tour. His ground crew, incidentally, now call him 'Land-away Andy'.

If that's all they called us, it showed commendable forebearance. For the last five trips they had waited long hours throughout the landing sequences, ready to marshal us in to dispersal. All in vain. They had been lumbered with an aircraft which was undoubtedly plagued by gremlins. Now it looked like they had inherited the squadron jinx crew. I wouldn't have blamed them if they had called us something stronger.

Memory recalls an incident, soon afterwards, filed under the heading 'Old Len Shows The Professional Touch.'

We had set out in daylight to attack a railway marshalling yard, not very deep inside Germany, which was known to be holding supplies for the retreating German armies. We flew again in N-Nan, whose gremlins by this time had been exorcised. With the arrival of early springtime and much improved flying weather, Bomber Command were now ranging as freely by day as by night. The advent of long-range Spitfire and Mustang fighter support meant that we now went virtually unchallenged by the Luftwaffe, and though the flak batteries were more concentrated, our casualty figures had dropped drastically. It all seemed to have happened within the space of a week or two.

Old Len was undoubtedly one of the old school of bomb-aimers, brought up in darker days, when lightly-armed bombers rarely ventured over Germany in daylight. All his bombing had been done at night, or in cloud conditions, and he had seldom had the satisfaction of aligning an actual target in his bombsight. Today, the prospect was that he would be doing just that.

As we approached our target, on an easterly heading, the large marshalling yard appeared in the shape of a bottle, with its neck to the south. Len soon noticed that the red markers were burning brightly on the ground exactly at the bottleneck, and this was the area being pulverised by the bombs. To the north however, the yard itself, comprising an area a mile long and a quarter mile wide, was as yet untouched; this heavy concentration of lines, sheds and rolling stock had not attracted a single bomb. It was not a situation to be tolerated by a professional.

'Left, left, skipper,' he called. 'Give me about thirty degrees left.'

Instinctively, Keith began to turn, immediately diverging from the path of the leaders whom we had followed closely throughout the trip.

'Where the hell are you taking us, bomb-aimer?' he called.

'We're going where we can do some real damage. They're just wasting their bombs back there. Steady now.'

Len continued his bombing run. We were getting further and further away from the rest of the force.

'Steady, steady . . . steady . . . Bombs Gone. Bomb doors closed. Hold steady for photograph.'

Len turned, and beckoned me into the nose. Together we peered down. For the very first time we would be able to see the strike of our bombs, instead of looking into the smoke and the glare of the markers. For many long seconds we waited, until the target appeared directly below. Suddenly there was a ripple of light, and there appeared simultaneously a neatly drilled row of holes across the yard at its widest point. There were sixteen bombs in the stick; the first one hit the near edge of the long line of wagons, and the last one burst exactly on the far edge. A perfect straddle. I congratulated Len with a pat on the head, and he acknowledged with a huge wink.

Even so, I was highly relieved when Keith swung the aircraft fiercely round, and we set off to rejoin our company; the flak bursts around us indicated that the ground gunners were giving us individual attention. I could not help but feel elation at what I had witnessed. After all, each operation cost a great deal in risk and effort, and counted for nothing if the end product, the bombing, was not completely effective. Though today's effort in itself meant little in the final aggregate, and was thoroughly destructive in context, yet it represented something always to be admired – a thoroughly professional job.

Then followed 'The Night of the Complete Cock-up.' Things started off well enough, with a Tannoy announcement in the afternoon that the squadron would be stood down until 0800 hours the following morning. That meant a liberty run into Brid for most of us. Better still, today was a Saturday, which indicated that most of us would end up at the popular Spa Ballroom. To crown it all, Denis gave the news that today was his nineteenth birthday, and we were all expected to share in the celebrations. He and George were soon changed into best blue, and on the first transport into town.

We all considered Bridlington to be a resort with a lot to offer, even out of season, and none of us would dream of going further afield for our pleasures. It had friendly people, cosy pubs, good Yorkshire beer, a couple of cinemas, and the Spa. The latter was undoubtedly the social focal point of the town, attracting the servicemen like flies to the jampot. Here we waltzed and foxtrotted around the large crowded ballroom, often to the music of a big-name broadcasting band. We partnered and shot a line to the local girls and the Waafs from camp and the army girls from the searchlight units and even the warworkers from industrial Yorkshire on their weekend breaks. Nondancers would sit, nursing their beers, in the plush seats of the balcony under the blacked-out dome roof, enjoying the lively ambience below. The town itself had a long air force tradition. Between the two wars, Lawrence of Arabia had served as a lowly airman at the RAF Marine Unit, which still operated from the harbour. In more recent times, many of our number had done their basic training and drilling in its streets. It was a place where we always felt at home.

Keith and I caught one of the evening transports, and called for our first drink at the usual aircrew rendezvous, the town centre lounge bar known as Ouston's. From here we crossed the road to the pub in whose back bar we had arranged to meet our two gunners.

The bar was noisy and crowded, and it was some time before we spotted George. He seemed to be on his own.

'What's happened to Denis?' we asked.

'I'm afraid he's had one too many,' said George apologetically. 'Everyone we met insisted on buying him a birthday drink, and you know he doesn't normally drink a lot. He's taking a rest on that bench under the window.'

'Taking a rest' was something of a euphemism. Denis was lying flat out on the bench in a state of unconsciousness. It was interesting to note that his face still wore its habitual smile.

It was plain that the faithful George considered himself partly to blame for his friend's intoxication. 'If we can get him to the Spa,' he said, 'I'll sit with him in the balcony with cups of black coffee, till he sobers up.'

Before we could pursue the matter further, the door opened to admit two burly RAF Service Policemen. They looked carefully around the crowded bar, muttered something together, then walked towards us. For the moment, we thought they had been called in by the landlord to remove our supine gunner, and we instinctively tried to shield him. One of them addressed himself to Keith:

'Are you all from 158 Squadron, Flight?'

'That's right, sport. What about it?'

'Our orders are to tell all squadron personnel that the stand-down has been cancelled, and they are to return to their unit immediately. Transport is waiting in the square outside.' We looked at him in astonishment.

'Is it a call for ops?' I asked.

'Our instructions are to tell all crews to report to Operations. That is all we can say.' He looked down at Denis, who now had one eye open, and eyed him dubiously:

'Is he alright?'

'He's OK. He's just having a kip. We'll see he gets back to camp.'

The SPs departed, to continue their search of the airmens' likely lurking places. I suppose it says something about the gregarious nature of the crews that within half an hour virtually the whole squadron was packed into the transports heading back to Lissett. It also says a good deal about the morale of the squadron, that nobody disappeared into the night to avoid what was obviously an imminent operation. We got Denis aboard without much trouble – the news had registered, and brought on a sobering effect. He intended coming with us, no matter what. Every trip he missed with us meant that he would have to hang on as a spare gunner at the end of our tour, to make good the deficit. He was already one trip behind us: now he pleaded with Keith not to add to it.

It was indeed an operation in the offing. Someone, somewhere, had blundered, necessitating this extraordinary round-up. Some time after the stand-down had been announced, the Command teletypes had been activated, giving details of a bombing mission in support of the army, involving a late night briefing and an early morning take-off. Fortunately, the news had reached us in town before the night's serious drinking had started. With one exception.

At briefing, it was announced that in view of the circumstances, spare crew members would be available to take the place of anyone considered incapacitated. We kept quiet about Denis; we reckoned the sobering-up process would be sufficiently advanced by the time we took off.

We eventually got out to the aircraft. Shortly before start-up time, the CO's Hillman zig-zagged across the dispersals with news that H-Hour had been put back by an unspecified period, and we were to remain by our aircraft until further instructions were received. We were still there in the chilly March pre-dawn – shivering, stiff-limbed, weary and fed up. Denis in addition was suffering from boozer's gloom, and occasional bouts of sickness in the grass by the dispersal.

Finally, a great cheer arose in the early morning air, as the pooping of red Very cartridges from the Control Tower signified that events had overtaken the need to take out this particular target. The trip was scrubbed. We were free to take to our beds.

We had lost out on a stand-down, a Saturday night out, a birthday celebration, a night's sleep and four more operational points. Denis had memories of a birthday he would prefer to forget. The night had ended as it had begun – with a cock-up.

Then there was the business of Our Pilot's Progressive Promotion.

Aircrew promotions to commissioned rank were rather generously handed out on the operational squadrons. In fact, on our own squadron, practically all the pilots and navigators were recommended, after proving they could cope efficiently with the demands of operational flying. They were granted without the preliminaries normally associated with the commissioning process – aptitude tests, background probes, selection boards and OCTU courses. The procedure could not have been more simple. One was recommended by the officer in charge of one's section, an application was submitted, an interview was arranged with the Air Vice-Marshal commanding the Group, who invariably rubber-stamped the recommendation, one received a grant of £50 to buy an officer's kit and uniform, one moved from the corrugated-iron Sergeants' Mess to the corrugated-iron Officers' Mess, and one exchanged the crew Nissen hut for a similar one on the officers' site. The whole process was sometimes so speedy, it could be accomplished between two successive ops.

When the time came for me to submit my own application, there was a slight snag. Keith had been informed that his commissioning would be held up until the recommendations of the board of enquiry regarding our accident were made known. I did not relish the idea of becoming the only officer in the crew, and leaving the friendly confines of the crew hut. I also felt that my transition to an officer's lifestyle would be more smoothly achieved in the more settled environment of a non-operational station. Accordingly, I asked if my recommendation could be postponed until near the end of my tour. It was not altogether an unusual request, and was granted without any trouble.

Some weeks later, Keith's automatic promotion from flight sergeant to warrant officer was promulgated. After completing one more op, his commissioning was approved, and he put up the thin blue braid of a pilot officer. Since it was policy to give captains of heavy bombers accelerated promotion on commissioning, by the time our next op came along the camp tailor had sewn on his uniform the thicker braid of a flying officer. He must have had the unique distinction, for what it was worth, of being the only bomber pilot to complete four successive ops with an increasing rank on each one.

Bill and Cyril had also by this time moved into the Officers' Mess, and I thought the time had come to join them. With twenty-five ops now registered in my logbook, the end of our tour was in sight. After returning from leave, I went to see the Station Navigation Officer to request that my application now be forwarded. Alas, I had left it too late. Instructions had been received, only days previously, that in view of the imminent end of the war, and the large number of aircrew officers who would soon be surplus to requirements, all commissioning from the squadrons was now ended.

I was of course disappointed, but not desperately so. In one respect, it was to work to my advantage. I had already decided that I would like to take up a career as a navigator in the post-war RAF, on a long term engagement. As a non-commissioned officer I was later able to commit myself to flying duties up to my forty-fifth birthday, something I would have been unlikely to achieve as an officer.

I had also learned that the end of the war was imminent – and that was official!

Not that this was something which could not be deduced by glancing at the latest war maps in the newspapers with their thrusting black arrows, or listening in to the latest BBC news bulletins. The allied armies were across the Rhine in force, and the Russians were homing in on Berlin. It was extremely difficult to understand why the Germans did not throw in their hand, to avoid further catastrophe.

Bomber Command had now reached the tremendous peak of its power, but, such was the situation in Germany, it had almost run out of suitable targets. There seemed little point in massing a four-figure force of heavy bombers to hit her already pulverised industrial centres, and the military situation was too fluid to offer much in the way of tactical targets in support of the army.

At the beginning of the month of April, we had carried out what was to prove to be our last night operation. We bombed the oil installations near Hamburg, on a clear bright night. The defences seemed badly co-ordinated. We counted more than twenty search-lights sweeping the skies in the target area, and though we were twice coned by them, we did not get the heavy flak follow-up we expected. It was as though the demoralised defenders were merely going through the motions. By the time we bombed, the conflagration was such that the Master Bomber was instructing crews to ignore the markers and aim for the fires.

Our crew went on ten days leave the next day. On the civilian front, the smell of victory was in the air, and people were already planning their celebrations. At home, I assured my family that for our crew the war was already over, and their long period of anxiety about me was ended. It was a very happy and relaxed break for us all.

On returning to Lissett, I found my reassurances were a little premature. The very next day the squadron went in force to Heligo-land – one of the earliest targets of the war was proving also to be one of the last. Our crew did not take part, but everyone got back safely, and voted the trip a piece of cake.

To my surprise, after a week of total inactivity for the squadron, another target was found for us. Not only that, but a maximum effort was called for. Maybe that was to give one or two new crews their long-awaited opportunity of crossing the great divide between trainee and operational aircrews, before everything folded up. At the late morning briefing the target was announced as the island of Wanger-ooge, which nobody had even heard of before. It was, apparently, the easternmost of the North Frisian Islands – a fortified base whose large guns controlled the sea approach to the German port of Wilhelm-shafen. The aiming point was a battery of powerful naval guns situated at the northern end of the small island. It was a reasonable enough target, but with a combined force of 400 Lancasters and Halifaxes involved, it seemed to present a degree of overkill.

There were no doubts at all that this would be our last operation in Europe. The Americans and Russians had already met at the Elbe, and posed effusively for the newsreels. After today there would be nothing left to bomb. Today's finale for us promised to be both a short one and an easy one. No wonder there was such a light-heartedness apparent at briefing.

It was a feeling I found I could not share. I seemed to have developed a premonition about today's trip – a deep uneasy feeling that our luck would run out today. The psychological factors involved were not difficult to pinpoint: they all concerned the expected early ending of hostilities. By some perversity that factor was outweighing in my mind all normally accepted laws of probability. I remembered reading about the unlucky soldiers in World War One, killed by desultry gunfire on the morning of 11th November 1918, awaiting the official cease-fire time of eleven o'clock. I thought too of our squadron crew who had done their thirty ops, each one preceded by prayers, and had then been shot down in their own airfield circuit. I had recently jumped the gun by assuring my parents that my war was already ended; wasn't that dangerously tempting fate? The fact that this trip seemed on the face of it to be the easiest of them all merely compounded the anxiety. Disaster usually struck when it was least expected.

Then there were the superstitious tendencies I seemed to have developed to an increasing degree lately. The silly business regarding my flying boots, for instance. Two year's wear and tear had made them almost unwearable. Both rubber heels had worn right down, and one of the soles was detached from the upper, yet I had no intention of replacing them. This pair had seen me through my flying training and the best part of a tour – I would be a fool to risk ending the good luck I had so far experienced. The fact that I knew I was being completely irrational didn't make the slightest difference. Not that I was alone in my superstitious indulgence. Even our phlegmatic skipper, before take-off, would always discard his necktie in favour of his lucky neckerchief; and Denis I knew would no more think of flying without Herman in his turret than he would of flying without his trousers! I am quite sure that it was all part of the anxiety neurosis which, although unacknowledged and certainly never talked about, gradually afflicted everyone to some extent as his flying tour progressed.

We moved off in the early afternoon of a bright spring day. Twenty-seven squadron Halifaxes snaked along the perimeter track in a noisy cavalcade, the sunlight glinting on the polished perspex and the spinning propeller arcs. An unusually large number of spectators, including civilians waving from the roadside near the dispersal, gave an unaccustomed air of occasion. One by one, at thirty second intervals, the aircraft lumbered along the main runway, eased into the air, then banked onto their easterly headings.

We climbed quickly to our bombing height of 9,000 feet – the first time we had ever operated below oxygen height. For some reason individual navigation was the order of the day, so I was soon engrossed in my work and able to put aside my misgivings.

It seemed to be no time at all before Keith was reporting sight of the flat chain of islands which made up the North Frisians, on our starboard bow. Soon afterwards Len reported the red markers going down ahead, in conditions of excellent visibility. All around us the Halifaxes began to converge.

I was watching events from the nose. I still hadn't been able to shake off the vague feelings of apprehension. I had a sudden impulse to clip on my parachute pack in case we had to bale out in a hurry, then decided against it, as a pointless exercise; the enemy were hardly likely to concern themselves with rescue attempts for any of us unfortunate enough to land in the sea. Up ahead, there seemed to be an unexpectedly large amount of flak coming up: the sky above the target was already darkening ominously.

We were still a few miles from the target, from which the black smoke was now rising, when we witnessed our first casualties. It seemed like one of the bombers ahead was either trying to avoid a close salvo of shellbursts, or had been violently flung off its course by a near miss. In an instant it had collided with another converging Halifax. Their wings seemed to lock, then both broke up under the impact and fluttered downwards in a flash of flame. No parachutes emerged from the falling debris.

There was no time for comment. Len had the target in his sights, and had begun his bombing patter.

'Keep it steady, skipper. Looks like a good prang. Bomb doors open.'

Now there was another distraction. A Halifax flying a hundred yards ahead, and slightly to our left, had started to climb sharply, as though to clear the lingering black smoke of the shellbursts ahead. Steeper and steeper became his angle of ascent. Having just witnessed an awesome collision, we all eyed these antics with some alarm.

'What the bloody hell is he playing at?' came Keith's tense voice. 'Keep your eyes on him, gunners.'

'Steady . . . steady . . .' Old Len on a bombing run was not to be diverted.

I was standing in the nose, with my feet astride the bomb-aimer's prone body. I had been gazing intently at the red markers glowing on the ground at the base of the towering smoke, which now hid half the island from view. Now my eyes were glued to the Halifax which, as we swept past it, seemed to be all but standing vertically on its tail. Just as Len was announcing our bombs gone, the bomber gave a convulsive stall, and spun downwards. It was only then that I saw the gaping hole in its fuselage by the mid-upper turret. It must have received a direct hit. The exploding shell must have shattered the controls, and by some freak of chance the elevators must have jammed fully upwards, precipitating the uncontrolled climb and the sudden death dive. Whatever the cause, the sight of its effect was something none of us would forget.

Below us, the smoke from the exploding bombs had completely obliterated the aiming point, but the anti-aircraft guns were still firing. The gunners were sticking most gallantly to their job, and one could only admire them for it. Soon they would be engulfed by the creep-back of the bombing; in today's grisly balance of the war account, their lives would be offset against the equally brave lives already lost in the air.

Once we were out of range of the flak, our spirits rose to a new peak. My earlier premonition had already receded from my mind like a vaguely remembered dream. Now I merely speculated if any of the three unfortunate crews we had seen spinning to their deaths had experienced any similar forebodings. There was unrestrained chatter on the intercom, and we gave a cheer as we saw the approach of the Lancaster force who were backing up on the target with even bigger bombs.

Denis was already looking to the future:

'Well, that's that, now bring on the Japs. D'you know what we should do now? Volunteer right away to go to the Far East as a crew. They can't refuse us – we're entitled to finish our tour if we want to. If not, we're going to find ourselves split up very soon.'

He was expressing the thoughts of us all that a time of transition was rapidly approaching. The end of a memorable era of comradeship and shared danger. Soon our paths would diverge, leading us all to destinations unknown. We landed back at Lissett after a mere four hours. Every squadron aircraft landed safely; some of them, including *Friday the Thirteenth* on her 127th operation, had added battle scars from the shellfire. The reverberating noise of the engines gradually subsided as one by one the aircraft taxied to their circular concrete pans and cut their engines. Ground crews fussed around with wheel

169

chocks and covers. I climbed out of the rear fuselage door, and enjoyed the sudden cool freshness of the early evening air on my face. All was now quiet and still, except for the crew transports criss-crossing the dispersals. In my mood of silent euphoria, I felt I should be marking the occasion by a gesture like kissing the ground or mumbling a prayer of thankfulness. A coach with its Waaf driver suddenly pulled alongside, and we all climbed aboard for the short ride to Operations.

As I sprawled in my seat, contentedly puffing on a cigarette, I glanced down at my well-worn flying boots. Really, I decided, I must get myself a new pair. These were in a disgraceful condition. I would exchange them at the clothing stores first thing in the morning.

13

THE AFTERMATH

W e had indeed played our last part in the long-running air war, but the official ending of hostilities in Europe proved to be a long drawn out and contentious affair – a presage of the decades of cold war to come. The German forces in north-west Europe had surrendered to Field Marshal Montgomery as early as 4 May, but no official stand-down was announced to us. Even after the German radio gave the news of a general unconditional surrender on Monday 7 May, it seemed the Russians were still stalling until they had ratified their own surrender terms in Berlin. On camp, all sorts of rumours were circulating – that negotiations had broken down, or even that we were planning to advance against the recalcitrant Russians. Later in the day, the BBC broadcast news that the following day, Tuesday 8 May 1945, would be a public holiday, and that Prime Minister Churchill would make an official announcement at three o'clock.

Here at Lissett, someone made the decision a little earlier. Just after eleven o'clock on the Monday evening, minutes after we had put out the lights in our crew hut, the station Tannoy blasted out the news.

> 'It's all over! The war in Europe is over – and that's official! Come along to your Messes to celebrate. Bar hours are extended indefinitely. On your way, look out for the fireworks display at the Control Tower.'

Hardly had the reverberations of the broadcast died down before we were on our way, with battledress hastily donned on top of our pyjamas. We joined the happy and animated stream of airmen crowding the narrow country lane leading from the living sites to the Messes. The atmosphere reminded me of the exodus from a football league ground after a resounding win by the home team. Over to our right, the pyrotechnics display from the roof of the Tower was already lighting up the sky. Stockpiles of signal rockets, illuminating flares and red and green Very lights exploded in rapid sequence, giving a noisy and colourful spectacle. It was like a Pathfinder-target marking exercise, seen from a new angle.

All the mess buildings were ablaze with light. After being conditioned by six years of enforced blackout, we found the sight of unrestricted bright light issuing from every window a startling one. As a symbolic gesture of this new freedom, in the open space in front of the Sergeants' Mess someone had started a fire fuelled by plywood screens and blackout curtains.

In the Messes the celebrations started, and continued until well after daylight began to filter through the uncurtained windows. At last the war was over, and where in England would the significance be greater, the relief more heartfelt, than on a front-line bomber station? Where would the celebrations be at their wildest other than on these bases, which had endured so much for so long at such a cost? Yet, though it became a night to remember, it was not the night of unrestrained revelry and drunkenness which I had expected.

True, the drinks flowed freely, with practically the whole station complement involved at some stage or another. True, our Mess regulations went completely by the board. Aircrew officers came along to join their NCO crewmembers at the bar, and some of the Waafs had been invited along – two of them, at least, wearing pyjamas under their greatcoats – causing one or two old sweats to mutter darkly into their beer. True, a company of colonials decided the occasion should be marked by the ceremonial burning of a Halfiax at its dispersal – preferably I-Item, with his history of niggling unserviceabilities. Such a plan however had been anticipated and forestalled by someone in authority. Sometime earlier, all the squadron aircraft had been towed to and lined up along the runway adjacent to Flying Control, with service police dog patrols on duty throughout the night.

In spite of all this, the festivities held a measure of restraint. The general feelings of thankfulness at having lived to see this day were inevitably tempered with thoughts of those who had not survived, especially those with whom we had been personally involved. Also, the present excitement could not disguise the fact that the way of life to which we had adjusted was now irrevocably ended, and in all probability peacetime would present problems of adjustment as yet unconsidered. The songs so noisily sung round the piano tonight were not the airmens' bawdy drinking songs but the refrains of wartime nostalgia. Perhaps now there really would be bluebirds over the white cliffs of Dover, and maybe the last all-clear had sounded for all time.

The following day was officially designated 'Victory in Europe Day.' The whole squadron had been instructed to attend a morning meeting in the main briefing room, at which the new station commander would impart whatever information he had regarding our future, and attempt

172

to kill off the wild rumours still circulating on camp. It was a bleary-eyed but intensely curious audience who assembled.

As most of us had expected, the main item of news was that the Halifax force would not be participating actively in the forthcoming onslaught against Japan in the Far East. Considerations of increased range and endurance meant the introduction of the new Lincoln bomber as the spearhead of the proposed 'Tiger Force.' However, No. 4 Group still had a part to play. As from the very next day, squadrons of the group would be transferred to the control of the RAF's Transport Command; they would then be trained for the task of flying out troops and supplies from the United Kingdom to India, for the duration of the Japanese war. If this came to us as a surprise, the next item left us flabbergasted. The aircraft onto which the crews would be converting for this new role was the Stirling – the poor relation of Bomber Command, long since phased out of operations due to its poor performance! The ungainly-looking Stirlings had been the first of the command's four-engined bombers, and had never been popular with the crews. Rumour had it that when the prototype arrived, the designers had been told to clip its wings, as the aircraft was too wide to fit inside a standard RAF hangar. This they had done, and it had resulted in a marked loss of performance, and an inadequate operational ceiling. Now they had been taken out of retirement, in preference to our well-loved Halifaxes. Nobody could tell us why.

No details had yet been worked out as to which personnel would be involved in the new venture, but I was ready to volunteer, and, if necessary, postpone my demob indefinitely. Many of our number would automatically be rejected. There would be no place for the bomb-aimers and the air gunners, nor for the Canadians, Australians and New Zealanders, who altogether made up about half our present aircrew strength. Indeed, the Canadian authorities, with commendable alacrity, had already indicated that all their countrymen would be posted away within days for instant repatriation to Canada.

Our crew came away from the meeting with plenty to think about. Later, we sat together in a bar in Bridlington, where flags and bunting decorated the streets, and discussed our future prospects. They seemed very uncertain. Keith said:

> 'I wouldn't mind giving this trooping lark a go, trouble is, if the Canadians are going home, it's almost certain we'll be going too. I hear Bill is already on his way. Just think, in a few month's time I could be back at university with a bunch of school leavers. And you lot think you have problems of adjustment.'

Both George and Denis, in an effort to avoid their impending redundancy, had already tried to volunteer their services for the Far East.

'They just laughed at us,' moaned Denis, 'and told us there were ten thousand gunners already ahead of us in the queue.'

No such problems on Old Len's mind. He had joined up at the beginning of the war, and could expect to be one of the first to be demobbed. As he sat placidly puffing his pipe, his philosophy was simple:

'I've enjoyed my service, mostly. Wouldn't have missed it. But I'll be just as happy back home in Brum in civvy street. If you youngsters want to soldier on, good luck to you.'

For the rest of us, we would have to take our chance.

As it happened, there followed a period of intense flying activity on the squadron. The following day, our crew had to forego the public holiday to carry out a ferrying trip to an airfield in the north of Scotland.

It was a beautiful May morning, with endless blue sky and crystal clear visibility, and we felt that we had the whole of Britain's skies to ourselves. As the rising ground of the Scottish Highlands eventually came into view ahead of us, I suggested to Keith that we should take a closer look at the scenic splendours. Pointing the nose at a narrow strip of water ahead, he descended rapidly, and soon we were skimming the surface of the loch at no more than fifty feet. It was an exhilarating experience to see the high ground zipping past on either side at a tremendous speed, and I gave enthusiastic V signs to the occasional startled loch-side angler. This, I decided is what flying is all about: a far cry from the mundane high altitude straight-and-level of the bomber stream. The loch bent sharply to the left, and as we banked to follow it we suddenly and startlingly found ourselves faced with a huge ridge of high ground directly ahead. Keith hauled back on the stick, and we shot up into the air. For a few agonising seconds I was convinced we wouldn't make it. Then, with our speed dropping off alarmingly, we staggered over the plateau with about five feet to spare. Sitting in the nose as I was, I had a momentary eyeball-to-eyeball confrontation with a mountain sheep, and it would be difficult to say which of us was the more terrified. Nothing was said, but I learned a lesson from the incident – how a short lapse into bad airmanship had almost achieved what the enemy had failed to over the last six months!

For the whole of the following week we found ourselves actively engaged in the current priority flying task – bomb dumping in the North Sea. Lissett's underground bomb dump at the end of the war held large stockpiles, and it was considered that the safest method of disposal was to load them aboard the Halifaxes, and drop them unarmed in deep water. So it was that day after day we set course from Flamborough Head, with our bomb-bays crammed with bombs of all sizes and canisters of incendiaries, for consignment to the depths some ninety miles out to sea. The sight of a row of harmless splashes appearing on the placid sea surface seemed to symbolise this new era of peace.

It was at this time that the dissolution of Andy's crew began, with even less ceremony than at our coming together exactly a year previously.

Predictably, Old Len was the first to go. He was told to hand in his flying kit, then proceed to his home on indefinite leave. From there, presumably, he would be called upon to undergo the process of demobilisation; like all who had served the full duration of the war, he was extremely pleased at the prospect. We heard no further news of him.

Our two gunners, and Dick our engineer, were also sent on leave, but went with rather less enthusiasm. At the tender age of nineteen, they were now redundant as far as their flying careers were concerned. They were to await a re-allocation board, which would decide the capacity in which they would be employed for the rest of their service. Even the prospect of retaining their present pay and rank failed to ease their disappointment.

Any hopes that even a nucleus of Andy's crew would remain were soon dashed. Out of the blue came a posting notice for Keith. With mixed feelings he learned that he was to join an all-Australian squadron, which would be converting onto American Liberator bombers in England, prior to active service in the Far East war.

Thus it was that of the seven crew members, only Les, our wireless operator – now retitled signaller – and myself were available for a final drink with Keith. The three of us spent a subdued evening in a country pub on the far side of the airfield, quietly reminiscing about our time together. Strange, that within a few weeks of peace arriving, we were already referring to our shared wartime experiences as the good old days. We wished each other good luck in whatever ventures lay ahead, and promised that we would all remain in contact.

If Keith's departure next morning signalled the end of an eventful chapter in our lives, there was every sign that a new one was about to start. Although the squadron strength had been decimated in recent weeks, new faces were appearing day by day. One had only to look at the new arrivals to see that the emphasis now was on experience. It was noticeable in many ways. They seemed that little bit older, more mature looking, even a little more smartly turned out – as befitting men who in the main had completed a tour of bomber ops plus a spell as instructors at the various training units. Another noticeable aspect was the number of aircrew wearing decorations beneath their flying brevets. Most of the newcomers were commissioned officers, so the strength of the Sergeants' Mess fell to less than half its former numbers. Les and I took the opportunity of moving out of our gloomy Nissen hut into better accommodation – single room quarters with their own fireplaces and washbasins. We felt we should improve our life-style if we were going to fly with this new élite.

After all surplus bombs had been despatched to the depths of the North Sea, the next flying phase involved the disposal of the aircraft themselves. The Halifax, that sturdy reliable workhorse, regarded with affection by all who flew in her, had now outlived her usefulness, it seemed. Two large airfields, High Ercall in Shropshire and Brackla in Scotland, had been nominated as the official graveyards, and to these bases we started to ferry the remaining aircraft. By the end of this operation, both places bore testimony to the appalling prodigality of modern warfare. Literally hundreds of bombers, some of them fresh from the production lines, were parked wingtip to wingtip in endless lines. Who knows what proportion of the nation's wealth and resources went into their construction? Now they were mere items of scrap metal, set slowly to deteriorate in the open air.

Late in June, before the last Halifax had left Lissett for its final resting place, I took off on one more mission over Germany. The flight was one of several self-styled 'Cook's Tours', laid on to enable us to view Germany's wrecked industrial heartland from low level. For the crews involved, it was undertaken more as a pilgrimage rather than as in any spirit of exultation,; already places like Duisburg, Essen or Dortmund were as evocative to us as were names like Mons or Ypres to our fathers. We carried several passengers, mainly ground staff personnel, who were intensely curious to see places they had only known as targets from returning aircrews over the years of attrition.

In the event, the extent of the devastation I saw was as startling to me as to any of the fitters and riggers viewing it from the cabin and the two turrets, or to the two Waafs lying in the nose. Bombing from a height of 20,000 feet had been a very impersonal business, which had given one little idea of its effect on the ground. Now, as we made a wide sweep of the Ruhr valley, I got the full picture, at little more than circuit height.

Below us moved an endless belt of urban desolation, a no-man's-land of ruins and rubble. Every building was an empty shell, every factory reduced to a trellis of twisted rusting girders. A moonscape so cratered it had completely distorted the course of inland waterways. There was no sign of habitation, no movement apparent. Had they given up all hope of reconstruction?

For anyone who had been in any way involved, it was impossible to view the scene without a variety of emotions flitting through the mind. Like, for instance, the young officer who was piloting the aircraft. I glanced at him, foolishly assuming his emotions would be on display. Flight Lieutenant Sloan was a relative newcomer to the squadron, but his story was well enough known. He had first visited the town we were viewing below, Dortmund, exactly two years previously. Then he had been a sergeant bomb-aimer, flying operations in a Wellington. His aircraft had been badly shot up, seriously enough for half his crew, including the pilot, to bale out. Sergeant Sloan had fought his way to the wheel, managed to gain control, and succeeded in extinguishing the fires. Thereafter, showing tremendous skill and guts, he had not only guided it back to England but had managed to put it down in one piece on a Lincolnshire airfield. His reward had been a pilot's course, a commission and a Conspicuous Gallantry Medal. Some of us wondered what you had to do to get a VC.

Whatever he was thinking as he gazed out of his window, my own emotions were probably a good deal more impersonal. In the skies above these and other ruined cities, more than 55,000 aircrew of Bomber Command, we were to learn, had perished in the six years of war. In a sense, everything around us was their memorial. They had been told what had to be done, and had done it well. Had their efforts achieved the results their leaders hoped and predicted? Surely nobody could have envisaged the endurance and resiliance of the German people, in the face of the continual destruction of their cities on such a scale. If then one granted them a measure of grudging admiration, what of sympathy for their present plight? None whatsoever. By chance, not half an hour previously, we had overflown the Dutch city of Rotterdam and seen the ruins of the city centre – destroyed by the Luftwaffe in 1940 as an act of terror bombing against an undefended target. I recalled the Christmas blitz, the Baedeker raids on cathedral cities, the indiscriminate rocket attacks on England. Now had come the retribution, and who would call it undeserved?

Having said that, in the few decades since the war ended, the Germans have rebuilt their shattered country in a manner few could have foreseen. It has been called the 'German Economic Miracle'. To those of us who saw what we did on that June morning in 1945, it has been nothing less than that.

Back at Lissett, a few days later, came a short interlude. Our two gunners turned up on a one day visit to attend the convened re-allocation board. Both young eagles seemed to have come to terms with the fact that their wings were about to be clipped, but neither could hide his disappointment when I met them afterwards.

'How did it go?' I asked solicitously.

'Worse than I expected,' said Denis, his customary grin deserting him. 'There were no jobs going that I fancied. Do you know what trade they offered me first of all? Cook and butcher! I ask you – can you see me as a cook and bloody butcher?'

I couldn't. The momentary image of Denis in a tall white hat, meat chopper in hand, was too incongruous to sustain. George was equally disconcerted:

'And I was recommended for a store-basher's job in the equipment section. Can you think of any job to send you round the bend quicker?'

'Did you have to accept them?' I asked. Denis replied emphatically:

'Not on your life. We went through the full list of trades available, and haggled a bit, and in the end settled for the same one – trainee pay accounts clerk. It seemed to be the best of a bad lot. We'll be going on a course together, and we'll probably end up at some far-flung overseas outpost for the rest of our time. They say it'll be at least another eighteen months before our demob number comes up. What a life. Win the war with a gun, lose the peace with a pen.'

I sympathised, genuinely. During their short-lived flying careers they had both been zealous and exemplary crewmen. The transition from the glamour and excitement of squadron life to the workaday routine of a pay office would not be an easy one. When Les and I shook hands with them for the last time, I was glad to see that Denis had soon regained his equal equanimity and enthusiasm.

'I'll drop you both a line when we get settled somewhere,' he said. 'I've got everybody's home address. One day, when we're all bald and fat, we'll try to arrange a reunion – maybe here in Brid. In the meantime, if any of the girls at the Spa ever ask what's happened to the tall good-looking gunner who did a devastating foxtrot, tell 'em I loved 'em all. Happy landings in Transport Command – and never forget how lucky you are.'

My own transition period was now well under way. By this time, the last of our Halifaxes had been unceremoniously dumped, and their replacements were arriving daily. The Halifaxes, dark, sleek and low-slung, had always seemed to blend happily with their surroundings – spreading their wings at dispersals like a flock of nesting birds. Not so the Stirlings. Their peculiar crouching attitude on the ground, along with their beaky noses, dorsal aerials and single large tail fins, gave the impression of a colony of early vertebrates settled in the dispersals. Moreover, they had come to us from the refurbishers sprayed pale blue in colour, which only served to emphasise their general ungainliness – like an old woman in a bright party dress.

Transport Command instructors had arrived, enabling the squadron pilots, co-pilots, signallers and engineers to begin their flying conversion programme. For the navigators there was first a short ground course, and the Chief Navigation Instructor made it plain from the outset that we were going to operate with a completely new rulebook.

'The procedures used in Bomber Command you can forget as soon as possible. As the Americans say, this is a whole new ball game. There is no target for tonight. We have no percentage losses. We do not press on regardless. Your sole concern now is the safety of the aircraft and its passengers. This is the RAF's new airline, and high standards of professionalism, discipline and dress will be demanded. You can start by skipping the Skipper – your pilot should now be addressed as Captain at all times. You will be operating on the UK to India routes, and special light-weight overalls will be issued for use in the air. Things like parachutes you can forget – you won't be carrying them.'

He paused until the general mutterings of his predominantly bomber crew audience had died down.

'For you navigators, it's back to basics. You won't be sitting behind curtains viewing your sophisticated radar sets any more. You'll have to dust off your sextants, and settle for a drift recorder and a radio compass as your navigational aids. Your operating heights will be below oxygen level, so you'll have a lot of contact with the ground. The weather on your routes is the thing which will probably give you most trouble, so this course is heavily biased towards meteorology and climatology. You should find your new task interesting and rewarding. And don't forget there's a war still going on, even if you're not in the thick of it.'

The course proceeded, opening up new dimensions.

We learned about the weather patterns of the Mediterranean, the Middle East and the sub-tropics. How, in this new sphere of operations, our windfinding routines would often involve us in the peculiar airflows of the Mistral, or the Khamsin, or the Sirocco. How our airmanship would be pitted against the flying hazards of the Intertropical Front or the Southwest Monsoon. Our notebooks began to read like pages from E.M. Forster or Somerset Maugham.

We were introduced to the bulky RAFAC, the Bible of the route-bashers. Crammed with essential information, from the frequencies of the Middle East broadcasters to the flashing light characteristics of unmanned Persian Gulf lighthouses; from the runway patterns of an international airport to the location of a landing strip of oiled sand in the desert. For us, positively *sine qua non*.

Then there was the important business of survival in the event of a forced landing on water, desert or jungle. At sea, assuming a successful ditching, the Stirlings offered two large wing-stowed rubber dinghies, and ancillary equipment which included a radio transmitter and a solar still for distilling seawater. No great problems there. In a desert landing, we were told, we should stay with the aircraft, utilise emergency food and water, and signal for help by any means available. Engine oil, mixed with dried camel dung, is considered an efficient smoke generator for signalling: not a lot of people know that. In the unlikely event of our becoming stranded in the jungle, it became a matter of knowing what you could eat, and what could eat you.

Finally, mention should be made of the small booklet issued to all the aircrew, to be carried on all overseas flights. Each contained pages printed in the script and language of all the Near East regions – Arabic, Kurdish, Persian – offering a reward for the safe return of a British serviceman. In the event of finding oneself, by some mischance, in the hands of such a tribesman, one handed him the appropriate page and hoped for the best. Our instructions, in English, on the back of each chit, ran as follows:

'Be very courteous and polite.
A personal present, e.g. your watch, to the headman, will create an atmosphere of goodwill.
Always remove footwear on entering dwellings.
Offer to share your food, if any.
IGNORE THEIR WOMEN!
Good Luck!'

Since some tribes were known to favour the castration of their captors as a matter of principle, the afore-mentioned pages were popularly known as 'Ghooli Chits.' Nobody could tell us whether they had ever been redeemed in recent times.

The ending of this interesting and informative course coincided with the astonishing news of the atomic bomb drops on the Japanese, and their subsequent surrender. The war was over. Where did that leave us now? We were soon informed – the end of hostilities would make no difference to our trooping project. The new requirements for priority releases, urgent replacements, compassionate leaves and the like, meant a continuing demand for the air trooping facility. I, for one, was delighted to hear it. Moreover, as if in confirmation, we could expect soon to be moving south, to an airfield more suitably endowed as a transport base.

Soon afterwards, I received a letter from Keith, saying that he was now in Brighton, awaiting an imminent passage back to Australia. The plans for his new squadron to convert onto Liberators had now been scrapped, and he wasn't sorry. They had already started their conversion course on an airfield near Cambridge recently vacated by the Americans, who had left the place littered with empty bottles and discarded contraceptives. He had never managed to develop any confidence in or affection for the Libs. In fact, he had incorporated a little prayer into his pre-take-off checks:

'Please God, make sure I clear those trees at the end of the runway.' Now he was happy to be on his way back to dear old Oz.

At the bottom of the page was written 'P.T.O.' I turned over to read the postscript: 'Did you know I have been awarded the DFC?'

No, I didn't know, but I was delighted to hear it now. The thought that any of the crew might have been recommended for a decoration had never entered my head, nor anyone else's I'm sure. My first thought was how pleased and proud his folks would be, compensation for their anxious years. For Keith himself, merited approbation for those difficult decisions, the determination with which they had been followed. And I had long held the belief that the dominions aircrews who had operated so far from their homeland and families deserved all the official recognition they could get.

With regards to crew awards, this proved to be far from from the end of the story. At a later date, I read on squadron orders that Old Len, our former warrant officer bomb-aimer, had also been awarded the Distinguished Flying Cross. The citation – the standard one on these occasions – reading:

'For courage and devotion to duty in air operations against the enemy.'

Another well-deserved honour. With his cheerful and conscientious attitude at all times, he had set an excellent example to the rest of us. Apart from this, he had finished the war only four trips short of two completed tours of ops.

Some weeks later, I received a letter from my father congratulating me on the award of my medal, which had just been announced in their local paper. I wrote back to say there must have been a mistake, probably a mix-up with the other crew awards. The very next day it was promulgated on orders that, as a flight sergeant, I had been awarded the Distinguished Flying Medal, with the standard citation. I was pleased, of course, but completely surprised. What had I done above and beyond the duties of a squadron navigator? We had always managed to find the right target, at approximately the right time, but so too had most of the others. I could recall no instance of outstanding bravery or proficiency in my operational career. This latest award meant that all three of our bombing and navigational team had now received a decoration. In those terms at least, it could be said that Andy's crew, plodding their way through an unfinished first tour on the least glamourous of the bombers, had finished in the same medal league as such crews as the Dambusters. And that really was something to write home about.

When the time came for the crewing up, there was no repetition of the free and easy mating process which had banded together Andy's crew. This time the preselected names appeared on the notice board, and we got together for the first time over a cup of coffee in the crewroom.

Flying Officer Les Creed, my new captain, appeared quite different from Keith. He was older, and a far more experienced pilot, with a tour of ops on Lancasters and a long spell of instructing behind him. My first impressions were of a sharp tongue, a keen eye, and a more volatile temperament than I had been used to before.

'When I was instructing,' he told us, 'I was considered a bit of a bastard. It didn't worry me. A few bollockings never did anyone any harm.' I took it that his crew would get their share of them when things didn't go right. I consoled myself with thoughts that my first impressions hadn't always proved right.

Jimmy Calvert, the co-pilot, was more my type. A long lean Yorkshireman, with an engaging twisted grin never far away, he had finished a tour on Halifaxes, and like our captain wore a DFC. It was a measure of Transport Command's newly-found prerogative for picking and choosing that we should have such an experienced man in what was basically a secondary crew role. His demotion to the right-hand seat did not seem to bother him at all. For him, this new transport venture was something to be enjoyed, while it lasted, as a bit of a lark, after the serious business of bomber ops.

I had hoped that Les Lamb and myself would remain in the same crew, but he had been nominated elsewhere. Bill Williams, our new signaller, was a flying officer who had previously served as a Signals Leader on a bomber squadron. Quiet and conscientious, with loads of experience, he would be an asset to any crew.

The fifth and final crewmember was Jack Harrowing, the engineer, a flight sergeant like myself. Very smartly turned out, he had the assurance and accent of a public school boy; in fact, he had joined the RAF at the age of fifteen. As one of the redoubtable ex-Halton 'brats', one thing was certain: he would have the best possible technical background for the job. He also had a dry sense of humour, and that street-wise quality, in relation to service life, which seemed to be bred into all the 'brats'.

I was well aware that in terms of age, experience and flying time, I was very much the junior member of this crew. It seemed to me to be quite a challenge.

Soon afterwards, we started our crew conversion onto the Stirlings. None of us found our new aircraft type appealing in any sense. In appearance, there was something decidedly unaesthetic about its long angular body, supported on the ground by a disproportionately heavy undercarriage. Access was gained by climbing a ladder to a small rear door, followed by an awkward passage along a sharply upward-sloping floor, and a laborious clambering over the two main spars, to reach the crew cabin. My first feeling was of relief that this was not the aircraft in which I had been called to do my bomber ops, and sympathy for my predecessors who had been. The cabin looked quite spacious, mainly because it lacked the more modern radar units and other navigational equipment. I was further disconcerted to find that the nose compartment, the only place for accurate map-reading, had been sealed off as a luggage storage; the ground could now only be viewed at a distance through the small side windows. There was, however, an American-style radio compass fitted near the navigator's table. This was a wireless receiver incorporating a dial and pointer, which would register reasonably accurate bearings on any particular radio beacon or broadcast station tuned in. This would no doubt prove invaluable when we found ourselves flying in the more remote areas of the Far East routes.

If I had registered a decided antipathy towards the aircraft, it was nothing compared with the active dislike expressed by our captain. Long accustomed to the virtuous Lancaster, he soon made known his feelings about the performance and handling characteristics of the Stirling. He would sometimes talk to it, as to someone he held in great distaste. On take-off, there would be a muttered 'Lift off, you great awkward brute:' on landing, 'Get down, you cow.' His summing up: 'I've never flown a brick shithouse, but this must be the nearest thing to it.' The aircraft sometimes responded in kind. During early conversion days, we once lost an engine at a critical phase of take-off; another time, the weighty undercarriage refused to retract, and we had to cut short a cross-country exercise. Altogether it did little for our confidence in or respect for the aircraft type our betters had foisted onto us.

The full conversion programme completed, it was time for the squadron to move on. The airfield chosen for our new role was at Stradishall, in Suffolk. It was a base built to peacetime specifications, which meant solid brick barracks, standard H-shaped Messes, permanent steel hangars, and refinements like trimmed lawns, flower beds and married quarters.

It was a fitting move. The airfield at Lissett had been conceived and constructed in the middle war years, with no concession to anything other than the most basic requirements. Not a single building on the camp had any look of permanence. Soon the concrete runways and dispersals would be torn up, and the fertile land returned to the farmers; the villagers would sleep at night undisturbed by the reverberating engines, and life would return to its normal tempo.

Even so, when we finally loaded our kit aboard the waiting Stirling, and carried out one last circuit before setting course for our new home, I experienced strong feelings of nostalgia. The squadron lived on, but below there was nothing to catch the eye, no movement, no symbol of farewell, no sign of what had been. Already it was difficult to visualise that these rural acres, drawn for a brief moment from the obscurity to which they were now returning, had launched assaults on countless enemy targets. That had been the effort. Nearly a thousand young men, from many lands, had taken off and never returned. That had been the cost. To those of us who had been involved and survived, this was a place which would draw many of us back in future years. A place where ghosts walked. A place of memories, good and bad, forever vivid.

14

A Passage to India

The time had arrived for us to embark our first-ever contingent of army passengers. It was some unearthly hour, long before the dawn. Our Stirling stood dark and silent on the perimeter track, as though shunning the light from the brightly floodlit parking apron only a few hundred yards away. The only illumination came from the pale moonlight and the guiding beam of our engineer's torch. The troops moved slowly forward, and climbed the aircraft steps in a silence which was quite unnatural. It emphasised the fact that they were extremely reluctant to be joining us.

The whole exercise had assumed the air of some furtive and nefarious cloak-and-dagger operation. To our passengers, that is exactly what it was.

The scene was set at a large military airfield near Brussels. Bordering its perimeter was a tented army transit camp, where rested several hundred troops awaiting air transport. Our aircraft was but one of many troop carriers recently arrived from England, assigned the task of airlifting them all as soon as possible as replacements to the Far East. These passengers on the RAF's immediate postwar airline were no eager seekers of pleasure or sunshine. They were Tommies already serving abroad, who had done their bit in defeating the Germans. Now, with the recent capitulation of the Japanese, they must have been justifiably thinking in terms of a speedy return home, and a not-too-delayed demob. Now we had arrived to wing them away another 5,000 miles in the wrong direction. I, for one, felt a great deal of empathy.

Once aboard, two dozen pairs of iron-tipped army boots slithered and skidded on the sloping metal floor, as they shuffled forward in the semi-darkness to fill up the twin rows of tubular steel and canvas seats. There came the sound of tin hats and rifles clanging hollowly on the bare metal of the fuselage, to be followed by muttered but emphatic four-letter expletives.

When they were finally settled, our captain introduced himself and gave his preflight briefing. Never a man to sugar the pill in any way, there was nothing to ease the general mood of dumb resignation, nor to inspire confidence in those about to fly for the first time. In fact, his words would probably serve as a good example to a modern airline pilot of exactly how not to address his passengers. He emphasised the risks of a ditching or crash-landing, the dangers of touching various switches and handles in view, the enforcement of the no smoking regulations and the desirability of remaining seated at all times.

> 'Stretch your legs, if you have to, but every time a passenger moves around I have to retrim the aircraft. Every time I have to retrim, I get more and more bad-tempered. And if the pilot isn't happy, nobody's happy. Oh, and if you have to be airsick – make sure you do it in your cardboard ration boxes, and not on the floor.'

Jack, our flight engineer and part-time passengers' steward, tried to give each passenger a reassuring wink as he began to distribute the boxed inflight rations of corned beef sandwiches and chewing gum.

'Cheer up, mate,' he addressed one particularly gloomy face. 'Remember, one day we'll be bringing you home just as quickly as we're taking you out today. And we haven't lost a passenger yet.'

'That's what they told 'em on the b . . . *Titanic*,' came the immediate response. It was enough to bring forth a muted ripple of approbation, and to ease the atmosphere. At least, someone was talking at last.

In due course we were airborne, on the first leg of the flight, as far as Malta. Here the aircraft would be refuelled, and a slip crew would be waiting to fly the passengers on as far as the next fuel stop in Egypt. Our crew would night stop at Malta, pick up another Stirling the following morning, then carry on eastwards. Our final destination would be Karachi in India, as it then was. Our return route would involve staging through Palestine instead of Egypt, and Tripoli instead of Malta. The whole trip would take us nine days, on what appeared to be an undemanding and interesting schedule by any standards.

Our crew had been looking forward to the trip, for several good reasons. It offered the prospect of sunshine and exotic new places, away from the austerity of war-damaged Britain, which the end of hostilities had in no way alleviated. Food was still tightly rationed, and after years of the bland wartime diet I had promised my stomach a grand gastronomical blow-out when the chance arose somewhere on this trip. The shops in England were still woefully short of anything which could be loosely described as a luxury item – hence the diversity of the shopping list prepared for me by friends and relations. Hopefully the Indian bazaars could yield such items as a pair of ladies' silver shoes for a bride-to-be, a supply of lemons, unlimited silk stockings or nylons, one of the novelty American pens with a ballpoint instead of a nib, and wines and spirits of any description. With each crewmember having his own list, which included bulky objects like an Indian carpet and a sack of rice, I began to wonder if we would have any room on board for army passengers on the return flight.

Jimmy, our regular co-pilot, was unfortunately indisposed, and his place on the trip had been taken by Bob Carter, a warrant officer pilot whom Jack and I knew well. He was an easy-going former Metropolitan policeman, conspicuous by a bushy air force moustache of quite impressive wingspan.

As we flew southwards across France, I soon found myself thoroughly enjoying the unaccustomed navigational routine. Flying in a transport aircraft offered a degree of freedom I had never experienced in Bomber Command. Here there was no bulky parachute harness or oxygen pipe to restrict movement; no rapid fixing cycle to keep one glued to the navigation table; no lurking fear of imminent enemy action to inhibit the mind. In the darkness I was able to navigate comfortably by merely taking compass bearings on various aerodrome light beacons which we passed. When daylight came, flying over the Mediterranean, there were sun shots to be taken from the astrodome, or radio bearings obtainable from a wide choice of stations. I had ample time to make occasional visits to the rear to check the passengers. One or two sick bags were in evidence, but morale generally seemed to have improved considerably, and most of the troops appeared ready to take an interest in life again.

It was about this time that Bill, our signaller, came up with some startling news picked up on the radio. Apparently, a Transport Command Liberator loaded with troops had taken off shortly after us and had crashed on the airfield, with a heavy loss of life. It was an inauspicious start to the RAF's major trooping commitment.

'For God's sake don't tell any of our passengers,' said Les, our Captain. 'I don't want any of them going LMF at Malta.'

Our flight proceeded without incident. Long before the sun had reached its zenith I had attained the navigators' blessed state of nirvana – final time of arrival checked and corrected, destination radio beacon indicating steady and dead ahead. Soon the island of Malta came into view, looking for all the world like a wrinkled brown leaf floating on a still blue pond.

At Luqa airport we handed over our charge to the waiting squadron crew, and booked our accommodation in the colony of white-painted Nissen huts which housed all transients. Two hours later, Jack, Bob and I were bumping down the hill on a crowded Maltese bus, heading for Valetta and a night on the town.

For me, this was the first of many subsequent visits over the years to the island, and I have never had to revise my first impression of its charm and interest, and the friendliness of its inhabitants. Indeed, on that crowded bus, we were startled to find villagers standing to offer us their seats, and their general happy chatter gave little evidence of their recent wartime privations attributable to their British connection.

When we reached Valetta, to my eyes the much bombed capital held none of the ugliness of European blitzed cities. Built entirely of honey-coloured limestone, its damaged buildings took on the appearance of ancient noble ruins. One felt that soon the fallen stone blocks and pillars would be reassembled, and one wouldn't even be able to see where they were joined.

This was Malta's heyday as a Royal Navy base. As we sipped a cool beer in the city centre square, hundreds of sailors mingled with the civilians who promenaded the main street. Black-clad matrons, formidable chaperones, took the evening air with their nubile dark-eyed daughters. The fleet was in, the Grand Harbour was cluttered with warships and their attendant craft fussing round them. There was an all-pervading atmosphere of relaxation and enjoyment about the place. Even later in the night, when many a jolly tar was returning to his ship three sheets to the wind, arms around his mates' shoulders and toes trailing along the ground, the atmosphere hadn't changed. The Navy lads seem to have long acquired the gift of getting drunk without becoming offensive. It all seemed a good natured business.

The three of us eventually found our way to Valetta's famous Gut, to join the Navy at play. Strait Street was a long narrow thoroughfare lined with ill-lit eating houses, cave-like bars and garish night clubs. As we walked its length, we were accosted by female voices from the shadows:

'Come inside, air force. Big eats. Fish and chips, egg and chips . . .'

'English beer here. Very cool, very cheap . . .'

'I show you good time, air force. Come inside and dance with me . . .'

The Royal Navy was Malta's bread and butter, and nowhere was this more appreciated than down the Gut. Bar owners vied with each other in proclaiming their allegiance to the senior service. The 'Lord Nelson' sign over one door gave way to the neighbouring 'Jolly Jack Tar', followed by the 'Pompey Bar' and the 'White Ensign'. Bar walls were adorned with faded pictures of great warships, many alas long consigned to a watery grave; dusty naval badges and cap bands festooned the bottles on the shelves. The three of us were conspicuously aware that we were the only patrons not dressed in navy blue.

We settled for one of the livelier-looking establishments. 'Egyptian Queen' was spelled out in coloured lights outside, and loud music issued from the doorway. Inside, a three-piece band on a raised platform performed strenuously; sailors and girls locked in tight embrace gyrated slowly round the dance floor.

We found ourselves a table, and were immediately joined by three of the hostesses. One of them, a small bird-like creature of indeterminate age, attached herself to Bob. She perched on his lap, and expressed great admiration for his moustache. 'A drink for the ladies,' said the hovering waiter, handing out three small green concoctions along with our beers. We paid for the round. Our companions were no great beauties, conversation soon flagged, and Bob confirmed to the girls that there would be no more drinks forthcoming. There came a sudden buzz around the room as a party of American sailors entered the doorway. Within moments all the hostesses homed onto them, in search of what would undoubtedly prove richer pickings. Before leaving us, Bob's companion lifted her skirts over his head, drew him to her in tight embrace, and indicated loudly to the whole room that his moustache was providing her with the ultimate in sexual pleasure.

Bob endeavoured to regain his composure, to the amusement of the sailors at the next table. This, they told him, was his introduction to 'The Sparrow', a local character well known in Navy circles. She could effortlessly out-swear a trooper or out-curse a master-at-arms, and bring a deep blush to a three-badge stoker. She had let Bob off lightly. The drinks supplied to the girls consisted merely of coloured water, but each arrived with a metal token redeemable at closing time for threepence. It wasn't hard to see why they hustled their drinks at such a pace.

We sampled further delights of the Gut, in company with the Navy, until a very late hour. Then, spurning the eager taxi drivers, we decided to return to Luqa by horse and carriage. Two of us seated up front with the driver, one with whip and one with reins, we galloped up the hill like something out of the *Ben Hur* movie. It rounded off a thoroughly enjoyable evening.

Malta today of course has changed its image. Independence has been achieved. The Royal Navy has long since gone. The Gut has long since closed. The island has established itself as a popular international holiday centre, with the British still the favourite visitors. I visited it recently, and enjoyed its sunny sedateness. How perverse of me, therefore, to prefer my memories of it as a noisy, war-battered, naughty, fun-seeking port of call. And how many thousands of ex-Navy men will go along with me, I wonder?

The following afternoon, fully rested and refreshed, our crew took over the incoming squadron Stirling. Yesterday's sad news about the crashed Liberator was confirmed. It had not affected the morale of today's passengers. They were all Gurkha troops bound for India, who, before re-embarking, paraded smartly in front of the aircraft, with much shouting of orders and stamping of feet. Their round adolescent faces were inscrutable as ever, but they were obviously a good deal happier to be with us than our previous contingent. To these passengers, heading eastwards meant heading homewards.

There is not a lot one can write about a flight from Malta to Egypt. Half the trip is flown over featureless deep blue sea, and half over the equally featureless dull brown desert. Only where the two merge has nature relented, to provide a delightful pastel palette of aquamarine, turquoise, mauve and pearl.

Our destination was the RAF base at Cairo West. This eventually appeared below us as a dark tarmac parabola of runways and taxiways, set in the desert sand some twenty miles from the city. Here we landed, once again to hand over the aircraft to the waiting slip crew, and to settle in for a night stop.

We three NCOs were accommodated in a tattered bell tent with sandbagged walls, and beds covered in mosquito netting to keep at bay the pestilential sand-flies. Our first thought was to leave behind these grotty surroundings in favour of a night out in the city. Unfortunately, no transport was available. We were forced to throw ourselves onto the resources of the Sergeants' Mess. Fortunately, as we found, there are far worse ways of spending a sticky evening than on an open verandah, sipping cold Stella beer in the company of lively demob-happy sergeants.

A peculiar feature of the camp, to our eyes, was a wired compound containing German prisoners of war – bronzed veterans with blue eyes and sun-bleached hair, dressed in faded khaki shirts and shorts. In addition to the various camp duties they performed, most of them were engaged, with true Teutonic industry, in turning out saleable items from scrap material. How strange to find myself bartering cigarettes, the international currency of prisoners everywhere, with a formidable-looking member of the Afrika Korps, in exchange for a stylish pair of sandals made from leather strips and part of an old rubber tyre.

We were due to resume our journey the following day, this time carrying a contingent of Indian troops on repatriation from their Middle East wartime theatre. The flight from Cairo to Karachi was of some twelve hours duration, which meant a fuel stop at the RAF staging post at Shaibah, in southern Iraq. So high were normal daytime temperatures here that the Stirlings were only allowed to land at night, to avoid overheating the engines. This was why, when we eventually set course for Cairo, the domes and minarets were casting long evening shadows over the sprawling city.

After nightfall, I spent much of my time with my sextant, shooting the stars which were diamond bright in the clear desert air. Below rolled hundreds of miles of dusty plains and rocky hills, without a single distinguishing feature until we reached the windings and loopings of the Euphrates, clearly visible in the moonlight. We turned to follow its course towards Basra. The powerful flashing red pundit at Shaibah was discernable more than forty miles away, and the reek of the oilwells reached our nostrils even before we landed there.

I had been particularly interested in visiting Shaibah, even if only for this short scheduled fuel stop. A time-serving airman of my acquaintance had described it as a nightmare posting, the dread of every pre-war airman. Such was its intense heat, discomfort and sheer boredom that all consigned there ended up sand-happy or suicidal. Even today, no canteen sing-song was complete without a few verses of the plaintive dirge beginning 'I've got those Shaibah blues.' I was curious to see this hellhole. Not only that, I had recently learned that one of my old schoolmates was currently serving there, as a ground wireless operator. Tonight I was going to surprise him.

Even now, in the middle of the night, when we opened the aircraft doors we were met by a wave of hot air which set the nerve-ends tingling. Looking around, not a blade of grass or vegetation broke the monotony of this flat expanse of scorched earth. The buildings we could see were half buried in the sand, to give some sort of insulation against the scorching sun.

After we had all taken a meal in the transit dining room, served by silent Arab waiters, the crew reported to Flight Planning. Here we were advised by the local met man that early morning fog was forecast at Karachi, and he was advising a two hour delay. Les agreed. As a result, whilst the other crew members relaxed in easy chairs under the fan in the crew room, I now had ample time to seek out my school friend.

I eventually traced him to his billet, one of the underground huts, where he was sound asleep. He was delighted to see me, after recovering from the shock, and we chatted happily for half an hour about old times. I was frequently distracted by such happenings as a large lizard darting up the wall, and a huge beetle dropping from the thatched roof and trampolining heartily on the top of his mosquito net. I shook his hand as I prepared to leave.

'Well,' I said, 'in view of all I've heard about this place, I'm glad it isn't driving you round the bend.'

'No danger,' he replied. 'There are too many compensations here.'
'Compensations? Like what?'

'Oh, lots of things. Every Saturday night, for instance, we get a special treat – the English football results read out over the station Tannoy. And we now have a strip of grass by the flagpole which we are allowed to walk on anytime we please; it's made of plastic, but it's the right colour. Then I enjoy chess games with a friend of mine; he's been posted down the Gulf to Sharja, but we still play by wireless. You've probably noticed there are no women around these parts; on the other hand, we have some of the best-looking camels in the Middle East. So, you see what I mean?'

Hmm. I left him by expressing the hope that one day we would have the pleasure of his company on one of our return flights. And the sooner the better!

We took off before dawn, on the final stage of our journey. The coastline of the Persian Gulf was dotted with a profusion of accurately charted lighthouses, many of them unmanned, which made for easy navigation. After crossing the moonscape of the Oman Peninsular we were over the placid waters of the Arabian Sea. For the next thousand miles we would have the barren coastlines of Iran and Baluchistan on our left to guide us to India.

I noticed that approximately half way along this coastline there appeared on my chart the symbol of an airfield, virtually the only point of interest along its great length. My RAFAC informed me that it was an emergency landing ground, by the name of Jiwani, operating a low-powered radio beacon for navigational purposes, and manned by a small detachment of RAF personnel. We were all intrigued at the thought of a base so isolated that the nearest town was five hundred miles distant. Our pilot was interested enough to reduce height to get a closer look as we approached it.

The airfield appeared as a flat patch of bare ground, with oiled lines in the sand to denote a runway. There was something oddly pathetic about its sole facilities – a lone radio mast, a limp windsock and a small cluster of huts. One felt instant sympathy for the poor devils who manned it.

'Let's see if there's anyone awake,' said Les.

He called them up on the RAFAC listed frequency. There was no immediate reply.

'They probably only keep a limited listening watch,' said Bill, our signaller.

'I don't blame 'em,' said our captain.

Suddenly a loud cheerful voice came over the air:

'Hallo, Rafair One Six Four. This is Jiwani Tower. Sorry for the delay in responding to you. Reading you strength five. Can we be of assistance?'

'No thanks,' said our captain. 'This is just a social call. We were wondering how you exist in a God-forsaken hole like this.'

'Oh, we sleep and smoke and sometimes fish, and slowly go round the bend. But thank you for asking.'

'How do you get your supplies? Who looks after you?'

'Most weeks we get an Anson in from Mauripur with mail and rations. We get by.'

'The thing is, we've just started a regular service out here from the UK. If it would be any help, we could easily airdrop you a bundle each trip – up-to-date newspapers and magazines and suchlike.'

'Thank you very much. We'd be very grateful.'

'Anything else you can think of?'

There was a slight pause.

'You'll laugh at this – but apart from my local barmaid, I sometimes get a craving for some lovely crisp Sussex apples.'

'I think we might be able to manage the apples.'

Was I hearing things – apart from some strictly non-regulation radio patter? Was this really our brusque no-nonsense captain displaying such empathy and consideration? Was this the unexpected soft centre under the hard exterior? Apparently so, since this was to prove to be no idle promise. Before future trips, a reinforced sack of papers and periodicals would be painstakingly scavenged from the Officers' and Sergeants' Messes at Stradishall; with apples added as available, it would be stowed in the aircraft until ready to be airdropped from low level, as promised.

It was on this friendly note that we resumed our eastward journey.

We eventually reached our destination, the large British base at Mauripur airfield, a few miles from Karachi, about mid-morning. It appeared as an untidy complex of runways, hangars, hutments and tented encampments, set amid arid scrubland. Our landing here was not without incident. On final approach we ran into a flock of the local kitehawks. Bob in the co-pilot's seat was shaken out of his end-of-flight lethargy when his windscreen suddenly became opaque with a mess of blood and feathers. In spite of this late distraction Les made his customary good landing, and we taxied to the concrete apron by the terminal building.

Hardly had the propellers stopped rotating before Indian officialdom took over. First, a civilian boarded the aircraft, sternly bade us all remain seated, and with a spray gun proceeded laboriously to disinfect the whole interior. Presumably, having plenty of bugs of their own, they were reluctant to import any western varieties. Next, in the terminal, we had a long wait while another official inspected our certificates of immunisation against cholera and yellow fever as minutely as if he suspected we were already plague-ridden, and these were clever forgeries. Finally, the customs officers searched our kit, and informed us of the dire penalties meted out to any persons found smuggling gold into the country. By the time all these formalities were completed we were visibly wilting. It had been a long hard night, we had been without sleep for thirty hours, and the day was hot and humid.

Eventually we procured a lorry which dropped off Les and Bill at the Officers' Mess, and Bob, Jack and me at the Transit Mess. Here a dignified Indian with a grey beard introduced himself as our bearer, and conducted us to our billet in one of the transit tents. He returned bearing sheets, pillow cases and mosquito nets, which we accepted gratefully. All we wanted was to strip off our sweat-stained khaki and collapse onto our beds until the cool of the evening.

We hadn't bargained for the camp followers.

Firstly, an elderly Indian shuffled into the tent, his sandals flip-flopping on his thin feet. 'Dhobi, sahib,' he said, solemnly handing me a tattered envelope. Inside was a sheet of paper, folded and unfolded so many times that it was almost in four pieces. I managed to decipher the handwritten lines:

'To whom it may concern, this is to certify that Bahardur Khan has been my dhobi-wallah for a year, and I have always found him reliable and honest. Signed: J. Johnson, Flight Sergeant, RAF'. On the strength of this, we entrusted him with our soiled khaki uniforms, to be returned the morrow morn without fail, washed, pressed and lightly starched.

Our next visitor was a rather shifty looking character bearing a bulky suitcase, from which he began to peddle his wares. The more we disclaimed interest, the more the floor became spread with cheap toiletries, ornaments and general bric-a-brac. We finally got rid of him when Bob picked up one of his brass ornaments and explained in exact clinical detail what he intended doing with it if the fellow did not pack his wares and leave us in peace.

We resumed our prone positions on the beds. Minutes later a turbanned head peered into the tent, and a cheerful voice called out: 'Char-wallah, sahib.' The voice's owner entered, with his portable tea urn and tray of rice cakes. This time we were tempted, but declined his services on closer view of the flies encrusting the cakes.

Finally I drifted off to sleep. But not for long. A persistent voice impinged on my consciousness. I opened my eyes to see a figure at my bedside dressed in a grubby dhoti, and brandishing what appeared to be a large surgical scalpel. I shot up, startled. The voice came again: 'Good day, gentlemen. Do any of you suffer from corns, chilblains or veruccas? I am also qualified to cure hard skin and other afflictions of the feet.' We were spared further details of his pedal expertise by the sudden entry of our bearer. Without a word, he took our visitor by the back of the neck and propelled him out of the tent door. Silence reigned again.

Jack, for one, had given up thoughts of sleep. 'We might as well stay awake,' he said philosophically. 'Someone's bound to call and offer us his daughter!'

The next day was our rest day, and the three of us caught a bus into town for shopping and sightseeing.

If this was India, it hardly came up to my expectations. There was little scent of exotic blooms or eastern spices: rather a pungency of cow dung and bad sanitation. No profusion of high-born beauties in richly-hued saris: more a variety of street beggars, some with grotesquely malformed limbs, and one, an elderly woman, completely naked. The bazaars however were impressively colourful and surprisingly well stocked. I was able to satisfy my full list of shopping requirements.

Later we found an expensive looking restaurant which offered an extensive menu, air conditioning and smart turbaned waiters. The time had come for me to indulge in my pre-planned course of sheer gluttony. It was a meal to remember. A meal one could only dream about in food rationed England. A bowl of rich soup, a delicately grilled fish, a dish of fresh prawns, and half a chicken on a bed of spiced rice. As I gently removed a sliver of chicken from the bone, Bob watched me and remarked: 'Did I ever tell you of my time in the Thames river patrol, when we found this body floating in the water? I grabbed its arm to try and lift it out and the flesh just slid off the bone. Watching you with that chicken just put me in mind of it.'

'No,' I said. 'You haven't mentioned it before, and thanks for mentioning it now.' The truth was that for some minutes now my stomach had been transmitting occasional distress signals, indicating that the ingestion of this rich fare, after years of wartime diet, was causing problems for my digestive system. Bob's indelicate remark was a triggering mechanism. A sudden wave of nausea hit me, and I found myself rushing desperately towards the toilets. I made it, but only just in time. Seconds later, the whole four courses came up in one long retching surge.

When I later paid the bill, which amounted to about half a week's pay, I pondered the question of how much one tips the waiter for a meal which one has just flushed down the toilet in its entirety! It's one of those experiences one laughs about later. Much later.

The following afternoon, we left the sub-continent on our return trip to England. This time the Tommies were on their way home, and it was a pleasure to see their delight. Most wore the slouch hats and jungle green of the 14th Army, and the majority were returning home on compassionate grounds. Compared with the men of the Desert Army, who appeared lean and bronzed, these troops looked thin and sallow faced. They were in good heart however, and had not lost the soldiers' rueful sense of humour. As we settled them in their seats, one joker was giving a comical parody of Churchill's VE Day broadcast:

> 'The war in Europe is over. Well done, chaps. Soon we'll have you back with your families. I'm told we still have a forgotten army fighting in Burma. For them I have this message. You may fall out for a ten minute smoke.'

En route, we passed the time of day with our unseen friend at Jiwani, and landed at Shaibah after dark for refuelling. My school friend was waiting, with the parcel and mail I had promised to take home for him. Four hours later, we landed at Lydda airport, in Palestine as it then was, for our night stop.

Palestine, the Holy Land, at this period was experiencing a particularly unsettled phase of its turbulent history. With three years to go before the creation of the state of Israel, Britain held the Mandate, and with it the thankless task of attempting to reconcile the conflicting interests of Jew and Arab. Normally, as British servicemen, we would not concern ourselves with such political matters. Now, however, our troops were becoming the targets of the local extremist organisations, and there was a great deal of ill-feeling in evidence.

We ourselves soon experienced an example of the anti-British feeling currently fashionable in the Jewish community. Our five crewmembers had caught a bus into Tel Aviv that morning, and, after ogling the extremely attractive girls displaying themselves on the beach, called in one of the small seafront bars for a cold beer. The proprietor seemed to be in two minds whether or not to serve us, and then did so with obvious reluctance. At the same time he launched into a bitter tirade against the British Administration. He himself was a prewar Jewish immigrant from Nazi Germany; now, he claimed, his fellow countrymen were being denied access because of stupid quota restrictions. He then railed against the brutal British soldiers who were actually turning back what they callously called the illegal immigrant ships. It was all too much for our captain, a man not without strong views of his own.

'Look, mate,' he glared. 'When you've finished ranting about these brutal British troops, remember one thing. If it hadn't been for them, your chums wouldn't have been aboard those ships in the first place. They would have been heaps of ashes at the bottom of the gas chambers!' His forceful point must have been considered and conceded: when we finally left it was handshakes all round.

One could not fail to be impressed by the industry of the Jewish settlers in this part of the country. Housed in neat hutted encampments, they had transformed former desert areas into vegetable plots and large citrus groves. Tel Aviv was the very epitome of a modern city, and the civilian section of Lydda airfield already showed signs that soon it would develop into an international airport.

Early next morning we picked up the incoming Stirling, and set course on the penultimate flight, as far as Tripoli, in Libya. So far we had experienced no mechanical troubles of any kind, in spite of our captain's gloomy predictions that the Stirling was not designed to operate in hot dusty climates, and would soon be found wanting. However, when we were over the Med some 250 miles outbound, Jack reported a serious malfunctioning of the starboard inner engine. Soon afterwards, Les had no option but to close down the engine. This meant that, according to the book, we would have to land as soon as possible.

'Navigator, give me a course for the nearest airfield with RAF servicing facilities,' he called.

That was why we now found ourselves heading for Cairo West, where we had night-stopped on the outward trip.

Some half an hour later we made our three-engined landing there. The Engineering Officer and a sergeant fitter were waiting to inspect our unserviceable engine. Their verdict was soon given – a complete engine change was necessary. This would have to be flown out specially from England, so we would be stuck here at least a week. In consideration of our army passengers, who of course were desperately eager to get home without delay, I tried not to show my delight at the prospect of a paid holiday in Cairo.

Three hours later, we three NCOs were spruced up in our spare uniforms and successfully thumbing a lift into town on the main road outside the camp. We had arranged for our passengers to be picked up by another aircraft, found a suitable stowage for our kit and shopping loot, drawn an advance of pay in Egyptian currency and collected a five-day leave pass. We intended to make the most of this unexpected bonus.

My first impression of Cairo was that in addition to being the largest city in the Middle East, it was without doubt the noisiest. Quite apart from the loud pleadings and wailings of the street vendors, there was a sustained cacophony of blaring car horns and clanging trams like I had never heard before. Its bustling pavements were crowded with servicemen of every Allied nationality. It occurred to me for the first time that since this was obviously the region's premier leave centre, accommodation might well be at a premium.

Two hours after our arrival, we stood disconsolately outside the YMCA on the central Soliman Pasha Street. In our search for lodgings we had tried every service club and hostel marked on our street guide – the Tedder Club, the Red Shield, the Toc H and others. The large YMCA Hostel had been our last hope, and the answer there had been the same as everywhere else: 'Sorry, we're absolutely full up.' We could not afford to stay in the city centre hotels, and the cheaper lodgings were all in the out-of-bounds areas. It looked like we would soon be hitching a ride back into the desert. What a desperately frustrating situation.

We had tried to ignore the fellow in gown and fez who had latched himself onto us. He had walked behind us, exclaiming: 'Hello there, sergeants. You looking for beds? I find for you – very clean, very cheap.' His importuning had been as unwelcome as that of the others who had dogged our steps – the persistent street vendors, the purveyors of dirty postcards and the young shoeshine boys who darted about our feet. His furtive air, and the affliction of a dreadful squint, did nothing for his credibility. It was obvious he was trying to lure us to some bug-ridden hovel in the smelly back streets, for his own purposes. We were not that green.

It was mere curiosity which prompted me to ask him how far away was this place. 'Very near,' he replied. 'I take you there in two minutes.'

Since we were standing in the city centre, it must be situated in a reasonably respectable area, I figured. What could we lose by taking a look? After all, we were desperate. I told him to lead on, and we would follow.

His estimation of two minutes was not wildly exaggerated. He soon led us to the rather imposing entrance to a tall modern block of flats, set in a pleasant tree-lined avenue, and beckoned us inside. 'Hang on,' I called. 'We're only poor sergeants. This is too expensive for us.'

'No, no,' insisted our cross-eyed acquaintance. 'Very cheap. Madame is my very good friend. You'll see.'

We entered, dubiously, and followed him into the lift. He took us to the topmost floor, where there was a small hallway, and a door leading into a large lounge. The lady of the house, middle aged and European looking, came to greet us, and engaged our guide in rapid conversation in Egyptian. Then she smiled at us and said we were welcome to stay in the apartment for a few days; she happened to have a room with three beds available. The place was nicely furnished, and spotlessly clean. It would suit us perfectly. But first was the question of how much we would have to pay. With true navigators' caution, I put the question to her.

She spread her hands and shrugged her shoulders. 'How much would you pay at one of your soldiers' clubs?'

'About twenty-five piastres,' I said. That was about five shillings in English money.

'Then you shall pay me the same. Twenty-five piastres each per day, for bed and breakfast.'

We couldn't believe our good fortune. High class accommodation in a city centre pension for the price of a bed in a crowded servicemens' dormitory. What incredible luck. We were still congratulating ourselves an hour later, having settled in our bedroom and showered in the large adjoining bathroom. Various tongue-in-cheek theories were propounded regarding Madame's benevolence, ranging from her being a raving Anglophile to a panting nymphomaniac with designs on our bodies.

She put an end to our idle speculation when she invited us to join her over a pot of tea, before we set off to explore the city night life. She explained that she was Greek, and ran the pension with her Egyptian husband. She was well disposed towards the British, and let her spare room to British servicemen at cheap rates since she had always found them well behaved. Two other bedrooms were occupied by her permanent residents, four young Egyptian ladies of impeccable family. These girls were employed as cabaret dancers at an exclusive night club frequently patronised by King Farouk himself. They worked late hours, and we would probably never even meet them. She gave the impression of being rather snobbishly proud of her high-class residents, and had appointed herself guardian of their moral and general well-being.

Next morning we had an early breakfast, then set off on a day's sightseeing, accompanied by our cross-eyed friend, Abdul by name. We had tipped him well the previous day, and, as a further reward, had booked him as our guide for the next few days. It proved a wise investment. Not only did he conduct us patiently around many places of interest, but he kept at bay the numerous street hawkers with effective streams of Arabic invective, which was an entertainment in itself.

I found Cairo exciting and fascinating. A city of startling contrasts. Which other city in the world offered wide tree-lined boulevards and narrow jumbled bazaars; elegant shops in chrome and neon alongside monuments of awesome antiquity; a skyline etching mosques and churches, temples and synagogues; streets where camels and donkeys vied with trams and taxis – and smells as varied as the sights themselves? For three days we did the tourist rounds, from morning till night. We shed our shoes to look around the alabaster Mosque of Muhammad Ali, and gazed with wonder at the mummies and Pharaonic remains in the Cairo Museum. We sipped Turkish coffee in the bazaar with Abdul's shopkeeper friend as he tried to sell us silks and perfumes. We saw the Sphinx by starlight, and the inner chamber of the Giza Pyramid by torchlight. I could happily have spent a month absorbing the atmosphere of this most cosmopolitan of cities.

We spent little time in the apartment. Late one evening we managed to catch a glimpse of our fellow residents, who were leaving for work as we arrived home. They were very attractive girls indeed, elegantly groomed and dressed, and we were very impressed. One of them in fact could have passed for a young suntanned Ava Gardner, then in her heyday as a movie queen. They looked exactly as Madame had described them, extremely high-class girls. No wonder they had caught King Farouk's eye.

Sunday morning arrived, giving every indication of becoming a particularly hot day, and we decided to forgo the sightseeing. We arose about midmorning and went into the commodious bathroom. Bob took a shower, standing in the bath, while Jack and I shaved in the washbasins. The far door suddenly opened, to admit young Ava Gardner, dressed in a silken dressing gown which revealed more than it concealed. For a moment there was complete silence. When any young girl in dishabille, and particularly one of gentle breeding, is suddenly confronted by three male strangers, one of whom is completely naked, certain reactions may be expected. Perhaps an embarrassed scream, or at least a squeal or giggle, followed by a rapid exit. In this case, none of these things happened. The girl coolly addressed herself in perfect English to Bob, who was still standing in the bath, modestly attempting to cover himself.

'I don't wish to hurry you, but will you please let me know when the bath is free?'

She strolled back into her bedroom, and we looked at each other – intrigued to say the least, at such feminine sangfroid. Minutes later, our ablutions completed, we tapped on her bedroom door. The girl opened the door wide. There were two double beds in the room, one of which held two sleeping figures. In the bed she had recently vacated was a sleeping man. The uniform spread on the floor alongside denoted that he was an officer of the United States Air Force.

We were not so naive that the implications of the scene did not register pretty quickly.

'What's the score here?' I found myself asking.

The colloquialism must have puzzled her.

'The score? Ah, you mean how much? It's five Egyptian pounds short time. For all night you must arrange with Madame.'

After the surprise involved in this encounter, the humour of the situation hit us shortly afterwards. Back in our own bedroom, Bob summed it up:

> 'Would you credit it? We've been here four days, and only just clocked we've been living in a bloody knocking shop! The lads at the nick will never believe it. She's conned us beautifully. Don't you see, she lets off one of her rooms to servicemen as a cover for all the comings and goings in this place.' 'No skin off our nose,' said Jack, like a true airman. 'We're the ones getting the bargain.'

Who could argue with that?

We decided to remain indoors for the rest of the day. That afternoon we settled at a table in the lounge, with a few bottles of cold beer, to watch the operating procedures of a well run illegal brothel.

The four girls and the two Americans had left the apartment by lunchtime. Soon afterwards one of the girls returned, and crossed the lounge on her way to the corridor leading to the bedrooms. Half a minute later, the lift outside discharged the first client of the afternoon. He had been well briefed. As we quietly watched, a hand came through the letterbox and retrieved the key hanging on the string inside, the door was opened, and the man followed the same route to the bedroom. He seemed to be a rather senior policeman, who eyed us dubiously as he passed our table.

Business became quite brisk as the afternoon wore on, and we lost count of the progressions. Most of the clients were army officers, which made us think the girls' rallying point must be one of the nearby officers' clubs. Our own service did not go unrepresented; a young pilot officer, obviously newly-commissioned, entered with the furtive air of a man who felt he was taking a risk and knew he shouldn't really be here. His guilt feelings were so apparent it was quite comical. He did not see us in the shade until he was almost abreast our table. Then he stopped in his tracks, his face registering complete embarrassment.

'Oh, er, sorry chaps,' he stuttered. 'I didn't know there was anyone waiting.'

'That's all right, old chap,' I said. 'We live here.'

It was too much for him. I could read his thought process. What's going on here? Are these sergeants running this place? Is it a set-up? He suddenly turned about, hurried through the door and scampered down the stairs.

'First time I've been mistaken for a pimp,' said Bob. That started us laughing.

'At least we've saved him a fiver,' I added. We laughed louder.

'Unless he paid in advance,' said Jack. We collapsed.

Madame came from her room to investigate such hilarity. We knew now what went on in this place. Madame knew we knew. We knew Madame knew we knew. Somehow it made no difference to our friendly relationship. In fact, she soon returned with a tray of sandwiches for us.

That evening the three of us, by now flat broke, went for a last stroll. When we returned about ten o'clock, there were signs of trouble. In the lounge Madame was engaged in a loud harangue with a sergeant bearing the orange shoulder flash of the South African Army. He had turned up uninvited – and very drunk. After being refused admission he had turned nasty, and was starting to throw ornaments around the room. Madame's husband, a small insignificant figure, was useless, and she turned to us for assistance. Our arrival, apparently as preferential customers, inflamed him all the more. Since we could not pacify him, the three of us struggled and managed to bundle him into the lift, slam the gates and despatch him to the ground floor. We waited, almost certain he would be back. His ardour must have cooled, however, and we were not troubled again. Madame was grateful, and we got our reward. No, not a free sample on the house. A supper of egg and chips, with a bottle of wine.

'You know,' said Bob reflectively. 'By the strict letter of the law we have become accessories to the running of an illegal brothel. And me a London bobby.'

Next morning we said our goodbyes, and hitched a lift back to the airfield. Les and Bill, our two officers, told us that they too had had problems in finding accommodation in Cairo. As a result, they had spent most of the time hanging around their Mess on camp. They listened to our story with some envy.

'Nothing like that ever seems to happen to us,' said Les. 'You peasants get all the luck.'

The engine change on our Stirling had been completed on schedule, and after an air test and compass swing we were ready to resume our homeward flight. All our original army passengers had been accommodated on other flights, so twenty-four lucky airmen whose demob date was near found themselves getting a speedier return to the UK than they had ever anticipated.

We flew westwards for six hours, covering in that time almost exactly the ground gained by General Montgomery and his 8th Army in months of hard slog, from Alamein to Tripoli. From our height there was nothing whatever to see of those years of desert war. This desert was nothing like the romantic image of golden sand and green oases – just a drab vista of dun and grey, of rocky outcrops and dried-up *wadis*.

Our destination was the RAF staging post at Castel Benito, situated in the desert south of Tripoli. A former base of the Italian Air Force, it had been named after Mussolini, and built as a showpiece by the prewar colonists. We found it a surprisingly well-appointed place, with solid buildings of stone and marble in the Italian style, which had withstood well the frequent bombings and strafings by both sides. It had well tended gardens, with clusters of palms and groves of oranges, and an open air pool. We were accommodated for the night in substantial stone barracks, with comfortable beds. How strange that having slept soundly for the last few nights in the centre of noisy Cairo, tonight in the desert I couldn't sleep at all for the continual barking of dogs in a distant Arab encampment.

The final stage of our journey home seemed interminable. Over the Med, the strong northerly airflow of the Mistral was blowing in our face, cutting down our groundspeed dramatically. Over the French Massif we came in for some severe buffeting, and had to make wide detours to avoid thunderstorms. The old Stirling was stretched to the limits of its safe endurance before we finally reached Stradishall. I had never before realised just how rich and green was the English countryside.

Looking back, this had been a trip to remember, in all respects. In my case, it had also proved to be something of a watershed. I had long been pondering my future – whether to try to make my way in civilian life, or to take a chance on signing up for the postwar RAF. I had enjoyed my flying immensely, but it had been wartime flying – giving an excitement, exhilaration and sense of purpose which peacetime flying would be unlikely to provide. This trip had proved to me that flying still had its allure. Never before in my life had I crammed such experience into such a short time. My job as navigator still offered challenges, not least against wind and weather. The RAF still had bases worldwide – and in Transport Command my already expanding horizon would be limitless. On a less altruistic plane, my access to the overseas bazaars coupled with the continuing austerity at home, gave possibilities of profitable future entrepreneurship. The decision needed no further soul searching. While most others about me assiduously ticked off the days to their demob, I hurried to the Orderly Room to sign the paper which would delay mine for the maximum of eighteen months. Later, when the RAF made clear the options for long term service, I would further commit myself.

We carried out several more flights to India, but it was obvious that the Stirling's role was coming to an end. Increasing unserviceability meant more and more of them littering the staging posts, and there was a fatal crash at Castel Benito later in the year. There was talk of the new Avro York, designed specially as a transport aircraft and reputedly with the navigators' comfort and convenience in mind, coming into full squadron service. It came as no surprise to hear that the Stirlings would be phased out by the end of 1945.

Sadly, we learned that 158 Squadron would be disbanded as from 1 January 1946, and its remaining personnel transferred elsewhere. It was not a squadron with a long history and deep-rooted traditions. Formed originally in 1918, it had been disbanded only months later, and had not been reactivated until the middle of the Second World War. For that reason, it was inevitable that it would be one of the first to go when the RAF began to contract to peacetime strength.

The squadron crest bore a linked chain, with the motto: *Strength in Unity*. Nothing could have been more appropriate. The strength had shown itself by the squadron's splendid record of operational achievement in the air war against Germany. The unity was just as plain to see. Aircrews and groundcrews, airmen and airwomen, regulars and volunteers, Britons, Canadians, Australians, New Zealanders, and others, had all joined in common bond.

From my own experience, it had always been a happy squadron, with high morale. Though most of the aircrews counted their time on the squadron in months rather than years, their attachment to it was every bit as great as a soldier to his regiment, a sailor to his ship. All of them, and all those who supported them on the ground, would look back on their service with immense pride in their achievements. Fifty years on, the squadron ex-members would still be coming together regularly in celebration of a rare comradeship and in remembrance of lost friends. They would continue to do so until age had taken its final toll.

15

POSTSCRIPT

I reproduce here a selection of letters received by me about this time, which add in some degree to my story

ACTON, LONDON.
Dec. 1945.

Dear Harry,

You will no doubt get a big surprise to receive this letter, a voice from the past. I thought I had lost your home address, but it turned up unexpectedly, so I thought I would write to find out how you have fared since we last met.

You will also be surprised to hear that I have been in civvy street some time now, having obtained a medical discharge from the RAF. I was unfortunate enough to be on the receiving end of one of the flying-bomb attacks on London, not long after returning from S. Africa. I was pretty badly knocked about and was in hospital a long time, but am OK now. I am hoping to take up a teacher's training course in the near future.

Hitler certainly had it in for me. Did I ever tell you that before I joined up a bomb fell just behind my home? Fortunately it did not go off, otherwise I wouldn't be here. When they dug it out they found chalked on the bomb 'For Tommy'. Question is, how did they know my address? . . .

I have heard once from our mutual friend Ronnie, the muscular Christian. Did you know he got the job of navigating a mighty Anson carrying wounded troops to hospitals in England from Normandy after D-Day? So the RAF don't always put square pegs in round holes . . .

Hope to hear from you soon with all your news of how you helped win the war,

Your old oppo,

Tom.

BUCKINGHAM PALACE

1621875 Flight Sergeant H. Lomas, DFM.

'I greatly regret that I am unable to give you personally the award which you have so well earned. I now send it to you with my congratulations and my best wishes for your future happiness.

George R.I.

No. 361 M.U.
RAF INDIA COMMAND.
Jan. 1946.

Hiya, Pal,

First of all Harry, congratulations on your DFM. Just think of it, three gongs in the crew, and maybe it would have been four if George or I had clobbered that Jerry who shot us up.

As you can see for my sins I have landed out here in India, way out in the wilds in typical northern jungle country with the nearest town (Patna) more than twenty miles away. I am sweating my time out in the Pay Accounts here. The old stagger juice is in very short supply, but there are plenty of spirits available so it doesn't take me long to get airborne . . . What else can I say about this place? Nothing, so let's talk about something interesting.

I am in touch with all the crew at present, and also two of the girls from Rufforth. George and I got split up at last. I hear the lucky devil got a posting to London. Did you know that Dick was now a flight sergeant discip in Singapore, can you imagine it? . . . I often lie on the old charpoy thinking wouldn't it be great to get back to the old exciting days of ops. If ever we were needed again I'm sure we could rake up all the old crew. I often think of the good times we had at the Wellington in Moreton in the Marsh and the Spa at Brid, and all the other hostelries. What wouldn't I give for a night out at any of them right now. I still have Herman the Airman with me, do you remember him?

If ever you are unlucky enough to be in this part of the world, come and see me and I will fix you up with an advance of pay. Hope to see you again when I get back to Blighty. Happy landings.

Your old Tail-end Till,

Denis.

POLLARD STREET
MANCHESTER
Jan. 1946.

Dear Mr Lomas,

Thank you for your letter informing us that you have further postponed your release from H.M. Forces.

Please let us know when you have a definite date when you will be taking up your old position with us. If you decide to terminate your employment, let us know as soon as possible so we may return Pension Fund contributions.

Yours faithfully,
H.G. pp Manager.

WALLSTONECRAFT
SYDNEY N.S.W.
Feb. 1946.

Dear Harry,

Thanks for your last letter, and congrats on the gong. I have been on a week's holiday in Melbourne, and found letters from you, Dick and Denis on my return. Also a letter from your mother and father thanking me for a food parcel I sent them some time ago.

I am still on disembarkation leave, and managed to bum a flight to Melbourne to see what prospects were for pilots with Australian National Airlines. No chance, there is a waiting list as long as your arm, and you also need a second class navigator's ticket and Morse at twenty words a minute. So it looks like I will eventually be going back to university. I was amazed to find how primitive the flying is back home, about ten years behind the times. The aerodromes at Melbourne and Canberra are just huge open paddocks, no runways, peri tracks, radar or anything, and they navigate on a beam and a radio compass only. By the way, I have met Bill Strachan in Sydney. I don't see a lot of him as his home is on the other side of the harbour. He has been home since last July, and also has a DFC.

Well Harry, after all the big build-up I have always given Australia, I find I am almost ready to catch the next boat back to England. The cities here are as dead as Julius Caesar, there's hardly any beer, and the bars are only open from 4.30 to 6.00pm. To make it worse at present you can't buy cigarettes for love or money. Luckily I brought about 2,000 home with me, but when they are smoked I will probably be picking butts up from the gutter. The weather is uncomfortably hot both day and night, and I often wish I was back in the old village pub sipping cool beer till 10.30pm.

No more news for the present, but in closing let me just say what a great experience it has been for me going overseas and meeting up with you blokes. When we first crewed up, being the only Aussie, I didn't know how things would turn out, but now that it's all over I'd say that I wouldn't have swapped you for any other crew. We had a few ups and downs but we went along well, and I certainly enjoyed our time together as a crew. If ever 158 Squadron should extend its routes, you know where to find me.

Happy Landings,
Your old mate,
Keith.

16

THE REUNION

The longer we awaited our guests, the more my wife Joan's nervousness increased. Her feminine forebodings, which I had tried to dispel, were returning in full force. Do you think they'll find the house small and cramped? Will it be too cold for them? Will they object to my smoking? Do Australians really like steaks for breakfast? I had tried to reassure her on all counts. They are on an overseas holiday, and will be anticipating a completely different life-style. This is English summertime, and certainly no cooler than an Australian winter. Keith, when I knew him last, was a twenty-a-day man like most of us. As for breakfast, he had baked beans or dried egg like the rest of us, and glad of it. Yes, I know that was in wartime, but honestly, as far as I know, the Aussies nowadays eat more or less the same as we do; except maybe for rabbit pie.

To tell the truth, in spite of the assurances to my wife, I was growing a little nervous myself. After all, it isn't every day you are called upon to greet someone to whom you were once close after a gap of over forty-two years. That period is over half a lifetime, and people can change dramatically. The last time I had seen Keith, my wartime Australian skipper, had been soon after the end of the war, when the crew had disbanded. Was he still the same easy-going fellow? What if we found we had become as complete strangers? What if we had nothing to say to each other? Or what if our two wives didn't hit it off? I had been trying to think of something to say when they arrived on our doorstep which would be suitable to the occasion without sounding too pretentious, but so far nothing had come to mind.

Our forthcoming meeting had been arranged quite fortuitously. Keith and I had kept in touch for a period after we had parted, but as with most wartime friendships the correspondence eventually lapsed, and we lost touch completely. After many years I reached an age, which I think comes to all of us, when I felt a compulsion to renew old acquaintance-ships, a nostalgic yearning to revive the memories of younger days. I tried without success to trace and meet former members of my wartime crew.

I found that there was an active 158 Squadron Association which held regular reunions of former aircrews and ground staff, splendidly organised by a former pilot, Bluey Mottershead. (No connection, let me add, with the Bluey previously encountered at Moreton in the Marsh). My wife and I became members, and though we met none of my old crewmates, three of Bill Strachan's crew were regular attenders. Ed Richards, Johnny Wakefield and Arthur Tait I remembered well enough; Cyril Keeton, their former navigator and my old friend, alas had been killed in a tragic accident at home, I learned. Ed's wife, Brenda, a resourceful lady who by dint of well-directed letters, phone calls or even newspaper ads had helped Bill's crew keep in touch, promised to help dig out my own crewmates. It was partly due to her efforts that in due course Keith had been contacted. Now Keith and his wife Helene had travelled from Sydney on a European holiday, during which they proposed to attend this year's squadron reunion at Bridlington. Prior to this, they would be spending a week at my home in nearby Driffield. Today was to be our first meeting.

My wife peered through the curtains as a car pulled up outside the house.

'They're here,' she called excitedly. We hurried out to greet our two guests.

I would have recognised Keith anywhere. His features had hardly altered, his hairline had barely receded, his easy grin was unchanged. He walked towards me with his distinctive loping stride, instantly taking me back to that evening at Moreton-in-the-Marsh when he had walked purposefully into my hut in search of a navigator. I instinctively looked for the forehead scar, his souvenir of our crash in *Lili Marlene*, but time seemed to have erased it. His wife followed him from the car; casually smart, younger than I had expected, a friendly smile on her face.

'Welcome back to East Yorkshire, Keith,' I said, as we shook hands.

'It's been a long time, Harry. But I said I'd be back, one day.'

All those years between seemed suddenly to have melted away. It was just like a normal meeting of old pals who haven't seen each other for a while. I should never have doubted that it could be otherwise. We introduced our wives, with friendly kisses, then went indoors for a celebratory drink. Within minutes we were laughingly confiding our mutual earlier misgivings. Helene had dreaded finding herself amongst stiff and formal English strangers, while Keith declared that the very thought of a steak for breakfast was enough to give him indigestion.

The reminiscences carried on for the rest of the day. Keith and I seemed to have quite a lot in common. We had both married at the same late age in life, and taken partners a good deal younger than ourselves.

We both had grown-up families, without yet attaining the status of grandparents. We had stopped smoking at the same age, and taken retirement together – Keith from an executive position, myself from a more humble banking job. And it seemed we had both caught the nostalgia bug at approximately the same time.

Plenty of coincidences there. But none more so to Keith's mind than the fact that I had finally settled in a Yorkshire town only a figurative stone's throw from our wartime airfield at Lissett; in fact, the hospital where our crewmate Ken died all those years ago I can see every day from my window. But then, experience has taught me that in life no coincidence is too inconceivable, no irony too rich to contemplate. For instance, I learned today that over the years Keith's business affairs had on occasion brought him to London, where he had desperately and vainly sought contact with any of his old crew. Just as I myself had visited Australia during my Transport Command days and been unable to make contact with Keith. I was able to quote to him the ultimate irony. Only three years after he and I had devoted all our energies to dropping bombs on the Germans, I had found myself engaged for eighteen arduous months in flying food and fuel to the beleaguered Berliners in what became known as the Berlin Airlift. When one surveys Germany's present-day economic dominance, I sometimes find it difficult to get things into historical perspective.

Of immediate concern to Keith was what news I had of our former crewmates. I had to report that even Brenda had been unable to come up with anything concerning Old Len, our veteran bomb-aimer, and Dick, our flight engineer, who was thought to have emigrated. She was however in touch with Les Lamb, our wireless operator, and longtime friend of her husband. Les was now a Canadian citizen, a store-owner in Ontario, where he had raised his family. He would dearly have loved to be joining us for the reunion, but an impending business sale made it impossible. I had gazed at the photograph of himself which he had sent. Was this ample bespectacled gentleman with the shining pate really the muscular young fellow with the dark wavy hair that I remembered?

There was more success with the news that George Tuohy, our one-time mid-upper gunner, had been contacted at his home near London, where he was still in employment as a printer. He had never been in contact with any of his comrades before, but was now looking forward to our forthcoming reunion with excited anticipation.

My quest for news of the one remaining crewmember, Denis, our rear gunner, had received an unexpected boost when a perusal of Bluey's extensive lists of ex-squadron personnel produced his name and a Midlands telephone number for contacting. Armed with plans for our forthcoming get-together, I had rung the number without delay. It was a woman's voice who answered.

'Hallo,' I said. 'Am I speaking to Mrs Denis Till?'

'You are'.

'I wonder if I could have a word with him.'

A pause. 'Who is this speaking?'

'Tell him it's an old wartime friend from Andy's crew.'

Another pause. 'I'm afraid I have to tell you Denis died of a heart attack seven years ago.'

Somehow the news came to me with a shock as though we had been in day-to-day contact since the war. I could only mumble my regrets, and apologies. Then we talked on for several minutes. Denis had died in his prime, much respected by all who knew him, a caring member of the community, a Samaritan. He had often talked to her of the comradeship of the war years.

All this I now told to Keith, and we both agreed that this was yet another of life's ironies. Denis, the baby of the crew, was the one known to have died before his time: the one who had first enthusiastically visualised an eventual reunion would be the one most missed.

We talked together until late into the night, spanning the long years we had been out of touch.

The next morning we started out on my prepared itinerary with a visit to York. This fair city held pleasant memories for us both. It was the place we had sought our recreation when we were stationed at the training airfields nearby. We made our way to Betty's Bar, once the homing point for all 4 Group's aircrews out on the spree; where the talk was always of ops and prangs and popsies, in the accents of Birmingham and Belfast, Sydney and Saskatchewan. Today, the basement bar was closed and shuttered; in the select tearooms above, the local matrons selected their cream cakes and discussed the day's shopping. We moved on to the riverside pub where we had once stumbled out of the blackout and found ourselves in the lively rallying point of the Free French airmen; today, it was just another bar. Only the historic charm of the city was unchanged.

We ended the afternoon with an enjoyable visit to the recently-opened Yorkshire Air Museum at nearby Elvington aerodrome. Of the thousands of Halifax bombers built during the war, not one had been preserved for posterity. Here, local aviation enthusiasts were remedying the situation by attempting to reconstruct one from spare parts and salvaged wrecks, and we wished them every success.

Browsing amongst the various exhibits, we came across some odd little items which we could associate with our own personal experiences.

There was, for instance, a copy of the signal sent by the American commanding general to our station commander at Lissett, thanking him for his hospitality when a whole group of USAAF Fortresses were diverted there in November 1944. I remembered it well. I had lost a couple of pounds in the all-night poker school held that night in the Sergeants' Mess billiards room. You could say that it was my own contribution to the hospitality.

I also read, for the first time, some details of Operation Gisela, the German intruder operation over England on 3 March 1945, in which our crew had been heavily involved. I had long sought details of the losses involved on that traumatic night, without success. Today I learned that RAF losses had been high – some twenty-four bombers, mainly Halifaxes, having been shot down over eastern England. I also learned that the Germans lost a similar number of their aircraft, mainly due to bad weather and fuel shortages on their return flight. At the time, we would have been glad to know that.

We continued to follow the trail next morning. I had arranged lunch for the four of us at the Blue Post at North Frodingham, the village inn where we had taken refuge after *Lili Marlene* had crashed in the adjacent field. Nobody there remembered those days, and indeed, as we sat in the comfortable chairs amidst the horse brasses and thick-pile carpets, it was difficult to associate the place with the rough wooden pews and stone floors onto which we had trodden mud and dripped blood on that occasion.

It was impossible to pinpoint the spot where our plane had come to rest and burned to cinders, since the whole area was still under cultivation, and no scars remained. As we left the scene, I got into conversation with a lady who was tending her garden at a nearby cottage, and asked her if she remembered the night of the bomber crash.

'Indeed I do,' she replied, in the broadest of Yorkshire accents. 'I remember it as though it was yesterday, though I was nobbut a bairn at the time. It must have been on a Saturday night, 'cause I remember the chip shop was open. It was black as pitch 'til this fire started. They said it was a burning bomber, and a miracle it hadn't hit the cottages. I could hear all the bombs and bullets going off. There was only my mother and me at home – my dad was fighting in the desert – but she went off to have a look. She'd been a nurse, and wasn't afeared of seeing blood and bodies. She saw them bringing the men to the ambulance. Ever such big men they were, she told me. One of them was so big, he couldn't fit on the stretcher. She thought one of them was dead.'

I realised then that she hadn't yet associated Keith and me as two of the men so clearly defined in her story. On being so informed, she was

213

shocked into silence for some moments. 'Nay,' she said. 'Fancy that. And you both looking so well!'

It was an interesting insight into the event as seen through other eyes. We hadn't realised before that we had gone into local folklore as young giants who had dropped from the skies and so nearly blown the village apart.

On then to the airfield at Lissett, or what remains of it.

There can be few places in the land with the power to evoke such mixed and strong emotions as a disused wartime airfield on which one once served. I suppose it is all to do with the awesome contrasts between past and present which it instantly brings to mind. There is the sort of poignancy one feels when viewing a war cemetery, or some ancient bloody battlefield. As I gazed around, the present receded in a bitter-sweet memory of youthful days. This crumbling foundation and moulding brickwork must be where we gathered in noisy concourse to brief and plan our missions; this long straight rutted cart-track where heavily-laden bombers lumbered into the air; this sagging concrete pile the humming nerve centre of it all. Along the quiet lanes to the scattered domestic sites, the former Mess complex was now a grassy paddock where cattle eyed us with vacant bovine stare; the old living quarters mere heaps of brick and rust amidst the thicket. Could this really have been the setting of those momentous days? Had it all been just a trick of memory? Could this be a place of pilgrimage?

Driving home, we didn't talk much. We had been overtaken by the past. Nostalgia can breed its own sadness.

Next day, we let Helene choose the outing, to give our wives a change from the pursuit of things past. We drove to the beautiful Yorkshire Dales – the so-called 'Herriot country' whose delights were known to our friends through books and television back home. We savoured the English countryside at its best, with features like ancient village churches, meadows bounded by rustic dry-stone walls and distant vistas of purple heather of particular appeal to antipodean eyes. We dined on grilled trout in a cool stone-built inn on a hillside, under the benign gaze of a stuffed owl on the wall.

The squadron reunion was scheduled to span three days, beginning on the Friday evening. The four of us drove into Bridlington for the initial informal get-together, in a seafront bar-restaurant taken over for the night.

Bluey, ever the faultless organiser, was at the door to greet each arrival and provide each one with a pinned name-tag, in the knowledge that the recognition of former comrades after a gap of up to four decades usually needed some form of prompting.

214

THE REUNION

We had recently seen the changes time had wrought on our old airfield at Lissett, the sad decay and delapidation. Now, what of the men who had flown and serviced its aeroplanes? What state of preservation were they now in?

Pretty good, was the immediate impression. The men who met our gaze in the noisy crowded lounge were all of advanced years, mature of face and grey of hair; the dash and vigour of their squadron days had gone, but they were upright of bearing and square of shoulder. In their neat suits and blazers, with regimental ties predominant, there could be little doubt that this was a gathering of former servicemen. They were complemented by their well-dressed and coiffured wives. The years had not treated these people harshly. They were representatives of the generation whose youth had spanned the years of Depression and uneasy peace, whose later teenage years had been blighted by the dangers and deprivations of wartime. Education, careers and family life had been subjugated to the extraordinary demanding life-style of the war years. Had any of this left its mark? Not a sign of it. The impression was of a company who had been successful in their careers, and who had comfortably met the challenges life had presented. It was almost as though nature had compensated them in their later years.

As we moved into the room, the face that immediately caught my eye could belong to nobody but George. It was almost exactly the face of our young gunner portrayed in the crew photograph in my pocket – the hair still thick and dark, brow unlined, smile unchanged; probably the youngest-looking man in the room. With a loud whoop of recognition he bounded across to us, his wife Jean in tow, positively radiating delight. 'I can't believe it,' he cried, frantically pumping Keith's hand. 'Forty years out of touch – now three of us together again. Marvelous. Absolutely marvelous!' It was the sort of enthusiasm I remembered from George of old, and set the tone for the evening.

I am sure there are people with some misconceptions about what a present-day reunion of war veterans is about. Anyone who thinks it is some kind of beer-hall bacchanalia or jingoistic jamboree is way off the mark. There is surprisingly little in the proceedings which is in any way militaristic; there is no glorification of war, no stories of bravado or derring-do, no divisions of former rank. We were here in the spirit of camaraderie; we are here to reminisce, and recall a little of our youth; we are here because we have a genuine interest in each other; we are here to remember our missing comrades. The drinks flow freely, and the hubbub of conversation is loud and sustained, with some of the accents from beyond the bounds of the British Isles. 'Do you remember . . .?' starts a hundred stories – and the things remembered are the funny foolish things

215

that remain in the memory. The night old so-and-so was trapped in the Waafery; the time a live sheep dressed in a sergeant's tunic turned up in the Mess. We are all together in the nostalgia business.

The three members of Bill Strachan's old crew, who now came to greet us, along with their wives, to my mind epitomised the whole spirit of these reunions. Johnny, one-time bomb-aimer and retired Midlands headmaster, Arthur, former rear gunner and lifelong Yorkshire miner, and Ed, ex-wireless operator and still the cheerful Cockney extrovert; three men who in ordinary circumstances would have had little in common. Yet each year they assiduously seek each other's company, maintaining those comfortable bonds of comradeship established so long ago. Next year they hope to realise their ambition of a full crew reunion. Bill has promised to join them from Australia sometime during his retirement, and tonight it is to Keith they turn to apply the final pressure on his return home.

At some later stage of the evening we began to circulate. Keith chatted to one or two remembered acquaintances from the pilots' section, while I found a navigator's face here and there which I recognised. Strange how the memory can play tricks. The former Navigation Leader, with whom I must have had constant dealings in my squadron days, had now rather embarrassingly faded completely from my mind; yet another fellow I had barely known was now instantly recognisable from his voice alone. I came across my old friend Dai Johnson, once a pale dark-haired Welshman, now the very image of a ruddy-faced white-maned countryman. I reminded him of the day his aircraft had been hit by shrapnel, and he had suffered the shock of being suddenly drenched with glycol from the ruptured tank above his head. He had forgotten the incident completely!

The following afternoon, Saturday, Bluey had laid on a couple of coach outings for those members weekending in Bridlington. There was a trip to the RAF Cemetery near Harrogate for those wishing to pay their respects at the graves of former squadron members, mainly from the dominions, who were buried there. For those not so inclined, there was the option of a visit to one of Yorkshire's more eminent stately homes. We availed ourselves of neither, since we were entertaining lunchtime guests at home.

We resumed the social scene in the evening. Helene and Keith, along with our local friends Christine and Richard, accompanied us to our rendezvous at Brid's Spa Ballroom, so well remembered by us all. Our Squadron Association had booked tables bordering the floor for an evening of dancing to the music of Joe Loss and his Orchestra – to whose music in this self-same hall we had danced during the war years.

216

The setting was exactly as I recalled it – the huge domed roof, the brilliantly floodlit stage, the crowded galleries – with but one exception. Now the ladies were a little more mature, and their partners were not almost exclusively dressed in air force blue with shiny buttons. The dapper figure of our master of ceremonies seemed unchanged. He greeted us warmly from the stage as the opening strains of *In the Mood* faded, and said how well he remembered playing for us in those stirring wartime days. He took up his baton and led us through a medley of old favourites. As we moved round the floor to the sentimental strains of *Anniversary Waltz*, *We'll Meet Again* and *Jealousy*, the music made me feel I was twenty-one again. I found myself thinking of Denis, with whom I always associated this place. If ghosts walked here tonight, one would be his tall figure weaving across the floor under the rotating mirrored lights.

Sunday dawned bright and sunny. This was the day for more formal business, the day we honoured our fallen comrades. By mid-morning some three hundred of us were gathered at Lissett's ancient village churchyard. We circled the stone memorial, recently erected to commemorate our three-year sojourn in this small hamlet. A former squadron pilot, now in holy orders, led the simple open-air service. Then we stood in silent remembrance of our comrades. On the fringe of our company, bare-headed villagers joined us in our tribute. For two minutes all that was heard was the sigh of the wind in the trees, and the occasional clinking of medals; the bright ribbons standing out against the sober suiting, and the crimson poppy wreaths resting against the grey granite added a vivid splash of colour. Each of us was lost in his own thoughts. From the field beyond the fringe of trees, nearly a thousand young men of many nationalities had taken-off never to return. It seemed right that it was now at this place, now so calm and peaceful, we should stand in proud remembrance.

By request, the coaches waiting to convey the party back to Bridlington made a symbolic detour. Slowly they made their way along the narrow mile-long track which was all that remained of the airfield's main runway; on either side the corn had grown high. To the right, the small green hill marked the site of the old bomb dump; to the left, the flat expanse of the flight dispersals. Eventually nature will obliterate even these relics. Maybe hundreds of years from now people here will dig up bomb casings or spanners or tail fins and wonder what to make of it all.

The final and more formal part of the reunion took place again at the Spa, miraculously transformed overnight from a ballroom into a large dining hall. Group Captain Tom Sawyer, the popular former station commander at Lissett, was the guest of honour at the top table, along with the local bishop and the lord mayor. The bar was opened, and a buffet lunch served.

A few short speeches followed. All visitors from overseas were personally introduced by Bluey, and Keith and Helene stood to take a bow, along with an impressive number of others from Canada, Australia and New Zealand. There followed the sad recital of the names of those members known to have passed away since the previous gathering.

There remained an hour or so to browse around the hall, or to make final contacts. Keith, in what was to prove a day of surprises, found himself in conversation with a former flight commander who had also flown over from Australia, and in fact lived not a great distance from him in Sydney.

Around the room were stalls offering a selection of topical books, photographs and other squadron memorabilia, but of more immediate interest was a table display organised by a local friend of mine. Brian Gillard had never served in the RAF, but had always maintained a fanatical interest in aviation matters, and pursued an extraordinary hobby – the searching for and excavation of crashed wartime aircraft. His trophies, a selection of which were here on display all cleaned and labelled, were the various aircraft instruments and components dug up with the aid of metal detectors and hard graft. Most of his successful digs had involved Halifaxes of 4 Group in the local area, of which there were unfortunately rich pickings. *Lili Marlene* had been one of them.

It says much for the diligence of his researches that he had managed to contact Keith, as the captain of one of his excavated bombers, a good deal sooner than I had. He had already sent photographs out to Australia, and on hearing that Keith was coming over for the re-union, had planned another memento. I myself had already received from him as a souvenir a highly polished portion of one of Lili Marlene's engine components. Today, after I had introduced Keith, he presented him with the pilot's instrument panel reconditioned as new, suitably inscribed, and beautifully mounted on wood. Coming more than forty-two years after the demise of *Lili Marlene*, I think I can say it was the most unexpected present Keith has ever received.

Soon it was time for the party to break up. There followed the long ritual of last goodbyes and final handshakes. The reunion had been enjoyed by all, particularly by George, who was emphatic that the survivors of Andy's crew should never lose touch again. We walked out into the sunlight, and for a moment it seemed strange to find ourselves amidst the ambience of a modern seaside resort again. It was Keith and Helene's last night with us. We all wished they could have extended their stay, but their booked flight back to Australia was awaiting them in London. We settled down at home for an evening of quiet retrospection, over a glass or two of whisky. At exactly nine o'clock the phone rang, and I answered it. 'It's someone asking for you, Keith,' I told him. Puzzled, he took the receiver from me. It was a trans-Atlantic call, right on cue, from Les, our old wireless operator, speaking from Ontario. If, on the evidence of the photograph he had sent, his appearance had changed considerably since we had last known him, his voice had changed even more so. The remembered homely Lancashire accent had been supplanted by a broad Canadian drawl, which I could hear clearly as he expressed his regrets to Keith for being unable to have made the crew reunion a four-some. They chatted for several minutes, spanning the events since they had last heard each other's voice, more than forty years previously. It was a fitting ending to a day of surprises for Keith.

Afterwards, we carried on our conversations. I posed a question to him which I had sometimes pondered but never asked. What had been the motivation for young men like himself who had happily travelled thousands of miles to England, to fight a war which must have seemed remote and of no direct concern to them? Not only to fight, but to do so as flyers, where the known odds against their ever returning home were stacked against them.

He thought about it for a moment, then said:

'I don't want to sound sentimental in any way – no Aussie would. You must remember that times were different then. My generation was brought up very much in the tradition of the British Empire. My father had never been to England, but it was always 'the old country' to him, and it just seemed natural that we should join in Britain's fight. Then of course there was this flying business. The attraction of learning to fly was probably stronger among Aussies than most other nationalities. In my own case, the thought of learning to fly a Spitfire was more than enough motivation on its own.'

'In the event,' I said, 'you had to make do with a Halifax. That must have come as a cultural shock.'

'I soon came to terms with that. The old Hali was a great aeroplane. What worried me was the thought that I was responsible for six other lives, all strangers, all Poms. I didn't have a clue how they would react to me as their skipper, or whether I could handle them. When we first got together I was nervous as a kitten.'

'You managed to hide it well enough.'

219

'Then I must have been like the swan on the lake: all serene on top, but paddling like the clappers down below just to keep afloat. After a while of course we gained our confidence. We learned to trust each other to do his job properly, and to work together. And that was what being a bomber crew was all about.'

Our guests left us next morning in their hired car, for their drive to London. Joan and I accompanied them as far as the Humber Bridge. In their short stay with us we seemed to have established bonds closer than anything I had expected. The goodbyes, however, were neither awkward nor protracted. We had been invited to spend a long holiday with them at their Sydney home, to be shown something of their country. From the way our two wives had had their heads together, it was purely a matter of finalising the date when we would be flying out there.

I must have known something that far back day in May 1944 when Andy's crew had first come together. I had written in my diary that day:

'Crewed up today. I think we'll all get on together. Maybe we've started something today which could last us for the rest of our lives . . .'

INDEX

148, 162, 163, 174, 175, 177, 178, 206, 211, 215, 218
Tuohy, Jean, 215

U.S. troops, 71–74, 77, 128

VE Day, 172
VERY pistol, 57, 79, 120, 164, 171

Wakefield, Johnny, 210
Wangerooge, 166

Watson, Flt Lt Jack, 115
Weather conditions, 42–43
Weather patterns, 179
Wellington, 65, 76, 77, 78, 86, 177
West Freugh, 55, 62, 63, 65
Williams, Bill, 182, 187, 114, 202
Window, 84, 118
Winterbottom, Frosty, 13, 55
Woodbridge, 144

York, 81, 212